P9-DMF-560

Crossing the Pond

The Native American Effort in World War II

War and the Southwest Series

Series editors:

Richard G. Lowe, Gustav L. Seligmann, Calvin L. Christman

The University of North Texas Press has undertaken to publish a series of significant books about War and the Southwest. This broad category includes first-hand accounts of military experiences by men and women of the Southwest, histories of warfare involving the people of the Southwest, and analyses of military life in the Southwest itself. The Southwest is defined loosely as those states of the United States west of the Mississippi River and south of a line from San Francisco to St. Louis, as well as the borderlands straddling the Mexico-United States boundary. The series will include works involving military life in peacetime in addition to books on warfare itself. It will range chronologically from the first contact between indigenous tribes and Europeans to the present. The series is based on the belief that warfare is an important if unfortunate fact of life in human history and that understanding war is a requirement for a full understanding of the American past.

Books in the series

FOO—A Japanese-American Prisoner of the Rising Sun

Wen Bon: A Naval Air Intelligence Officer behind Japanese Lines in China

An Artist at War: The Journal of John Gaitha Browning

The 56th Evac Hospital: Letters of a WWII Army Doctor

CAP Môt: The Story of a Marine Special Forces Unit in Vietnam, 1968–1969

"Surrounded by Dangers of All Kinds": The Mexican War Letters of Lieutenant Theodore Laidley

Crossing the Pond

The Native American Effort in World War II

Jere' Bishop Franco

V. 7 War and the Southwest Series

University of North Texas Press
Denton, Texas

First edition 1999
10 9 8 7 6 5 4 3 2 1

Permissions:
University of North Texas Press
PO Box 311336
Denton TX 76203-1336
Phone 940-565-2142, Fax 940-565-4590

The paper used in this book meets the minimum requirements of the American National Standard for Permanence of Paper for Printed Library Materials, z39.48.1984. Binding materials have been chosen for durability.

Library of Congress Cataloging-in-Publication Data
Franco, Jere' Bishop, 1948–
Crossing the pond: the native American effort in World War II / Jere' Bishop Franco.
p. cm. – (War and the Southwest series)
Includes bibliographical references and index.
ISBN 1-57441-065-2 (cloth : alk. paper)
1. World War, 1939–1945—Participation, Indian. 2. Indians of North America—History—20th century. I. Title. II. Series.
D810.I5F73 1999 98-44928
940.54'03—dc21 CIP

Design by Angela Schmitt
Cover photos courtesy National Archives

Dedicated to
my children
Brie, Luke, John, James
and
my husband
Arturo

Contents

Preface

"Crossing the Pond" is a term which Native Americans used to describe the process of being transferred overseas for military duty during World War II. This was both an event and a duty taken quite seriously by American Indians who participated in every aspect of wartime America. On the American home front Native Americans gave comparable and sometimes exemplary contributions to civilian defense work, Red Cross drives, and war bond purchases despite a severe labor shortage on most reservations. Their story, however, reaches far beyond these normal, mainstream activities. Native Americans also resisted a serious propaganda effort by Nazi spies, discovered themselves stereotyped in the media as uncivilized and exotic, and in return, offered their own views of white society. Finally, American Indians took advantage of the wartime and postwar era to gain political, economic and educational opportunities.

Nevertheless this is not a treatise on assimilation and acculturation. In every respect, Native Americans never lost the view of themselves as Indians and as tribal members. Furthermore the majority of American Indians intended to return to their reservations after the war, where they believed they would participate in "a better America" as the "First Americans." The significance of their participation can be summarized as role modeling. They provided role models not simply for a later generation of American Indians, but also for a generation of non-Indian Americans.

Native American veteran leadership has been largely discounted in the last four decades. Today few people are aware of the contributions made by Native Americans in the war, with the exception of the occasional history buff who has heard of the Navajo Codetalkers. Because of this lack of awareness, Native Americans are still confronted with sterotypes shaped by the white media and corporate America. On a more positive note, however, young American Indians, who have always been taught their history through oral histories and family traditions, now have the opportunity to learn their history in high school classes and college courses.

This book would not have been possible without the help of many friends, both professional and personal. Among the professionals, I owe immense thanks to several archivists who took a personal interest in this project. While researching in the Washington, D. C., National Archives, I met Richard Boylen, who helped me locate some valuable information on tribal resources. Unfortunately we were unable to locate any information in the Federal Employment Practices Commission that summer. A couple of years later, I received an unexpected package from Richard containing information on an unfair employment complaint from a Native American. Because Richard was gracious enough to remember my research, this information became a vital aspect in the chapter on Indian laborers.

Through the Tigua Indians of El Paso, Texas, I became acquainted with Jerrald Anderson, a Pentagon employee who was also studying Native American war participation. For several years, we shared research material and anecdotes. At the Santa Fe Records Center, archivists Lee Goodwin and José Villegas spent their valuable time reviewing the contents of their files, copying letters and photographs, and sending the material to me. It was enormously helpful in a year when my youngest child had two serious hospitalizations, and travel was out of the question. The material they furnished provided the foundation for the chapter on the Santa Fe Indian Club. In the computer department at the University of Texas at El Paso, education major Susan Snell patiently aided my efforts to scan the manuscript and make disk copies.

After the American Heritage Center in Laramie, Wyoming, offered me a travel grant to use their resources, Archivist Rick Ewig was kind enough to ask me to return to Wyoming's World War II Commemoration to speak about the Wind River Reservation. Again they paid my travel and an honorarium. This was the only financial aid received during my entire research. I can truly say that the state of Wyoming gave me one hundred percent of my research funds.

Several colleagues have provided invaluable support. At the University of Arizona, Paul Carter and Harwood Hinton in the History Department, and Tom Holm in the American Indian Studies Department, have aided my research efforts by offering scholarly advice. I owe the most thanks, however, to Richard Cosgrove, who gave me personal advice and encouraged me to succeed.

I wrote this book out of love for Native American history, and no one understands that love better than my family. For my cousin, Marcie Bowling, who always believed in me even when I didn't believe in myself, I have the utmost gratitude. For my children, Brie, Luke, John, and James, who literally "grew up" with this project and listened to countless stories about my research, I offer my whole-hearted appreciation. Finally, for my husband, Arturo, who encouraged me to pursue my doctorate, who never allowed me to acquiesce, and who, upon learning that my book had been accepted for publication, demanded to know what my *next* project would be, I can only say, "this is for you."

Introduction

Native American history has traditionally been compartmentalized into three categories: federal policy, Indian/white relations, and white viewpoints of Indians. For several years the area of federal policy was dominated by Francis Paul Prucha and Vine Deloria, Jr., who described the increasing bureaucratization of Indian affairs throughout the nineteenth and twentieth centuries. Indian/white relations typically consisted of white and Native American warfare as depicted in Robert Utley's *The Last Days of the Sioux Nation*. Robert Berkhofer's *The White Man's Indian* exemplified the quintessential stereotypical viewpoints of Native Americans by the mainstream society from the Columbian period to the era of movies and television. All other works, whether discussing education, pan-Indianism, or reservation lifestyle, appeared to fall under the rubric of at least one of these three areas.

In the past decade, however, several books have been published which seem to defy clear-cut categorization. Granted, these new works do fulfill some of the criteria for one or another of the traditional three categories. Although they do include the usual issues subsumed under policy, education and legislation, for example, and probably offer a few new white viewpoints concerning Native Americans, it is the area of Indian/white relations which has undergone the most dramatic transformation. Warfare between Native American tribes and American whites is no longer represented as a delineating thesis. The most recent research instead explores the reciprocal relationship between Indians and whites when they confront battle as colleagues and not as enemies. As oral histories, interviews and letters are increasingly employed, historians now encounter Indian viewpoints of whites, as well as white viewpoints of Indians. Focusing on the apprehensive and complex attitudes which accompany the onset of war rather than on actual military strategy, historians have begun to explore the ambivalence which occurs when a society suddenly realizes it is fighting *with* rather than *against* a particular group of people.

In *Between Two Fires: American Indians in the Civil War*, Laurence Hauptman explores the diverse reasons for Native American enlistment in both the northern and southern armies. Hauptman agrees with Tom Holm that Indians enlisted for reasons that included economics, status, and their need to feel useful to the white community. Furthermore, he concludes that American Indians chose military service in order to ensure their own future survival. Utilizing military records at national and state levels, Professor Hauptman researched log books, muster rolls, pension records and regimental books in the East, the Midwest and the South, in order to gain an in-depth personalized account of Native American participation in the Civil War.

Thomas Britten, *American Indians in World War I*, contends that "an examination of Native American roles in World War I is essential if one hopes to understand the evolution of Indian societies, cultures and federal Indian policy in the early decades of the twentieth century." Britten forcefully describes an American public which exhibited high expectations of Native Americans as soldiers and, at the same time, manifested racial stereotypes which would be resurrected in the next world war. Indian experiences in World War I are so similar to those in World War II that it seems futile to recount them. These similarities, however, which include significant home front contributions, only prove that Indian lifestyle had changed remarkably little in the intervening years despite high level administrative changes in the Bureau of Indian Affairs. Basing his research on several Doris Duke Oral History Collections in New Mexico, South Dakota, Utah and Oklahoma, Britten reminds readers that Native Americans had a longstanding duality in their warfaring tradition, both their own and that experienced through American institutions, particularly in military schools and in the U. S. Army as scouts.

Alison Bernstein's, *American Indians and World War II: Toward a New Era in Indian Affairs*, also devotes time to the American Indian experience both in war and on the home front, but she goes further in describing a political dialogue on the national level concerning the role of Native Americans during the international crisis. Professor Bernstein relied strongly on archival collections including those of John Collier, the American Civil Liberties Union and the National Association of Indian Affairs, and contrasted these viewpoints with research from congressional documents to present an intensive analysis of the wartime debate concerning American Indian assimilation. She effectively argues that "World War II had a more profound and lasting effect on the course of Indian affairs in this century than any other single event or period."

Tom Holm's *Strong Hearts, Wounded Souls: The Native American Veterans of the Vietnam War* draws heavily on first-hand oral interviews with veterans to encapsulate the experiences of American Indians in this devastating war. Using psychotherapeutic techniques to evaluate the predominance of post-traumatic stress disorder in Native American veterans, Professor Holm, a Cherokee Vietnam veteran, discovered that this methodology also led to a "deeper appreciation of our own Native American traditions and ceremonies." He places the Native American experience not only within the context of the longest undeclared war in America's history but also within the context of the anti-war movement.

These historians have varied theses and employ differing methodologies to disseminate their viewpoints, but they have one common thread. They are not interested in Native American servicemen and women simply as another useful component in military strategy. They have instead related the uniqueness of the American Indian role in America's wars. In a recent article published in *Western Historical Quarterly*, Sherry Smith argues that this declining emphasis on the military aspect of Western History has created a void which cannot simply be replaced with a "race-class-gender trinity." Rather, Professor Smith contends that advocates of the "New Western History" approach should analyze *relationships* between ethnic groups, the military, and the government in order to achieve a more balanced historical perspective.

Perhaps this is the inherent problem in confronting the new research. None of it seems to fall strictly under the rubric of "Western History." *Between Two Fires* tells us more about Indian viewpoints of slavery than about Native Americans in the West; *American Indians and World War II* gives us a nationally-based and not a regionally-based political perspective on Native Americans; Britten's work, which compares the treatment of Native Americans with the treatment of African-Americans and Mexican-Americans in World War I, could be used in the broader context of ethnohistory as much as American Indian history; and Tom Holm's Vietnam treatise could be subsumed under the anti-war movement or the civil rights movements of the 1960s. It is as if Native American studies as a subject, particularly this new research, has outgrown the boundaries of traditional definition. "Native Americans and Wartime" can no longer be solely claimed as a prerogative of Western History, and it does not solely subsist within the *policy-viewpoints-warfare* triad. It has moved beyond regionalism and prior classification to achieve national and even international implications.

Obviously much is left to be done in this new genre concerning research and analysis. Several national and state archives have yet to be explored, state historical societies have untapped resources in manuscript and oral history collections, and local libraries often have surprising collections of personal reminiscences in the form of letters and diaries. Furthermore, twentieth-century historians, operating within the most documented and recorded era of mankind's history, have a wealth of resources in as yet unused radio transcripts, films, and documentary television footage.

Further evaluation is also necessary. While the initial stories have been told, comparative studies, such as tribe versus tribe, whites versus Indians and regional comparisons, have not been attempted. In addition, the viewpoints which our allies and enemies abroad had of Native Americans, and vice-versa, would be an intriguing project. The roles played by Native American women, who have countless untold stories of their participation in the war and on the homefront, also need to be explored. These are the challenges for future studies and future historians.

It is my hope that with this study, I have contributed to the historiography of "Native Americans in Wartime." Without apology I accept that it is incomplete. Perhaps no historical work is ever complete. That is the ultimate challenge.

The Swastika Shadow over Native America: John Collier and the AIF

"I understand that Colin Ross, whom you know, is a Nazi and you should be governed accordingly." With this terse note, Secretary of the Interior Harold Ickes informed Commissioner of Indian Affairs John Collier that the latter had unknowingly dealt with a German agent of Hitler's regime. The 1939 incident embarrassed Collier and highlighted the bizarre relationship between Collier, Native Americans, and pro-Fascist groups. This relationship developed when the American Indian Federation (AIF), an assimilationist pan-Indian organization dedicated to the abolition of the Indian Bureau, turned to pro-Fascist, anti-Semitic groups for funding and for help in criticizing Collier's patriotism and alleging his Communism. Following their own hidden agenda to undermine the Roosevelt administration, these Fascist groups—which included the German-American Bund, the Militant Christian Patriots, and the Silver Shirts—drew the AIF leaders, especially Alice Lee Jemison, into a complex, controversial conspiracy.[1]

This alliance between Nazis and Indian Bureau critics degenerated when several participants experienced exposure, prosecution, or deportation. Failing to attain its goals, the AIF nevertheless distracted the Commissioner from business-as-usual with a continual barrage of publicity and demands for Congressional Committee Hearings. Although Collier asserted that the Federation had no grounds for criticism, the constant attacks on his patriotism and the management of his administration eventually led to his participation in a massive drive to recruit Indians for Selective Service registration.[2]

The majority of these critics had opposed both the newly-elected president, Franklin Delano Roosevelt, and the man he chose to head the Bureau of Indian Affairs, John Collier, because Roosevelt and other New Deal reformers intended to reverse government policies which they considered to be detrimental to Indian tribes. The public first learned of these abuses when President Herbert Hoover released the reports of the 1928 Merriam Commission, revealing that the 1887 Dawes Act allotting lands to Indian reservations had nearly destroyed tribal cultures in order to achieve a policy of assimilation. It had not only failed to acculturate the American Indian, but it had almost decimated their tribal economies. National polls revealed that Indians earned less than half that of the white population, and Congressional committee hearings uncovered disturbing statistics of checkerboarding, illegal leasing, and questionable sales of Indian land which resulted in the loss of over ninety million acres. In addition, Native American health had deteriorated, as evidenced by the fact that nationwide, Indians held the highest rates of infant mortality, tuberculosis, alcoholism, and trachoma. Native American children, other victims of the Dawes Act, had been forced into boarding and mission schools for decades, but nationally still possessed the lowest high school graduation rates and the highest illiteracy rates. Progressives and New Dealers alike intended to rectify these injustices.[3]

After Roosevelt was elected, Senator Burton K. Wheeler, Democrat from Montana, cooperated with the American Civil Liberties Union and John Collier to guide through Congress the Indian Reorganization Act of 1934. This act intended to reverse many of the policies of the Dawes Act, including the right of a tribe, if they voted to come under the jurisdiction of the act, to return all individual allotments to tribal ownership for communal benefit. The Wheeler-Howard Act, as it was sometimes termed, also provided for an Indian Arts and Crafts Board to encourage the revitalization of Indian culture and skills, the building of day schools on reservations to encourage more attendance, and a revolving loan fund for tribal enterprises.[4]

John Collier appeared to be the ideal man to serve as Commissioner of the Indian Bureau and thus, head of the Indian New Deal program. Widely traveled, well-educated, and a prolific writer, he had developed personal relationships from all walks of life. From 1907–1920 Collier had served as a community organizer with the People's Institute in New York City, where he helped immigrants assimilate into the American mainstream. He used this experience to his advantage in San Francisco as the Director of Social Science Training at the State Teacher's College. A native of Georgia, the new commissioner had graduated from Columbia University in New York, where he developed a liberal, humanistic philosophy. During the 1920s, he and other eastern intellectuals such as D. H. Lawrence, Mabel Dodge and Georgia O'Keefe, had visited Southwestern Pueblo villages in New Mexico, where they encountered unique Indian cultures. Almost mystically impressed with the heritage of the Pueblo, Navajo, and Zuni, Collier later incorporated many of their tribal values into his Indian Bureau policies. Branded as "intensely serious, idealistic, and feisty," Collier remained, above all else, dedicated to the success of the Indian Reorganization Act.[5]

Ironically it was Collier's intense dedication and single-mindedness which through the years resulted in a storm of opposition from tribes, Congressmen, and various other groups. By far the most vocal Indian opposition to the Bureau of Indian Affairs came from the American Indian Federation. Certainly many tribes had grounds for criticism of the Indian Bureau, such as the New York Seneca and the Southwestern Navajo, who openly rejected the Indian Reorganization Act, and the California Mission

Indians, who claimed that the Wheeler-Howard Act had been forced upon them. While Americans on the fringes of mainstream politics flirted with both left-wing and right-wing ideologies, some of these radical groups joined organizations in criticizing the Indian Bureau for failing to advance the American Indian economically, educationally, and medically. A counterpart to extreme right-wing groups which burgeoned in the Depression years, the American Indian Federation organized in 1934 in reaction to the Wheeler-Howard Act. This group, which adhered to the policies of Dr. Carlos Montezuma, a former Apache Indian Bureau physician who believed in abolishing the Bureau, elected Joseph Bruner, a full-blood Creek from Sapulpa, Oklahoma, with business interests in oil and real estate, as president. Collier, however, believed that O. K. Chandler, a Cherokee from Oklahoma, held the real power in the group.[6]

Chandler's motives for opposition to the Indian Bureau could be traced in part to old grievances with the department. In 1933 he had lobbied the new commissioner for a position with the Indian Bureau by offering to report on Oklahoma officeholders in whom the Bureau had expressed an interest. After sending some recommendations, generally negative and unsubstantiated according to Collier, he then extolled the virtues of the Indian Bureau to the Solicitor of the Department of the Interior, Nathan Margold. "You enter the Indian Bureau through the front door now," Chandler wrote Margold. "The Solicitor of the Interior Department is honest, has legal ability, and horse sense." Despite this flattery, Collier refused to grant Chandler an appointment.[7]

Collier's reservations about Chandler stemmed from several sources. He claimed that the previous Indian Bureau had denied Chandler Civil Service status for trading with Indians, a privilege not accorded to government employees. Although Collier refused restoration of status, this failed to stop Chandler from urging the commissioner to send checks belonging to several Oklahoma Indians directly to himself. Asserting that these Indians were "clients," Chandler charged a fifty percent commission for collecting checks. After reviewing the circumstances, Collier again refused to cooperate.[8]

By 1934 Chandler had relinquished his goal of obtaining employment with the Indian Bureau and had instead become one of its vocal critics. In the spring of 1934 Joseph Bruner had issued a public statement accusing Collier of advocating Communism and atheism on Indian reservations and in Indian schools. Joining forces with Bruner, Chandler helped form the AIF in Washington, D. C. on June 8, 1934. Two months later they held the first national conference in Gallup, New Mexico, which was attended by Native Americans from New Mexico, Arizona, California and Oklahoma. After electing Bruner president, the group formulated plans to continue its opposition to Collier and the Indian Reorganization Act. Citing Collier's past relationship with the American Civil Liberties Union and Roger Baldwin, considered by the AIF to uphold the ideals of Communism and atheism, the Federation requested a hearing with the House Committee on Indian Affairs.[9]

Held in February, 1935, the hearings offered Chandler the opportunity to exhibit the tactics the AIF would employ throughout the decade. While Bruner and colleagues openly testified and criticized the Indian Bureau, Chandler operated behind the scenes, writing articles and sending petitions to Congressmen. Bruner received valuable aid from the newly-elected Federation secretary, Alice Lee Jemison, a forthright speaker at the hearings. Born in 1902, the half-Senecan Jemison had been raised in a white community. Briefly married to another Seneca, Verne L. Jemison of the Cataraugas Reservation in New York, Jemison left him in 1928, taking their two children. Her marital status remained vague throughout the years. In 1938 she claimed to be married to a Washington, D. C. taxi driver, but two years later she once again named Jemison as her husband. In addition, her tribal status remained unclear. At times she claimed to be Cherokee.[10]

Jemison and Bruner agreed that the basic issue was "the bill which the Bureau forced through at the very close of the last session of Congress [in 1934]." The Federation Secretary expressed her fear that the construction of the bill would allow transients on Indian reservations to vote favorably for passage. She specifically cited her own Seneca Reservation which housed Cayugas, Onondagas, Mohawks, and Oneidas, in addition to legitimate tribal members. Because of this mixture, she suspected that the Seneca Nation would accept the Wheeler-Howard Act, which she considered exploitative. Testifying about Collier's nature, she added:

> My people always regarded Mr. Collier as a man who was trying to push himself forward, trying to exploit the Indian, trying to solicit funds for his organization, by holding forth to the people the Indian in his primitive state. . . . We looked upon him as a man who was soliciting money at the expense of ignorant Indians and spreading propaganda to the effect that these Indians must be kept as wards, poor savages that they are.[11]

Bruner agreed that Collier was spreading propaganda by further charging that the Commissioner published *Indians at Work*, an interdepartmental pamphlet, "to publicize himself and not to promote the welfare of the Indians of the government." Furthermore, Bruner asserted that Collier practiced "isolating, segregating and race-prejudice commitments." He referred particularly to Collier's attempts to revive Indian traditions with the establishment of an Indian Arts and Crafts Board. Bruner concurred with Jemison that certain groups coerced the Wheeler-Howard Act through Congress. "The fundamental ideas of the commissioner's plan or program are Communistic," he declared, "and had their origins in . . . the American Civil Liberties Union . . . prior to the commissioner's appointment." He further stated that the ACLU had been "constant defenders of Communists throughout America."[12]

Bruner also criticized Collier's character. American Indians, he insisted, liked their commissioner "to have a good reputation." Producing evidence which revealed that Collier harbored atheistic, radical sympathies, Bruner attested that these values were not in accordance with Native American traditions. Indeed Collier's background, lifestyle, and friendships did suggest an atypical environment. While working in New York as a social scientist, Collier had befriended such personalities as Mabel Dodge, who conducted a fashionable Fifth Avenue salon for intellectuals. At these salons, Collier met Isadora Duncan, the free-style dancer who enjoyed a comparably free lifestyle; John Reed, the radical editor of *The Masses*; and Walter Lippmann, Harvard social critic. These stimulating friendships—combined with a privileged southern background, an eastern education at Columbia University, and a penchant for humanitarian reform—enabled the Commissioner to develop an eclectic and complex philosophy of life which was easily labeled as liberal.[13]

Bruner exploited Collier's vulnerability as a free-thinker by producing two poems which Collier had written in earlier years. The first poem eulogized a Spanish anarchist, Francisco Ferrer; the second he had written to Isadora Duncan, an avowed atheist. Bruner asserted that these poems proved that Communism and atheism had infiltrated the Indian Service. Answering these charges, Collier admitted that he favored an international and interdisciplinary approach when dealing with American Indians and had solicited advice from various professionals in other countries. In 1934 the commissioner paid Dr. Moises Saenz, an educator with the Mexican Indian Program, a fee of $1,500 to visit Washington, D. C., and advise the Indian Bureau about instructional methodology. Furthermore Collier hired Mexican-trained women to organize community centers for Arizona Indians. Bruner objected to any use of Mexican-trained professionals, because Mexico required teachers to sign an oath stating that they were atheists. His reasons for objecting to Collier's use of professionals from Turkey, China, and even Canada and the territory of Alaska remained obscure but seemed to result from xenophobia.[14]

During the February 1935 hearings, Bruner found another valuable witness in Frederick Collett. Because he was white, Collett had been unable to join the AIF, but his organization, the Mission

Indians of California, had aided in establishing the Federation. In 1910 Collett formed the Indian Board of Cooperation in San Francisco, named himself executive representative, and began researching California Indian treaties. Ordained in 1911 as a Congregational minister, Collett occasionally preached but never held a pastorage. By 1934 he had uncovered eighteen treaties, and immediately brought suit for the Indians in the United States Court of Claims. Despite the fact that he considered his work "eleemosynary," the missionary collected thirty-six dollars or more from each Indian who expressed an interest in the court suit.[15]

Collett, who resented Bureau interference in his claims' suits, also desired to abolish the Indian Service. He particularly objected when Congress, with Collier's support, passed the Jurisdictional Act, which named the California Attorney General as the Indians' legal representative. The missionary felt that the twelve million dollars awarded in the suit should be paid directly to the Mission Indians and not held in trust at the discretion of the Secretary of the Interior. Finally, Collett brought a legal suit against Collier for claiming in an April 15, 1935 issue of *Indians at Work* that the missionary had been disbarred from the Indian Service. Collett asserted that he had never made application to appear before the Interior Department and therefore could not be disbarred. When the *Washington Times* printed Collier's remarks about Collett, the missionary sued the newspaper for libel.[16]

At the 1935 hearing, some Congessmen also aligned with members of the AIF in their attacks on Collier and the Indian Bureau. John Steven McGroarty, California representative who had been a lawyer, journalist, and businessman, agreed with Joseph Bruner on such basic issues as terminating federal aid, lifting restrictions on Indian land, and taxing Indian land. Usher Burdick, Republican representative from North Dakota, had been raised among Sioux Indians. His background included not only political positions, such as North Dakota Lieutenant Governor and District Attorney, but also experience in ranching and farming. Burdick, part Indian, showed considerable sympathy for Indian witnesses and questioned Collier's attitude toward the AIF, which numbered over 1,140 members. "The Commissioner seems to be very hostile to any organization of Indians that seek[s] to appear before the Committee," he commented, "and I was wondering why that antagonism."[17]

Collett found a powerful and influential benefactor in Senator Burton K. Wheeler, the Democratic Senator from Montana who had originally sponsored the Indian Reorganization Act, but for reasons he never fully explained, soon became a staunch advocate for repeal. Although Assistant Commissioner William Zimmerman attributed this about-face to "personal spite and resentment," Wheeler justified his reversal because of reservations concerning the bill. "I must confess," he reminisced years later, "that there was one bill I was not proud of having enacted." Claiming that he had introduced the bill at Collier's behest without reading it, the Senator asserted that he disapproved of many provisions, including the separate judicial system for Indians, the replacement of the old tribal council with executive officers, and what he felt was the undue influence of mixed-bloods who exploited the full bloods.[18]

Collier, however, began to suspect that Collett had gained some influence over the Senator, who openly endorsed the missionary's request for private attorneys in the California Indian Claims Case. Wheeler, nicknamed "Bolshevik Burt" for his opposition to the powerful Montana Anaconda Copper Mining Company, had gained a reputation in Washington as an independent champion of the underdog. In a strange twist of fate, Wheeler's political ideologies closely mirrored Collier's own beliefs. Previously an advocate of Russian recognition, the Senator generally opposed big business, favored the working class, and represented the Populist-Progressive tradition. Now viewing Collier as the entrenched bureaucrat, Wheeler supported Collett's interests with all the political clout he could muster.[19]

Anxious to dispel his image as antagonistic, Collier carefully defended his policies. First, he explained that "floaters"—Indians who moved on and off the reservation—could not vote on the Wheeler-Howard Act, because only Indians legitimately registered on tribal rolls were allowed to vote. He further defended the Indian Reorganization Act and the Indian Bureau as examples of Indian self-determination by stating:

> Summary abolishment or renunciation of government responsibility is neither politically nor legally practicable. . . . [W]e [have] to work out within the guardianship or trusteeship some objective whereby we could substitute Indian self-rule for the dictatorial management of the federal government.[20]

Second, Collier justified his use of Mexican professionals by emphatically denying any knowledge that Mexican teachers had to take an oath of atheism. Furthermore, he argued, Indian schools followed no such policy. The commissioner continued throughout his tenure to profess great admiration for Mexico's Indian policy in land reform, literacy and health, all issues high on his agenda. When pressed to explain his personal beliefs, however, Collier hesitated. Discussions of his religious and political affiliations obviously rendered him uncomfortable. While he reluctantly admitted that he considered himself to be religious and denied being an atheist, he proved even more evasive when questioned about his association with the American Civil Liberties Union. "I do not remember whether I was [a member]," he stated, "but I am wholly in sympathy with that organization . . . because it is devoted to one cause, the establishment of the constitutional rights of free speech and the free press against all attacks."[21]

Impassioned constitutional arguments won Collier many allies. Abe Murdock, Democratic representative from Utah and a Mormon, had served as County Attorney and City Attorney of Beaver, Utah, before entering Congress. He expressed the sentiment that many of the complaints lodged against the commissioner were immaterial, particularly those concerning his political beliefs. Murdock patiently explained that one might eulogize a man like Francisco Ferrer in a "general" way while remaining unconverted to his anarchistic philosophy. Knute Hill, representative from Washington and a former teacher, lawyer, and farmer, reacted strongly to "unsubstantiated" complaints from the AIF and suspected that the organization was ridiculing Congressmen for being "duped" by Collier. "We were not coerced," he sternly lectured Bruner. "We knew exactly what we were doing. We and not Mr. Collier passed that law." Murdock spoke up in agreement.[22]

By the end of the February 1935 hearings, the AIF had established the basic framework of confrontation which they would continue for several years until just before the attack on Pearl Harbor. Through the use of publications, conferences, and congressional hearings, they constantly reiterated their basic themes that Collier and the Indian Bureau espoused Communism, atheism, and tribalism. From 1935 until 1940, Collier fought mainly on the defensive. His forays into the offensive yielded not so much an exoneration of his administration as an exposé of a Fascist propaganda network among Indian Bureau critics.[23]

After the hearings, Collier wasted little time initiating investigations of the Federation's witnesses. His inquiries about Jemison proved particularly fruitful. Jemison herself claimed that the Senecas had questioned her motives for five years but now considered her so reliable that they had once paid her one hundred dollars. William Harrison, Special Agent at the New York Agency in Salamanca, New York, disagreed and informed his superior that the Seneca Council had not authorized Jemison to represent them at the hearings. "Mrs. Jemison seems inclined to agitate and to be on the off side," Harrison told Collier.[24] Conflicting but equally damaging information came from John Snyder, a Seneca attorney in Irving, New York, and a strong Collier supporter, who told Collier he suspected a conspiracy involving Jemison. He reported that she had failed to mention the Wheeler-Howard Act to the twelve Seneca councilmen who signed the petition she presented at the hearings. The lawyer detailed a relationship between Jemison, several white town sites on the reservation power lines, and gas companies who had secured "grants of questionable character." Snyder proposed that the persons involved in this issue opposed the Indian Reorganization Act because it would authorize the Indian Bureau to investigate their practices. In a further complication, Snyder suspected that the Lattimer Law Office, for whom Jemison had once worked, represented the Niagara and Hudson Power Company, which had vested interests on the Seneca reservation. Through Jemison, charged Snyder, Attorney Joe Lattimer had tried to secure the endorsement of the Seneca Council for the post of Commissioner of Indian Affairs. Snyder, however, had prevented this recommendation. "They seem to be working to create the Department's prejudice against New York Indians," Snyder concluded, "so that nothing will be done for them."[25]

In 1936 Collier uncovered more questionable practices, these concerning Bruner. For some time Bruner had designated himself "principal chief" of the Creek Nation, but Collier found that "at the tribal election of the Creek Nation held September 14 last, Mr. Bruner was not even among the candidates who trailed at the election." The commissioner also discovered evidence that Bruner had performed the same kind of "collection" system practiced by Chandler. After identifying certain Indians to whom government checks were due, Bruner would offer to collect the money for a fifty percent commission. If an Indian failed to pay, Bruner would "dun" him by letter.[26]

Collier's first discovery of a link between the AIF and Fascist groups occurred in July, 1936, when the Federation held its national conference in Salt Lake City, Utah. The commissioner contacted Field Representative Floyd La Rouche, stationed at the Carson Indian Agency in Stewart, Nevada, and requested that he attend the conference. La Rouche's reports to Collier contained critical reviews of participants and proceedings, identifying Bruner as "a good natured and not-too-intelligent" front, and Chandler as someone who "until recently kept himself in the background of the Federation, [but] now frankly runs the show. Nothing of the Cherokee is visible in this zealot." La Rouche further added that nothing Indian seemed to be visible at the "aimless, leaderless and drab" conference. Other observers, he claimed, noted that some of the older Indian participants seemed "bewildered and disappointed" at the speeches, which "rambled hither and yon aimlessly."[27] La Rouche further questioned the real purpose of the convention and believed that the financing came from "some unnamed organizations who sought to use the activities of this paper organization (and the tremendous energies of Mr. Chandler) to advance certain undisclosed purposes of their own." The agent noted that fewer than thirty people attended the convention, that only a few of those in attendance were Indians, and that out of the one hundred speeches presented, only a few even mentioned Indians. Instead, the convention seemed dedicated "to a death battle against John Collier," and it eventually emerged as "a thinly-disguised segment of a national anti-Communist drive."[28]

Certainly the convention literature, available through printed speeches or pamphlets, appeared to support La Rouche's viewpoint. Pamphlets such as "Negroes in America," written by James Ford and James Allen, hinted at racial bias, a viewpoint subscribed to by some AIF members. That fall, for example, Bruner complained when the Indian Service appointed May Parker, a Black nurse, to serve at the Sequoyah Orphan Indian Training School in Talequah, Oklahoma. Citing the laws of Oklahoma requiring school segregation, he demanded her removal. Furthermore, Bruner criticized Indian textbooks which supposedly stated that Thomas Jefferson and John Tyler had fathered children by their slave mistresses. In response, the Interior Department refused to change either their personnel or their textbooks.[29]

Much of the convention literature revealed strong anti-Semitic and pro-Fascist philosophies which were also at odds with Interior Department policy. "Communism with the Mask Off," a speech written by Dr. Joseph Paul Goebbels and delivered in Nuremberg on September 13, 1935, at the 70th National Socialist Party Congress, exhibited the Fascist fixation concerning the threat of a Communist dictatorship in Germany. American writers also condemned domestic threats to nationalism. Gerald Winrod, a Baptist minister who had never held a pastorate, visited Germany in 1934. Thoroughly infatuated with the new Führer, he immediately converted to Hitler's cause. When he returned to America, he began publishing two pro-Fascist, anti-Semitic and anti-Catholic journals. At the convention Winrod distributed an article describing Franklin Roosevelt's presidency as a dictatorship, and later endorsed the Federation's anti-Indian Bureau stand by publishing articles written by Chandler and Jemison. By 1938 Winrod's Fascist sympathies had became so pronounced that he alarmed mainstream politicians when he endeavored to run for the Senate. Although Winrod was an outspoken critic of John Collier's administration, John Hamilton, Chairman of the Republican National Committee and another strong Collier critic, refused to endorse him because of his extreme racism.[30]

After the convention, the Federation continued making contacts with pro-Fascist groups. A smaller conference, held later the same year, also addressed few Indian issues, according to Collier's informants. In Lewiston, Idaho, Federation officers met a representative of William Dudley Pelley, who would prove to be a significant ally. Pelley, a native of Asheville, North Carolina, possessed a rather eclectic background with many similarities to Gerald Winrod. On January 31, 1933, one day after Hitler assumed power in Germany, Pelley created and headed a nationwide American organization called the Silver Shirts of Christian American Patriots. Pelley modeled his group on Hitler's Brown Shirts, an anti-Semitic, militaristic organization. An ordained Protestant minister, Pelley published a journal called *The Liberation,* which he used to attack the Jewish population, calling for their nationwide disenfranchisement, disbarment from professions, and segregation from society.[31] In 1935, a North Carolina court fined Pelley for publishing and distributing his pro-Fascist, anti-Semitic literature, which they claimed appealed to the "basest prejudices." Because copies of *The Liberation* were available in Germany, the court claimed that "sinister foreign sources" financed the literature. After paying the fine, Pelley continued his attacks on Roosevelt's administration, which he claimed was dominated by "Jew Kissers." Pelley's slurs represented a peculiar segment of the population, including some members of the AIF, who believed that Roosevelt's administration had too dearly embraced Judaism and Catholicism. After making contact with the Federation at the Idaho conference, Pelley began pubishing articles in *The Liberation* attacking the Indian Bureau.[32]

Encouraged by this support, Federation members increased their efforts to receive aid from more legitimate organizations in 1936, but failed to gain endorsements from recognized mainstream groups. An initial attempt was made when the Reverend Floyd Burnett, Federation Chaplain, approached Mrs. Richard Codman, State Chairman for Indian Citizenship with the Daughters of the American Revolution in Fair Oaks, California. Codman, a strong Collier supporter, harbored suspicions about Burnett, who had recently been disbarred by the Board of Missions from his missionary post at the Sherman Institute because he was using school equipment to disseminate anti-Collier literature. She immediately warned her professional colleagues of Burnett's intentions to gain approval for the AIF. Matthew K. Sniffen, the National Secretary of the Indian Rights Association, agreed with Codman in denouncing the Federation as exploitative and misleading.[33]

Edith Murphey, State Chairman, Indian Welfare, California Federation of Women's Clubs, harbored even stronger feelings about the Federation. Asserting that the Indian Service had recently discharged many of the Federation's members, Codman argued that the largely mixed-blood group desired to "profiteer and graft on the older Indians." Murphey then advised one of her district officers not to speak at the Federation Convention in an official capacity, which prompted that officer to complain to Burnett. Although the Reverend also appealed to Murphey's superior officer, the officer upheld Murphey's decision. Jemison also unsuccessfully complained when Murphey prohibited a Federation member from speaking at a 1936 Women's Club Meeting in California.[34]

Codman's and Murphey's resistance to the AIF stemmed, in part, from their antagonism toward Frederick Collett, with whom the Federation had created strong ties. Although Collett still maintained some Indian clients, his following had declined. Collier supporters attributed this decline to a suspicion on the part of Native Americans as to Collett's true intentions. Mission Indian Stella Von Bulow stated that the missionary had refused to show members the contract for the Indian Board of Cooperation, because he said they would not understand it. When Collett further insisted that members must pay fees to share in the settlement, many left his organization. In March 1937, La Rouche obtained documents dated 1920, which revealed "a confederation between J. W. Henderson [an attorney from the Indian Bureau of Cooperation] and Collett." In these letters, the missionary asked his attorney what percentage he could make in presenting Indian claims. Furthermore, Collett asked for viable explanations to continue soliciting money from his clients. By 1940 this would amount to $181,000. He obtained the majority of these funds, $156,000, from California Indians.[35]

By 1937 the questionable methods of both the AIF and the Indian Board of Cooperation had created disillusionment among the California Indians. The Mission Indian Federation complained when Jemison presumed to represent them at a Congressional Committee Hearing, resisted when the Federation lawyer Thomas Sloan (an Omaha Indian) demanded that Indians dealing with him sign irrevocable contracts, and finally withdrew from the AIF. "Wherever this American Federation could do so," Murphey stated, "it has taken a leaf out of Collett's book and sowed the seeds of doubt and distrust . . . in the Indians' hearts." With thirty-two years experience working among Indians, she viewed Collett as an exploitative, unscrupulous agitator who was "not above collecting money from Indians who are dependent on County aid." Based on this evidence and because her sympathies lay with Collier, Murphey suggested to her national president that their group avoid siding with factions.[36]

Finding their efforts thwarted in developing mainstream alliances, the Federation soon gained attention from other sources. Henry Allen, a colleague of both Collett and Pelley, proved especially useful in introducing Jemison to financial contributors.

Throughout his twenty-eight-year career, Allen had served terms at Folsom and San Quentin Prisons, smuggled arms across the Mexican Border, and organized the American White Guardsmen (the United States unit of Mexico's outlawed Gold Shirts who were comparable to Pelley's Silver Shirts). Although the timing is unclear, it seems certain that he informed a wealthy industrialist, James True, about the Federation and about Alice Lee Jemison's writing abilities. True, a pro-Fascist, anti-Semitic, who had founded America First with Michael Ahearn and published four-page weekly industrial reports, also considered the New Deal to be both a Communist and a Jewish conspiracy. In October, 1937, he published an article written by Jemison, whom he referred to as "Pocahontas," and made an appeal on her behalf. Praising her as "a cultured woman of Indian blood and a skillful speaker and writer," he lamented that she could be impoverished, in poor health, without "even the bare necessities of life." The publisher raised sufficient funds to pay her six months' back rent in order that she and her children could return to their apartment. On February 23, 1938, True wrote to Allen thanking him for introducing Jemison. "She is a great character," he said, "and all the Indian patriots with her will be inspired and encouraged by the generosity of your friends (mine too) and the part you have taken in a very wonderful and beautiful work."[37]

Suspicious of such generous support, Collier enlisted the aid of Robert Marshall, an Interior Department employee. Head of the United States Forest Service, Marshall had also received criticism from the AIF because of his past association with the ACLU. Eager to cooperate, he asked a female friend to visit True's headquarters in Washington, D. C., and pretend to share an interest in his work. In the office, True showed Marshall's friend a cudgel with spikes. Referring to this weapon as a "kike killer," True maintained he wanted to patent it and assured her they had a smaller one for female Jews. The distraught woman immediately reported to Marshall.[38]

By early 1938 the Federation had increased its alignment with pro-Fascist groups. In February, Leslie Fry, a member of the Militant Christian Patriots, began publishing Jemison's articles in *The Christian Free Press*. Fry, a.k.a. Princess Shishmereff or Shishmarova who had previously worked with the British Secret Service in Russia, used Allen as an emisssary to send Jemison two payments of one hundred dollars each for her articles. Furthermore, when Jemison, unemployed at the time, purchased a car on July 13, 1938, Collier received documents from Naval Intelligence which indicated that German-American Bund sources had paid for the automobile.[39] Collier suspected that both the pro-Fascist organization and the journal—the latter of which criticized the "appalling, unsanitary, shameful conditions, due to abuse and maladministration" among California Indians—were financed by Elizabeth Stuart Jewett. Jewett, who had formed the American League of Christian Women in 1937, had connections to Henry Allen and William Dudley Pelley. Collier's sources alleged that the British had fired Fry for inefficiency, and she then became a Nazi propaganda agent. In turn, all of the above were associated with the American Nationalist Confederation headed by George Deatherage of St. Albans, West Virginia. Deatherage, born in Russia and educated as an engineer, advocated anti-Semitism, white supremacy, and armed resistance, in his role as the National Commander of the Knights of the White Camellia.[40]

By the summer of 1938, AIF members and Collett openly appeared in the company of pro-Fascist sympathizers. *The California Indian News* published by the California Mission Indians, criticized Collett for visiting Indian reservations in the company of Henry Allen, whom they called "a Nazi organizer and an ex-convict." Furthermore, in August the German-American Bund House in Los Angeles featured Winslow J. Couro, National Treasurer of the Federation, as a guest speaker at a meeting which an undetermined number of American Indians attended. By September, the Los Angeles German-American Bund displayed and distributed Jemison's circular, "The AIF," which advocated "dissolution of the Indian Bureau and the allocation of expenses appropriated for the operation thereof directly to the Indians." That year the Militant Christian Patriots and the German-American Bund joined the AIF in demanding a Congressional Investigation into American Indian conditions.[41]

The German-American Bund, headquartered in Chicago and claiming approximately 25,000 members, distributed propaganda material for Nazi Germany which they received through the World Wide Service. This propaganda agency of the Third Reich served individuals such as James True, William Dudley Pelley, and George Deatherage. Fritz Kuhn, the national president since 1927 and a native of Munich, left Germany after being twice arrested for theft. A chemical engineer at the Ford Motor Company in Chicago, Kuhn also earned three hundred dollars monthly as the Bund president. Considered by many to be Hitler's hand-picked officer, Kuhn had visited Germany in 1936 and contributed three thousand dollars to Hitler's "winter relief" fund. Other officials also maintained close ties to the Third Reich. Hermann Schwinn, who ran the west coast division of the Bund, had trained with Josef Paul Goebbels during a six-week propaganda course, and in 1936 Hitler personally praised him for his good work and effectiveness. At their meetings both Kuhn and Schwinn, reputed to be old Nazi party members, featured the Nazi salute, swastika, uniforms, and an initiation oath swearing allegiance to Hitler. Allen apparently had access to the highest offices of the German-American Bund, because at least once he carried a message from Schwinn to Kuhn, attended social functions with Dr. Gyssling, Los Angeles German Consul, and Dr. Von Kellinger, San Francisco German Consul, as well as speaking to a German-American group in celebration of the Austrian Anschluss.[42]

Another Federation member, E. A. Towner, a Portland attorney and hereditary Hoopa chief, gained attention on January 29, 1939, when the *Morning Oregonian* printed his activities in "A Report on Bund Activity in Oregon." Although the Warm Springs Indian Tribe in Oregon disclaimed any connection with Towner, a.k.a. Chief Red Cloud, the attorney had become a "more or less self-appointed travelling Indian delegate." Many Native Americans, however, declared they cared little for this "loud-talking individual," who actually "did not represent their sentiments."

Throughout the year, Towner, always dressed in traditional costume and displaying a swastika, delivered several speeches at Bund meetings in San Francisco, Los Angeles, Phoenix, Portland and other locations. Claiming that Jews controlled the Indian Service, Chief Red Cloud referred to them as "Children of Satan." He urged his listeners to join the reputed 750,000 Gold-Shirted Indians already active in North, Central, and South America who stood ready to fight against Jews and Communists in the event an insurrection occurred.[43] When speaking at Bund meetings, Towner often compared the German swastika to an ancient symbol used by Indians—the Thunderbird—and concluded that Native Americans also shared both similar governments and anti-Semitic attitudes. Although the Federal Bureau of Investigation claimed that Towner was "considered harmless," at a July 8, 1939, California Indians Meeting in Eureka, California, the attorney almost instigated a riot. Indian Service Field Agent Michael Harrison attended the meeting during which Red Cloud distributed material from the German-American Bund and William Dudley Pelley. The field agent reported that the Indian Rights Association group appeared "pretty heartsick over the whole affair," but "the Collett group were very enthusiastic." Referring to Towner as "a spellbinder and rabble-rouser of the first order," Harrison described the disgust of several members of the local American Federation of Labor. When Towner characterized President Roosevelt as "that dirty, stinking Jew in the White House," many of these union workers had to be forcibly restrained from rushing the stage and attacking the man.[44] Often praising Kuhn and Pelley, Towner also made extensive contacts within the German-American Bund. In the summer of 1939, he traveled to Washington, D. C., to meet George Deatherage. Towner especially approved the military preparedness approach advocated by Deatherage, Pelley, True and Allen.[45]

By the summer of 1938, after such visibility by AIF members, observers were questioning the Federation's financing in a manner similar to Floyd La Rouche's misgivings three years earlier. At the summer conference held by the National AIF in Tulsa,

Oklahoma, the Federation leveled the usual charges of Communism and atheism against the Indian Service. In the presence of a few Republican congressmen, the Federation demanded the resignations of John Collier, Nathan Margold, Harold Ickes, and Secretary of Labor Francis Perkins. Calling the conference "a dismal failure," A. R. Perryman, a Creek Federation member, concluded that Bruner "is not a bad sort . . . but is, I'm afraid, easily misled." In a line of reasoning similar to Floyd La Rouche's misgivings three years earlier, Perryman questioned the convention's financing. "There must be someone back of the movement that has some money," he remarked, "as it costs something to hold these meetings."[46]

Clearly the association with the AIF had well served the purposes of the Third Reich. The Federation provided German propaganda agencies with authentic Native Americans, such as Jemison and Towner, who criticized the United State government in cooperation with American pro-Fascist groups. As part of a Fascist intent to conduct a smear campaign in the United States, the Nazi propagandists promised that Germany would return expropriated land to Native Americans. Convinced that Indians possessed little loyalty to America, Goebbels predicted that they would revolt rather than fight Germany. In a further effort to create an alliance with American Indians, Germany declared that they considered the Sioux, and by extension all Native Americans, to be Aryan. The declaration resulted from a request by a German immigrant, descended from a Sioux grandmother, for German citizenship. Ruling that the immigrant fell within the pale for citizenship, this declaration legitimized Indians as Aryans.[47]

The declaration that Indians were Aryans prompted an immediate denial by Alex Hrdlicka. Hrdlicka, curator of physical anthropology for the Smithsonian Institution, an expert on North American and Central American Indians, and a published author, theorized that Indians migrated either across the Bering Strait or through the Aleutian Islands. Such a migration, accomplished possibly ten or twenty thousand years ago, would imply that Indians descended from either Russian or Chinese ancestry. Therefore, he contended, "by no stretch of the imagination can Indians be considered Aryans." It generated a more heated, sarcastic response from Collier. "Previously the Mormons had been denominating the Indians as 'The Lost Tribe of Israel'," he stated, and added in a paternalistically jealous vein: "Hitler is kidnapping them."[48]

Despite its association with the AIF, the Third Reich preferred to utilize its own agents whenever possible in dealing with Native Americans. In a more subtle approach than that employed by Federation member Towner, Germany attempted to send agents among Indian tribes, posing as anthropologists or writers, in order to learn their culture and languages. German propagandists were particularly interested in learning Indian languages, because they rightfully feared that America would once again use Indian radio operators speaking their tribal languages in the upcoming war as they had done in World War I. At the same time these agents could spread Nazi propaganda and undermine Roosevelt's administrative policies by publicizing unfavorable accounts of American Indian conditions.[49]

One such Nazi agent, Dr. Colin Ross, managed to ingratiate himself at the highest office, when on June 18, 1934, he visited Commissioner John Collier. Representing himself as a correspondent for several German periodicals, Ross told Collier that he had traveled the world studying "the administration of dependent peoples" and had now developed a "deep" interest in Native Americans. Quite impressed with Ross's qualifications, cultured bearing, and intellectual accomplishments, the Commissioner informed over a dozen Indian superintendents that the correspondent would soon be visiting their reservations and asked that they extend every courtesy to Ross and his family traveling with him. When Ross exhibited great curiosity concerning Appalachian whites, North Carolina Highlanders, and Georgia Blacks, the commissioner obliged with several letters of introduction to friends who could supply Ross with information and tours. Aided greatly by Collier, the correspondent completed his tour and returned to Germany.[50]

In 1938 Ross returned to America. Explaining to Collier that the data acquired four years previously had furnished material for his book, *Amerika's Hour of Decision*, he informed the Commissioner that he intended to gather more information for a new project. Ross had undertaken to research a film for the Degeto Film Company in Germany "which shall give a true picture of America." Assuring the commissioner that he had returned very much impressed with his Indian policy, Ross wanted to include reservations in his film. Convinced of Ross's sincerity and flattered by the praise, Collier again informed Indian agencies that the correspondent would return to photograph ceremonials and dances. C. F. Klinefelter, Collier's assistant, however, urged Collier to be cautious when dealing with Ross. After checking Ross's references, Klinefelter questioned Ross, who offered no plausible excuse concerning his substitution for the original filmmaker, a Mr. Krahforst. Klinefelter advised further caution when facilitating contacts for Ross.[51]

Meanwhile, the State Department had been investigating Ross for some time. On December 12, 1938, Ickes informed Collier that the State Department had declared Ross a spy, and they needed a photograph of the agent. Although the commissioner grumbled that he perceived no reason why Ross should not be informed about Indian affairs, he cooperated by suggesting to his superintendents, whom Ross still intended to visit, that they attempt to inconspicuously photograph the Nazi while he was standing with a group of Indians.[52]

Shortly thereafter, certain events publicly revealed Ross to be a spy. In January, 1939, S. K. Padover, an Austrian born professor of German history, analyzed Ross's book, *Unser Amerika*, and pronounced it to be Nazi propaganda. Describing Ross as an officer of the Stuttgart Propaganda Institute, Padover stated that the spy predicted that democracy would soon collapse in America, allowing Nazis to assume control. In his book, Ross had also asserted that Native Americans "would look forward to intervention" of this kind. He approved the "Indianization" in American policy and hoped it would develop into full political independence for tribes in the form of autonomous Indian states. As segregated communities, Native Americans would be more susceptible to Germany's "clever propaganda" which they would disseminate through American "redskins." After this and similar statements by Ross were published, the correspondent's popularity plummeted.[53]

By 1939 the entire Fascist network began to unravel. At the height of America's isolationist policy, Hitler had already seized Austria and Czechoslovakia. American intelligence branches, helpless to act overseas in the face of America's Neutrality Acts, responded by pressuring native Fascist groups. Several agencies, including Naval Intelligence, Military Intelligence, the Federal Bureau of Investigation, the State Department, the Post Office, and Congress, initiated investigations of all American-based Fascist organizations or individuals associated with them. Ross topped every list. A special "House Investigation on Un-American Activities," under Texas Representative Martin Dies, had begun hearings in 1938 which would continue for three years. Focusing on alleged subversive activities by Communist and Fascist agents operating within the United States, the Committee unearthed evidence for use by the Justice and State Departments. Several of those indicted had been involved in the Indian-Fascist network.[54]

Witnesses testifying at the Dies Committee on Fascist activities asserted that Ross, who had been under surveillance by the Military Intelligence Division since 1920, had operated as a Communist in Santiago, Chile, after World War I. When Hitler assumed power in Germany, he converted to Nazism. They further stated that Nazi consular officials had paid Ross and others to propagandize in America. Kuhn admitted that the correspondent had openly praised Hitler at Bund meetings and that on his filmmaking tour, the agent had illegally photographed specialized industrial plants and naval yards. After hearing testimony, the Committee recommended that Ross, who had since returned to Germany, "be prevented from ever setting foot again on American soil," because he had failed to report the full scope of his activities to the State Department. On September 20, 1940, the State Department officially informed the Secretary of War that Ross was a Nazi agent.[55]

When subpoenaed to appear before the Committee, Kuhn behaved in such an uncooperative manner that he insulted Congressman John Parnell Thomas, Republican representative from New Jersey. A veteran of World War I holding the rank of captain, Thomas described the Bund leader as "unruly, offensive, and evasive." Despite attempts to avoid incriminating himself, Kuhn confronted evidence provided to the Committee about the German-American Bund by Naval Intelligence. Because Hitler's invasion of Poland had created great disdain in America for Fascist symbols, the Bund already had discontinued the Nazi salute and swastika to avoid public criticism. Undeterred by smoke screens, Congressmen charged the Bund with being an agency of a foreign power. Furthermore, the committee learned that as a foreign-controlled agency, the Bund, in conjunction with the Silver Shirts, had received orders to support Republican candidates in order to stamp out the "red menace." Thomas recommended that material concerning the Bund should be forwarded to the State and Justice Departments for violation of Registration and Espionage Acts. In 1941 a federal grand jury sentenced Kuhn to Sing Sing Prison for sedition, and the German-American Bund disintegrated.[56]

The Committee targeted other groups related to the Bund, including the Militant Christian Patriots. Henry Allen became convinced that Leslie Fry and Elizabeth Jewett had double-crossed him when both fled the country, and this disillusionment rendered him a particularly talkative witness. Before the Committee, Allen implicated several other persons, including Jemison, Pelley, Deatherage and True. Under oath Allen admitted that he had arranged for Jemison to have articles published in Gerald Winrod's journal and that she had appealed to James True for funds. While still facing criminal charges in California for possession of a billy-club, Allen openly discussed militaristic plans developed by himself, Deatherage, True and Pelley. In July of 1942 a federal grand jury indicted twenty-eight American pro-Fascist sympathizers, including James True and Mrs. W. K. (Elizabeth) Jewett, but neither would serve time in prison. "A mistrial was declared when the judge died," wrote historian Glen Jeansonne, "and after the war ended, the indictment was dropped. Furthermore, Gerald Winrod was convicted of sedition in 1942, 1943, and 1944, but eventually a higher court dismissed the charges."[57]

William Dudley Pelley and his Silver Shirts suffered the same fate as the German-American Bund and the Militant Christian Patriots. Similar to the situation with Colin Ross, Pelley had been under surveillance by the Military Intelligence Division since 1934. By the fall of 1939 the Federal Bureau of Investigation, Naval Intelligence and Dies Committee were also investigating Pelley. Initially Pelley reacted offensively to allegations of subversive activities by filing a 3.5-million-dollar law suit against the Dies Committee for "alleged collaboration of the Republic," but he crumbled when the government mounted a counteroffensive. On October 20, 1939, Buncome County sheriff deputies in Asheville, North Carolina seized Pelley's files for violating a "blue sky" law. Charging that Pelley had published fraudulent representations, State Superior Court Judge Zeb V. Nettles asserted that the Silver Shirt commander was "seeking to further the cause of Naziism with himself as the dictator." Dies agreed with this assessment, stating, "The Department of Justice has a clearcut case to proceed against Mr. Pelley." In 1942 the Justice Department brought suit and Pelley was convicted of sedition. He served eight years in prison until his parole in 1950.[58]

While these agencies diligently examined Pelley's activities, Collier uncovered a conspiracy between Pelley and Collett. In 1938 Pelley had filed suit against Collier claiming that *Indians at Work* constituted misappropriation of public funds as "a propaganda medium for perpetuating the New Deal . . . to win the favor of the voters and to unlawfully influence Congress on pending legislation." A year later Collier discovered that Collett had suggested to Pelley that since both men had filed suit against Collier, there should be "an agreement between you and me whereby you will assign to me a fair share of any amount that may be recovered by the action." Before the plan could be finalized, Pelley parted company with his attorney, Harrison Fargo McConnell. He claimed that McConnell spent too much time writing pamphlets concerning the reorganization of the Republican National Committee. Collier, however, suspected that conditions "became too warm" for McConnell, because the Federal Trade Commission had initiated an investigation of one of his employers.[59]

By 1940 Collett's influence within the AIF and with California Indians had clearly declined as Indians claiming to be victims of Collett's claims settlements filed 154 depositions against him in a Washington, D. C., court. Furthermore, when Collett ran for a post on the central Democratic Committee of Los Angeles County, the California Indian Rights Association actively campaigned against him and informed voters that from 1920–1934, he had collected more than $800,000 from Native Americans.[60] Collett's influence with Senator Wheeler, however, appeared to remain intact, as the two men continued their association for some years. On December 2, 1940, a Senate Sub-Committee, composed of Senator Wheeler and Senator Elmer Thomas, Democratic Senator from Oklahoma, held hearings in San Francisco concerning the California Mission Indians. Michael Harrison, Indian Office field agent, attended one meeting and reported to Stella Von Bulow, Secretary of the California Indian Rights Association and a former Collett follower, that he considered Wheeler to be both hostile to Collier's administration and partial to Collett. Harrison claimed that Wheeler's remarks about Collett's organization amounted to "whitewashing" and that a nearby reporter queried "what was Wheeler getting out of it?" Senator Thomas displayed more partiality, said Harrison, and stated "off the record" that he believed the California Indians preferred to keep the Attorney General rather than hire private attorneys.[61]

By the early 1940s Collier worried that Collett's influence in California extended to John Wheeler, the Senator's son. Wheeler, an attorney, had joined the California branch of America First, fringe group dedicated to isolationism and organized in 1936 by pro-Fascist, anti-Semitic sympathizers James True and Michael Ahearn. Deeply committed to Native American causes, Wheeler had reportedly traveled the previous year to Mexico City as a representative of the newly-organized Federated Council of California Indians. Several California Indians complained to Collier that this organization merely served as a paper front for Collett. When rumors circulated that Collett had hired Wheeler as his attorney, neither publicly denied the charge.[62]

The AIF had also parted company with the majority of their Fascist allies by the early forties, in part because the pro-Fascist sympathizers were confronting their own investigations and in part because of a money-making scheme created by Bruner and Chandler. Two years earlier, discovering that Federation dues failed to generate enough income, Bruner and Chandler drafted a bill proposing that every voluntary member of the AIF who "agreed to accept the full responsibility of American citizenship" be given three thousand dollars as a final settlement of all claims against the government. Binding upon their heirs, the bill stated that the settlement was to be directly transferred from the Treasury to the Indians. In return the Indians would sign a receipt releasing the government from all prior and future obligations. Finally, the act specified that this agreement would have no effect upon "vested tribal property rights or tribal privileges." Furthermore, Chandler explained, people could receive money for their dead ancestors. Unanimously adopted at the 1938 Convention, the bill stipulated that only enrolled Indians were eligible. He urged Indians to send in their membership fee of one dollar per claimant and join the Federation.[63]

Indian agencies found themselves immediately inundated by requests for relatives' tribal roll numbers. Native Americans also requested addresses for tribal leaders which they intended to forward to the Federation. H. A. Andrews, superintendent of the Quapaw Indian Agency at Miami, Oklahoma, complained about the exploitative nature of the Federation's measure, because "oftentimes, such individuals do not have sufficient food in the house to keep them alive." Believing the association had violated a law which prohibited soliciting from Indians to secure government appropriations, he took steps to notify Collier.[64]

Many Native Americans obviously agreed with Andrew's assessments, and several came forward to give sworn affidavits concerning Federation attempts to solicit money. Some Indians disliked the pressure tactics employed when AIF leaders warned that those who failed to pay their "one dollar entrance fee" would be unable to participate in the settlement. One woman, describing herself as "an ignorant, weary, mother," appealed directly to President Roosevelt. "Mr. President," she wrote, "we do not think it right to have to pay when one is already a registered Indian." Believing they had received just treatment under the present administration, the Seminoles refused to sign the petition and adopted a General Council Resolution condemning the Federation's legislation.[65]

Despite these complaints, both Senator Elmer Thomas and Representative Usher Burdick introduced Senate 2206 and House Resolution 5921. Each bill was almost identical to the original proposed legislation, but Burdick's act carried a list of petitioners. The majority of the 4,640 signers resided in Oklahoma and belonged primarily to the Five Civilized Tribes, with the Cherokee constituting 2,907 of the signatures. Eighty California Mission Indians also signed.[66] Harold Ickes and John Collier lost no time in pressuring Burdick and Thomas to withdraw their bills. Ickes, a Pennsylvania-born Quaker, had graduated from the University of Chicago Law School, worked as a newspaper reporter, and also served as a lawyer. His progressive ideas led him to join several liberal organizations, including the NAACP, the ACLU, and the Independent Party. He argued that the Federation knew that its bill would never pass but instead felt that an actual House Resolution would aid their solicitation efforts. Many Indian groups joined in this condemnation of the bill. *Indian Truth,* a magazine published by the Indian Rights Association, printed an article in which editor M. K. Sniffen endorsed Ickes's viewpoint and described the bill as "a racket . . . based on rainbow promises."[67]

Apparently convinced by the opposition to his bill, Burdick withdrew his resolution for further study. Justifying his action on the grounds that he generally introduced bills for Indian groups, he claimed to have "the utmost confidence" in Ickes's honesty. Thomas proved more equivocal than Burdick. The Democratic Senator from Oklahoma had served thirteen years in his state legislature and two terms as a congressman before entering the Senate. During Collier's long tenure, Thomas and the commissioner had experienced a stormy relationship full of twists and turns. At one point, Thomas appeared totally committed to Collier and even told Navajo Tribal Council Chairman J. C. Morgan that Collier had done more for their tribe than anyone else. On another occasion, however, the Senator complained that the commissioner had "never considered the Indians of our state as deserving of much consideration."[68]

Refusing to withdraw his bill, the seasoned politician told Collier that he wanted to hold hearings to decisively "kill" the resolution. Privately, however, Thomas confided to an Indian Service employee that the bill had no possibility of passing Congress. On June 7, 1939, Collier received a further blow when Burdick reintroduced his bill as House Resolution 6714. Collier charged that the new bill would allow the Federation to continue soliciting funds while allowing Burdick to avoid identification with "the Federation's business adventure."[69]

The "$3,000 for $1" proposal, although it never became an act, had proved extremely lucrative, and it afforded the Federation an opportunity to repudiate former Fascist alliances. Until 1938 the Federation listed no dues-paying members, but by the middle of 1939, the group had accumulated $7,000. Heartened by these contributions, they felt sufficiently confident to openly disavow association with groups which were becoming increasingly unpopular. "We resent and we most vehemently deny," Bruner announced, "that there is any relation between the AIF and any group objectionable to a loyal, patriotic citizen."[70]

The break between the Federation and Fascist groups appeared to be reciprocal. "The '$3,000 for $1' bill embarrasses, not helps," commented Collier, "the fifth column program," referring to a popular media term for the Third Reich. By 1940 the AIF confronted investigations by the Federal Bureau of Investigation for racketeering and the Post Office for fraudulent use of the mails. A year later the FBI reported that the AIF had been previously investigated, that a number of investigative reports had been submitted, and that concerning a relationship between the Federation and Pelley, "there is some indication that such may exist." Nevertheless, the FBI concluded that "the facts did not warrant the institution of prosecutive action against the Federation, or its organizers or operators."[71]

In an effort to improve its image, the Federation began to endorse more neutral causes, such as obtaining Social Security benefits for Indians. Dropping its earlier rhetoric, it announced its "full cooperation, aid, support and loyalty" during the "national emergency." Their conversion to mainstream politics occurred at a propitious period, one month before the bombing of Pearl Harbor. With this statement, the Federation managed to enter the war as apparent patriots.[72] Furthermore, by this time Federation leaders were obviously viewing Alice Lee Jemison more as a liability than an asset. When Jemison resigned from the organization in 1939, she claimed to be dissatisfied with the fact that Federation leaders had betrayed the cause by trying to enlist Collier's support for their bill. Collier instead suggested that her fifth-column associations had become a handicap to the Federation.[73]

Unlike her colleagues, Jemison never wavered in her attacks on Collier. Perhaps the only witness to speak voluntarily before the Dies Committee, Jemison produced a one-hundred-page document in which she repeated the same charges of atheism and Communism she had leveled since 1934. Although she received some favorable press coverage as a "Seneca girl" fighting bureaucracy, Jemison's tactics also exposed her to criticism. Thomas called her "an agitator of the Indians," Mrs. Codman wanted to know who had "put her up" to testifying, and Richard M. Codd, Six Nations Confederacy attorney and Jemison's former employer, refuted her statements, asserting she knew little about the Indian situation.

Collier insisted that when she spoke before the Dies Committee, her statements "came back on the wire from Germany the same day."[74]

During her testimony, Jemison, also under investigation by Naval Intelligence, admitted that she had been paid by Allen, who was acting for the Militant Christan Patriots. She further claimed that Hitler personally chose her articles for publication in German magazines. While she continued to call James True her friend, she denied knowledge of any Bund members other than a casual acquaintance with a Bund organizer in Buffalo, New York. Throughout the war, while working at a Countryside School and then at the Census Bureau in Suitland, Maryland, she continued to lobby against Collier and advised Native Americans not to register for the draft. In 1947, the FBI initiated a "full field investigation" and learned that the Anti-Defamation League of B'Nai B'rith in Chicago, Illinois had designated her as a subversive individual.[75]

With the exception of Jemison, who continued to openly criticize Collier, the Indian Bureau, and Selective Service throughout the war years, America's entrance into the war effectively ended any Native American activity which might be viewed as unpatriotic. Perhaps to justify the success of his Indian Bureau policies or to dispel any remaining suggestion that he might harbor subversive tendencies, Collier exploited the immense participation of Native Americans in the military and defense work. In fact, the war years opened new avenues of opportunities for Native Americans educated and trained under many of the Indian New Deal programs. The enthusiasm exhibited by American Indians in World War II gained far more public attention than any propaganda campaign attempted by Nazi agents or sympathizers. Indeed the Nazi campaign to gain Indian allies was significant not because it failed to recruit large numbers of Native Americans to the Axis cause, but because large numbers of Native Americans ignored the Axis propaganda and wholeheartedly responded when their country was attacked. While the Germans failed to understand Native Americans or their love for a country which they still considered to be theirs, they also misunderstood the influence, or lack thereof, possessed by fringe groups and isolated individuals.

Finally, the effect of the AIF and its pro-Fascist allies should neither be overestimated nor dismissed as irrelevant. Although relatively few American Indians confessed to being swayed by speakers such as Towner, believing the charge of Communism leveled against Collier, fewer still expected the Third Reich to reward them with long-lost land. Nevertheless, the charges did result in distracting Collier from the administrative duties of the Indian Bureau. It contributed a conspiratorial mood to an atmosphere already rampant with distrust. Only the coming war would unite these diverse groups, as Congressmen, Indian tribes, and the Bureau cooperated to win the war against those who had only recently professed to be friends.

---

[1]Harold Ickes to John Collier, December 12, 1938, Record Group 75, entry 178, Office Files of Commissioner of Indian Affairs John Collier, 1933–1945, box 15, folder "Dr. Colin Ross," National Archives, Washington, D. C.

[2]In World War II, Collier would be able to boast of a ninety-nine percent Indian registration rate.

[3] Lawrence Kelley, *The Assault on Assimilation* (Albuquerque: U of New Mexico P, 1983); Francis Paul Prucha, *American Indian Policy in Crisis* (Norman: U of Oklahoma P, 1976); and Leonard Carlson, *Indians, Bureaucrats and Land: The Dawes Act and the Decline of Indian Farming* (Connecticut: Yale U P, 1981) describe the failures of the 1887 legislation. Checkerboarding was the practice of allotting non-contiguous acreage to Indian farmers.

[4]Donald Parman, *Indians and the American West in the Twentieth Century* (Bloomington: Indiana U P, 1994): 89–106, and Graham Taylor, *The New Deal and American Indian Tribalism*, give in-depth descriptions of the Indian New Deal. "Revision of Laws and Legal Status," Congressional Committee Hearings, House Committee on Indian Affairs, 78th Cong., 2d sess., House Resolution 166, December 1944, explores the results and opposition to the Indian Reorganization Act after ten years in operation.

[5]Brian W. Dippie, *The Vanishing American: White Attitudes and the U.S.-Indian Policy* (Connecticut: Wesleyan U P, 1982): 276; John Collier, "Indians Come Alive," *Atlantic Monthly* 170 (September 1942): 75–81.

[6]Hearings before the House Subcommittee on Indian Affairs, Congressional Committee Hearings, House Report 7781, 74th Cong., 1st sess., February 11, 1936, 863–71.

[7]O. K. Chandler to Nathan Margold, July 7, 1933; Chandler to Collier, June 1, 1933, May 9, 1933; Record Group 75, entry 178, box 4, folder "O. K. Chandler, Special"; Document 118198, Record Group 75, entry 178, box 6, folder "Alice Lee Jemison, AIF"; and Hazel Hertzberg, *The Search for an American Indian Identity* (Syracuse: Syracuse U P, 1971): 289.

[8]Document 118198.

[9]*Southwest Tourist News*, 5 (September 12, 1934), Record Group 75, entry 178, box 6, folder "Alice Lee Jemison, AIF"; House Report 7781, 14.

[10]House Report 7781, 29; Alice Lee Jemison to Mrs. William Walker, June 15, 1935; Jemison to John Snyder, Jemison Speech, January 17, 1938; Jemison to Congressman Rene De Rouen, June 10, 1939, Record Group 75, entry 178, box 6, folder "Alice Lee Jemison, AIF, Dies Committee, German Bund (Nazi)"; Michael Harrison to Collier, March 18, 1935, Record Group 75, entry 178, box 1, folder "Jemison . . . AIF"; Congressional Committee Hearings before the Committee on Indian Affairs, House of Representatives, 76th Cong., 3d sess., S. 2103; "An Act to Exempt Certain Indians from the Provisions of the Act of June 18, 1934," 48 Statute, 984, June 13, 1940, Vol. 891, 164; Federal Bureau of Investigation Report No. 121-6970 on Alice Lee Jemison, May 13, 1948.

[11]House Report 7781, 20, 29–37.

[12]House Report 7781, 18–19, 868; Document "The First American Fights Communism and Atheism in America," Record Group 75, entry 178, box 1, folder "AIF, 1935–1937."

[13]House Report 7781, 899, 868; Kenneth R. Philip, *John Collier's Crusade for Indian Reform, 1920–1954* (Tucson: U of Arizona P, 1977).

[14]Edward Spicer, *Cycles of Conquest* (Tucson: U of Arizona P, 1962) gives an excellent comparison of Spanish, Mexican, and American treatment of native populations; House Report 7781, 892–97.

[15]House Report 7781, 907, 953, 790, 798; Jemison to Walker, August 31, 1936, Record Group 75, entry 178, box 6, folder "Jemison . . . AIF."

[16]House Report 7781, 982; Jemison to Walker, August 31, 1936, Record Group 75, entry 178, box 6, folder "Jemison . . . AIF"; Hinchliffe Confidential Memorandum, May 15, 1939, Record Group 75, entry 178, box 15, folder "Silver Shirts of America."

[17]Serial Set 12938, *Biographical Directory of the American Congress, 1774–1971* (Washington, D. C.: Government Printing Office, 1971): 1377, 668; House Report 7781, 658.

[18]Zimmerman to Charles Dey Elkus, December 31, 1937, Record Group 75, entry 189, box A-M, folder "E."

[19]Richard T. Ruetten, *Burton K. Wheeler of Montana: A Progressive Between the Wars*, University of Oregon, Ph.D. Dissertation (Ann Arbor, Michigan: University Microfilms, Inc., 1961): 18, 30–31.

[20]House Report 7781, 49, 648, 651.

[21]House Report 7781, 659, 818, 895; Collier to Representative Virginia Jenckes, May 29, 1935, Record Group 75, entry 178, box 1, "AIF."

[22]*Biographical Directory*, 1119, 1454; House Report 7781, 38–39, 894, 899, 798.

[23]The scope of this chapter did not allow full exploration of the activities of the AIF. For example, from 1935–1939 they demanded several more Congressional Committee Hearings, complained when Congress refused to print their full remarks, and constantly presented resolutions to Congress concerning Collier's patriotism and demanding the repeal of the Wheeler-Howard Act.

[24]Jemison to John Snyder, June 15, 1935; Michael Harrison to Collier, March 18, 1935, Record Group 75, entry 178, box 6, folder "Alice Lee Jemison . . . AIF."

[25]Snyder to Collier, February 19, 1935, Record Group 75, entry 178, box 6, folder "Alice Lee Jemison . . . AIF."

[26]Collier to Senator Elmer Thomas, Document 118198, Record Group 75, entry 178, box 6, folder "Alice Lee Jemison . . . AIF."

[27]Field Agent Floyd La Rouche 1936 Document, July 24, 1936, Record Group 75, entry 178, box 1, folder "AIF, 1933–1937"; La Rouche to Miss Pomeroy, August 8, 1936, Record Group 75, entry 178, box 1, folder "Convention, 1936 AIF."

[28]La Rouche Memorandum, August 8, 1936; La Rouche to Miss Pomeroy, August 8, 1936, Record Group 75, entry 178, box 1, folder "Convention, 1936 AIF"; La Rouche 1936 Document, La Rouche to Collier, July 24, 1936, Record Group 75, entry 178, box 1, folder "AIF 1933–1937."

[29]E. K. Burlew to Collier, October 26, 1936, Record Group 75, entry 178, box 1, folder "AIF, 1936–1937"; "Memorandum on Convention Literature," Record Group 75, entry 178, box 1, folder "Convention 1936, AIF."

[30]Undated Document, Record Group 75, entry 178, box 15, folder "Silver Shirts of America"; Memorandum on Convention Literature, Record Group 75, entry 178, box 1, folder "Convention 1936 AIF," S. 2103, 155–56.

[31]Ibid.

[32]*The Asheville Citizen*, Asheville, North Carolina, October 20, 1939; "The Weekly Liberator," August 7, 1939, Record Group 75, entry 178, box 15, folder "Silver Shirts of America"; 1936 Unsigned Memorandum, Record Group 75, entry 178, box 6, folder "Alice Lee Jemison . . . Nazi"; Washington *Star*, May 28, 1938, Record Group 75, entry 178, box 2, "German-American Bund, Silver Shirts," John M. Allswang, *The New Deal and American Politics* (New York: John Wiley and Sons, Inc., 1978): 25.

[33]William Zimmerman to Abe Murdock, July 8, 1936, Record Group 75, entry 178, box 1, folder "Convention 1936, AIF"; Collier to Elliot Clark, May 26, 1936,

Record Group 75, entry 194, Office Files of Fred Daiker, 1929–1943, folder "AIF"; Floyd Burnett to Mrs. Richard Codman, February 6, 1936, M. K. Sniffen to Mrs. William A. Becker, October 14, 1936, Record Group 75, entry 178, box 1, folder "AIF, 1935–1937"; William T. Hagan, *The Indian Rights Association* (Tucson: U of Arizona P, 1985): x.

[34]Edith Murphey to Becker, October 20, 1936, Jemison to Murphey, August 10, 1936, Record Group 75, entry 178, box 1, folder "Convention 1936 AIF"; Jemison to Walker, August 31, 1936, Record Group 75, entry 178, box 6, folder "Jemison . . . AIF."

[35]Senate Committee on Indian Affairs, Senate 1651, Congressional Committee Hearings, 75th Cong., 3d sess., March 8–12, 1936, 34–58; Federal Bureau of Investigation Report No. 61-7587-603 on William Dudley Pelley, March 19, 1940.

[36]Murphey to Becker, October 20, 1936, Record Group 178, box 1, folder "Convention 1936, AIF."

[37]Document "To Americans Everywhere," October, 1936, Record Group 75, entry 178, box 6, folder "Jemison . . . AIF"; Senate 2103, 165, 325; Federal Bureau of Investigation Report No. 61-7587-652 on William Dudley Pelley, June 17, 1940.

[38]Robert Marshall to Collier, November 23, 1937, Record Group 75, entry 178, box 2, folder "German-American Bund, Silver Shirts of America"; Undated Document, Record Group 75, entry 178, box 1, "AIF, 1933–1937"; House Resolution 282, Special House Committee Hearings on Un-American Activities, 75th Cong., 3d sess., August 12, 1938, Vol. 893, 3538.

[39]Anne Mumford to Collier, March 28, 1938, Leslie Fry to Attorney General Homer Cummings, March 14, 1938, Undated Document "The German-American Bund," Record Group 75, entry 178, box 2, folder "German-American Bund, Silver Shirts of America"; House Report 282, Vol. 893, 1176, August to December, 1938, Vol. 894, 3526, May to June, 1939; Federal Bureau of Investigation Report No. 101-3d-044-5 on Mary Heaton Vorse, April 18, 1944, and Federal Bureau of Investigation Report No. 61-7587-675 on William Dudley Pelley, August 7, 1940, 8.

[40]Ibid.

[41]Ickes to Collier, December 12, 1938, Record Group 75, entry 178, box 2, folder "Bruner 1938 Oklahoma Racket"; Document "The German-American Bund," December 6, 1938, Record Group 75, entry 178, box 2, folder "German-American Bund, Silver Shirts of America"; House Report 282, Vol. 893, 1229.

[42]House Report 282, Vol. 893, 656, 1145–50, 1175, 1208, Vol. 895, 3706, 3773, 3827–28, 5185, 5511, 5492, 5200, 5524; Indian Bureau Release, November 23, 1938, Record Group 75, entry 178, box 6, folder "Jemison . . . Nazi"; Federal Bureau of Investigation Report 61-7587-605 on William Dudley Pelley, March 19, 1940, 103.

[43]1938 German-American Bund Document, Record Group 75, entry 178, box 2, folder "German-American Bund, Silver Shirts"; German-American Bund Meeting Document, May 19, 1938, Record Group 75, entry 194, box 1 "AIF"; Sander A. Diamond, *The Nazi Movement in the United States, 1924–1941* (Ithaca, New York: Cornell U P, 1974): 318; Federal Bureau of Investigation Report No. 61-7587-635 on William Dudley Pelley, April 29, 1940; Federal Bureau of Investigation Report No. 101-3044-5 on Mary Heaton Vorse, April 18, 1944; Federal Bureau of Investigation Report No. 61-7560-833 on Henry Allen, May 11, 1938.

[44]Harrison to Collier, July 11, 1939, Record Group 75, entry 178, box 2, folder "German-American Bund, Silver Shirts"; Federal Bureau of Investigation Report No. 61-7587-635 on William Dudley Pelley, April 29, 1940.

[45]House Report 282, Vol. 893, 1231, 2243, Vol. 894, 3456, 3464, 3526; Harrison to Pomeroy, October 13, 1941, Record Group 75, entry 178, box 5, folder "Michael Harrison."

[46]A. R. Perryman to A. C. Monahan, August 22, 1938, Ben Dwight to Monahan, August 22, 1938, Record Group 75, entry 178, box 1, folder "AIF, 1933–1937."

[47]Congressional Record, 77th Cong., 2d sess., A4385; Document "Regarding the Sioux as Aryans," August 7, 1939, Record Group 75, entry 178, box 15, folder "Dr. Colin Ross."

[48]Charles Coulton Gillespie (ed.) *Dictionary of Scientific Biography* Vol. VI (New York: Charles Scriber, 1942): 527–28; New York *Times*, April 25, 1942, 6:5; Collier to Bliven, May 4, 1939, Record Group 75, entry 178, box 2, folder "Bruner et al."

[49]Memorandum to Miss Sather, December 5, 1938, Record Group 75, entry 178, box 15, folder "Ross, German Nazi"; Collier to Superintendents, June 18–20, 1934, Record Group 75, entry 178, box 8, folder "Morgan Palmer et al."

[50]Ibid.

[51]Dr. Colin Ross to Collier, December 2, 1938, Collier to Ross, December 8, 1938, Collier to Superintendents, December 8, 1938, Record Group 75, entry 178, box 8, folder "Morgan Palmer et al"; C. F. Klinefelter to Margaret Dotson, December 5, 1938, Record Group 75, entry 178, box 15, folder "Dr. Colin Ross."

[52]Ickes to Collier, December 12, 1938, Collier to Superintendents, December 21, 1938, Record Group 75, entry 178, box 15, folder "Dr. Colin Ross."

[53]*The Forum*, January, 1939, "Der Balkan Amerikas," January, 1939, Miss Pomeroy to Collier, January 4, 1939, Record Group 75, entry 178, box 15, folder "Dr. Colin Ross."

[54]Frank Wallace to Ickes, December 5, 1939, Record Group 75, entry 178, folder "Silver Shirts of America."

[55]House Report 282, Vol. 893, 1150, Vol. 894, 6062, Vol. 896, 7190, February 7–10, April 2–4, 1940; Entries May 16, 1920, September 20, 1940, Microfilm 1194, MID 1917–1914, Roll 176, OCS, National Archives, Washington, D. C.

[56]House Report 282, 1175–76, 1208–13, 2134, Vol. 897, 1469, Appendix, 1941, Vol. 894, 3824, 5173–74, 6110; Harry Slattery to Secretary of the Navy, Record Group 75, entry 178, box 2, folder "German-American Bund, Silver Shirts"; *Biographical Directory*, 1806.

[57]House Report 282, Vol. 896, 1467, Vol. 894, 4028, 4134; Senate 2103, 329, Harrison to Collier, August 28, 1939, Record Group 75, entry 178, box 15, folder "Silver Shirts of America"; Federal Bureau of Investigation Report No. 100-41053-14 on Mrs. W. K. Jewett, April 14, 1943; Federal Bureau of Investigation Report No. 121-6970-1 on Alice Lee Jemison, May 13, 1948; Federal Bureau of Investigation Report No. 61-7560-833 on Henry Allen, May 11, 1938; Glen Jeansonne, *Transformation and Reaction, America 1921–1945* (Milwaukee: U of Wisconsin, 1994): 202–203.

[58]House Report 282, Vol. 894, 4529; Asheville *Citizen*, Asheville, North Carolina, October 20, 1939; La Rouche to Collier, August 19, 1942, Record Group 75, entry 178, box 15, folder "Dr. Colin Ross," Collier to Ickes, October 19, 1939, Record Group 75, entry 178, box 6, folder "Jemison . . . Nazi;" entry January 27, 1939, Microfilm 1194, MID, 1917–1941, Roll 176, OCS; Wallace to Ickes, December 5, 1939, Record Group 75, entry 178, box 15, folder "Silver Shirts of America"; "Silver Shirt Leader Seized," The Casper *Tribune-Herald*, April 5, 1942.

[59]Confidential Memorandum, May 15, 1939, Collier to Ickes, December 7, 1938, Record Group 75, entry 178, box 15, folder "Silver Shirts of America"; Codman to Collier, January 10, 1941, Record Group 75, entry 178, box 5, folder "Michael Harrison."

[60]Senate 1651, 34–58, Senate Committee on Indian Affairs, Senate 1424 and Senate 2589, Congressional Committee Hearings, 75th Cong., 1st sess., October 24, 1935, April 6, 1936, July 6, 1937, August 16, 1937, Vol. 549, 205, 216; Wallace Howland to Collier, September 5, 1940; "Don't Vote for Collett Document," Record Group 75, entry 178, box 5, folder "Michael Harrison."

[61]Harrison to Collier, December 4, 1940, Record Group 75, entry 178, box 5, folder "Michael Harrison."

[62]Collier to Harrison, October 20, 1941, Confidential Memo for Collier, May 20, 1940, Codman to Collier, January 10, 1941, Undated Deposition by Stella Von Bulow, Record Group 75, entry 178, box 5, folder "Michael Harrison."

[63]Document "A Proposed Bill," August 20, 1938, Record Group 75, entry 178, box 1, folder "S. 2206 and H. R. 5921."

[64]H. A. Andrew to Monahan, October 26, 1938, Record Group 75, entry 178, box 1, folder "S. 2206 and H. R. 5921."

[65]Affidavits by Dagenette and Fields, November 23, 1938, April 13, 1939, Letter by "Weary, Ignorant Mother," Record Group 75, entry 178, box 1, folder "S. 2206 and H. R. 5921"; Collier to Louis Fife, April 19, 1939, Samuel Simmons to Collier, May 1, 1939, Record Group 75, entry 178, box 2, folder "Bruner et al . . . 1938 Oklahoma $3,000 Racket . . . Dies Committee."

[66]Senate Report 2206, April 20, 1939, 76th Cong., 1st sess.; House Report 5921, April 20, 1939; 76th Cong., 1st sess.; *Biographical Directory*, 1806–1807.

[67]Ickes to Usher Burdick, April 28, 1939, Record Group 75, entry 178, box 2, folder "Bruner et al"; August 27, 1937, Biographical Sketch of Ickes, Record Group 48, entry 849, box 5, folder "Secretary Miscellaneous Correspondence," $3,000 for $1 Bill," *Indian Truth*, Vol. 16, No. 4 (Philadelphia: Indian Rights Association, April–May, 1939).

[68]Burdick to Ickes, May 1, 1939, Record Group 75, entry 178, box 2, folder "Bruner et al"; Elmer Thomas to Dr. Mary E. Tatman, May 11, 1937, Record Group 75, entry 189, box M–P, folder "Miscellaneous."

[69]John Herrick to Editor, New York *Herald-Tribune*, September 1, 1939, Record Group 75, entry 195, box 2, folder "AIF"; Collier to Ickes, June 22, 1939, Record Group 75, entry 178, box 2, folder "Bruner et al."

[70]Herrick to New York *Herald-Tribune*, September 1, 1939, Record Group 75, entry 195, box 2, folder "AIF," Congressional Record, 76th Cong., 1st sess., May 29, 1939, A8910; Senate 2103, 167–70; Unsigned Document, June, 1940, Record Group 75, entry 178, box 1, folder "AIF"; Federal Bureau of Investigation Report No. 121-6970-1 on Alice Lee Jemison, May 13, 1948.

[71]Federal Bureau of Investigation Report No. 61-7587-746 on The AIF, March 7, 1941; Congressional Record, 77th Cong., 1st sess., November 3, 1941, A4966–4967; Pomeroy to Harrison, June 26, 1943, Record Group 75, entry 178, box 5, folder "Michael Harrison."

[72]Ibid.

[73]Senate 2103, 167–70; Unsigned Document, June, 1940, Record Group 75, entry 178, box 1, folder "AIF."

[74]House Resolution 282, Vol. 893, 2436–37, Vol. 894, 4032; Codman to Collier, December 11, 1938, Record Group 75, entry 178, box 4, folder "Mrs. Richard Codman"; *Courier Express*, Buffalo, New York, November 23, 1938; Collier to Britt, June 15, 1939, Record Group 75, entry 178, box 2, folder "German-American Bund Silver Shirts."

[75]Senate 2103, 167–70; Unsigned Document, June, 1940, Record Group 75, entry 178, box 1, folder "AIF"; Federal Bureau of Investigation Report No. 121-6970-1 on Alice Lee Jemison, May 13, 1948.

John Collier, Commissioner of Indian Affairs, reading a "First Americans" broadcast on December 16, 1944 in Washington, D. C., in connection with the Sixth War Loan Drive. Commissioner Collier was introduced by PFC Cecelia Mix, MCWR, Camp Lejeune, North Carolina, the last living descendant of Chief Isaac Quino, last chief of the Potawatomi. National Archives 075-N-W0-W2.

Bringing Them in Alive: Selective Service and Native Americans

In 1941, armed with optimism and having declared Indians to be fellow Aryans, Josef Paul Geobbels, German Minister of Propaganda in the Third Reich, predicted that American Indians would rather revolt against the United States than fight against a Germany which had promised to return their expropriated land to them. Still unwilling to believe that their propaganda efforts of the 1930s had failed, the Germans further underestimated the Native American response to a declaration of war, which effectively resolved problems that had occurred during the registration process—viewed by many Indians as simply another example of meaningless, bureaucratic rule. Native Americans responded in unprecedented numbers to America's call for volunteers immediately after Pearl Harbor and continued throughout the war years, because they clearly understood the need for defense of one's own land.[1]

Well before Congress passed the Selective Service Act, the department of Selective Service began collecting data on the methodology of registering reservation Indians. This decision revealed that the government assumed that

Native Americans would prove to be the most difficult group in America to classify, register, and place for wartime service. Military officials constantly appeared perplexed by Indian citizenship status, and they often confronted situations where Indians immediately refused to acquiesce to white authority without substantial explanation. Furthermore, cultural clashes precipitated unusual policy decisions. Finally, interdepartmental questions of authority and jurisdiction arose between Selective Service, the Indian Bureau, and the Justice Department. These issues created an atmosphere of confusion and distrust for Indian registrants. Eventually, however, Native Americans responded to the draft with a one hundred percent registration rate, setting the standard for the rest of America.[2]

Commissioner of Indian Affairs John Collier had acquired a vast amount of knowledge of various Indian tribes from his early days as an advocate for Pueblo Indians in the 1920s, and he continued to do so through his tenure as commissioner in the 1930s. Nevertheless, his endorsement of the controversial Indian Reorganization Act had alienated many tribes. During Selective Service registration, this alienation would deepen when Collier was forced to choose between the welfare of tribal members and his own deep loyalty to the United States government.[3]

In early 1938 the Indian Bureau delivered to Selective Service a detailed list of all Indian Reservations, their respective states, the estimated number of registrants aged twenty-one to thirty-five, and the number of forms required. On January 1, 1939, the Bureau sent a revised list, much more detailed and grouped by age. Anxious to determine the exact status of these prospective recruits, Captain W. B. Palmer of the Joint Army and Navy Selective Service Committee conferred with Collier, who assured the Captain that under the 1924 Snyder Act, all American-born Indians held United States citizenship. A year and a half later Collier and his assistant, Fred Daiker, met with a Selective Service representative to determine how to best register Indians. Daiker, as Assistant to the Commissioner of Indian Affairs during World War I, had handled the registration of Indians during the 1917–1918 draft period and now presented several methods of registering reservation Indians.[4]

At this time Collier suggested that reservation superintendents, assisted by Indian personnel, conduct the registrations. Several unusual conditions pertaining to American Indian tribes prompted his request. For example, because of its isolated location and dearth of English-speaking Indians, the Alaskan Agency posed a particular problem. Collier also warned of a "rather slow procedure" on other reservations since the majority of Native Americans, being illiterate, would require much help in answering questionnaires. That fall, because of these "peculiar circumstances," the United Pueblo Agency actually began registration one month prior to the official date. Exhibiting the tight-knit efficiency and determination which characterized all Pueblo war efforts, the superintendent appointed interpreters to assist day-school personnel in successfully registering eligible tribal members.[5]

Despite the excellent example set by Pueblo registration, the Indian Service soon reversed its position in some cases and requested that state authorities handle Indian registration in California, Arizona, Oklahoma and New York. William Zimmerman, special assistant to the commissioner, cited as reasons for this change the lack of personnel and the close white-Indian integration in these states. Major Lewis B. Hershey, General Staff, Joint Army and Navy Selective Service Committee in Washington D. C., acquiesced to this request and added Texas and Louisiana to the list.[6] By the time Congress passed the Selective Service Act on September 13, 1940, the Indian Bureau and Selective Service had negotiated the major points concerning registration. On the same day, again citing insufficient personnel, Daiker asked that three more states, Kansas, Nebraska, and Mississippi, along with agencies in five other states, be added to the jurisdiction of state authorities. Feeling the full pressure of coping with the mainstream population, the Selective Service denied this request. Collier, always loath to relinquish authority, now revealed some suspicion of the Selective Service when he advised superintendents that they were to protect the rights of their tribal members concerning deferment and classification and "to see that the interests of the Indians are fairly and properly presented." For this reason the Indian Bureau requested that Selective Service literature, regulations, and news releases be sent to Indian superintendents, because the reservation personnel could explain procedures "more readily and with greater satisfaction than an outsider." Although Captain Robert B. Coons, Selective Service officer, considered this advice to be excellent, he cautioned that Indian Service employees must also respect the autonomy of state governors.[7]

Other agencies, in addition to the Indian Bureau, expressed concern that the registration process and actual draft might discriminate against Indians. Oliver La Farge, anthropologist, writer and president of the American Association on Indians, urged officials to consider the special status of Native Americans and plan to train them separately because of differences in their background. By differences he referred to Indian taboos against cutting their hair or eating fish, practices he considered "incompatible with standard military routine." He especially worried over their lack of English language skills and their unfamiliarity with Anglo customs. In general, however, he maintained that the Native American lifestyle suited Indians as well as or better than the average white for military service. "Military efficiency, as well as basic religious liberty, and common humanity," he concluded, "would best be served by training these men in a special corps where these peculiarities could be considered sympathetically."[8]

Many Native Americans agreed that their rights needed protection, particularly the Cherokees. After a one hundred percent registration had been effected in 1940, the Eastern Band of Cherokee in North Carolina requested the establishment of a separate draft board, because "we feel that any organization or group that would deprive a people of as sacred a right as the right of suffrage would not hesitate to deprive them of other constitutional rights." Justly proud of twenty-three volunteers serving out of a population of 3,400, the tribe proclaimed that "there is not a more patriotic people to be found anywhere in this country of ours than the Cherokees of North Carolina." Praising their patriotism but mindful of Coon's advice to be respectful of state government, Zimmerman suggested that they appeal to their state governor, and promised them bureau support.[9]

Disregarding minor differences to date, in January, 1941, Coons lauded the "excellent cooperation of the Office of Indian Affairs" for aiding in the registration process. Hinting at past problems, Coons conceded that "certain specific arrangements" had been necessary and would continue to be so. By this he meant that superintendents and Selective Service boards had drafted all available personnel, including Indian traders, school principals, and tribal members, to help complete questionnaires. On the Arizona Hopi Reservation these people, assigned as Associate Board Members, often traveled a full day on horseback to visit a registrant. Because their reservation covered New Mexico, Colorado, Utah, and Arizona, the Navajo designated eighteen places to register Indians for their July 1, 1941 registration. Furthermore, the Navajo Tribal Council issued a resolution in which it accepted the responsibility for assisting Selective Service.[10]

By October, the military had inducted 1,785 Native Americans into the Armed Forces. Having proven his willingness to cooperate in the registration process, Collier now felt justified in pressuring the Selective Service for information on his recruits. The commissioner explained that superintendents complained to him when they were unable to receive information on people from their reservations. "The Indians as a race have just cause to be proud of their 1941 record," the commissioner informed National Headquarters, "and we as a service feel that we should for various reasons obtain and keep as complete records as possible." Collier's various reasons included publishing *Indian Record*, a history of Native American wartime participation. Officials replied that because Selective Service kept separate records only on African-Americans, who remained segregated throughout the war, they could not furnish the requested information.[11]

By January, 1942, the Indian Bureau Health Director J. R. McGibony boasted that "under the present Selective Service Act, practically one hundred percent registration of Indians has been effected without difficulty." The Selective Service, however, disagreed that registration had been so effortless. They discovered that immediately after the enactment of the draft, military officials, superintendents, and Native Americans themselves, all seemed confused as to the status of Indians. When some tribes claimed they were not United States citizens, bewildered board members appealed to lawyers, to each other, and to the Indian Bureau. Collier unhesitatingly declared that every Indian born within United States borders was a citizen. Nevertheless, to settle the point, on October 14, 1940, Congress passed the Nationality Act granting citizenship to all Native Americans without impairing tribal property. Rather than settling the point, the act raised serious questions concerning tribal sovereignty and the government's jurisdiction concerning the drafting of Indians.[12]

Immediately after Congress passed the Selective Service Act, the issue of Indian wardship resurfaced, as did Alice Lee Jemison. In the fall of 1940 she circulated a petition stating:

> Indians are incompetent wards and as such cannot be conscripted for military service any more than the inmates of insane institutions can be conscripted, nor can they ever be until the Constitution of the United States is amended and the Bureau of Indian Affairs abolished.

Such remarks incurred Collier's full wrath. Zimmerman appealed to Clarence Dykstra, Director of Selective Service in Washington, D. C., to acquaint Jemison with "the impropriety or perhaps the illegality of her statements." E. K. Burlew, Acting Secretary of the Interior, reported Jemison's remarks to the Assistant Attorney General John Rogge and requested that she be prosecuted for criminal libel.[13]

Jemison escaped any serious consequences, as did her former colleague, Purl Willis. Willis, a white counselor for the Mission Indian Federation, had helped create the American Indian Federation but later broke with the group over monetary issues. Throughout the years Willis had played a dual role in Indian affairs, alternating between criticism of the Indian Bureau and informing on other agitators. A proponent of emancipation and the abolition of the Indian Bureau, Willis attacked the draft issue from a more subtle angle. In a fit of sophistry, he argued that if an Indian were a citizen, he could not be a ward. Conversely, if he were a ward, he could not be drafted as a soldier. Much as the Cherokees had done, he proclaimed the patriotism of the Mission Indians while seeking the "full protection" of the law. Cutting through the semantics, Collier declared that registration made no distinction between wards and non-wards. Furthermore, he informed Willis, the Supreme Court had ruled that Indian citizenship and wardship were compatible.[14] Willis remained unconvinced by Collier's stand and continued to counsel Mission Indians on their registration rights. During an investigation by William Palmer, United States District Attorney in Los Angeles, several Indians stated that Willis had advised them they were not subject to the draft. They testified that he based his remarks on a supposed letter from Collier. The commissioner again rushed to defend his position by suggesting that legal action proceed against Willis. Maintaining the loyalty of the Mission Indians, Collier remarked that the Indians desired to register but probably felt confused by "the false counsel" they had received.[15]

A final proponent of draft deferment for wards based his decision on deprivation of constitutional rights. John Hamilton, President of the National American Indian Defense Association and Chairman of the Republican National Committee, informed Dykstra that his organization protested "the drafting of American Indian wards living on Indian reservations under Federal Bureau jurisdiction." A long-term Collier critic, Hamilton challenged the constitutionality of the 1924 Snyder Act and charged that "destitute" and "deplorable" reservation conditions deprived Native Americans of all constitutional rights. The AIDA president suggested that Indians be allowed to serve voluntarily but not be subject to the draft.[16]

While these agitators discussed the issue of wardship versus citizenship, New York Indians presented the most complex and compelling argument of the period. Claiming that the Six Nations Indians were neither citizens nor wards, they asserted that tribal sovereignty prevented the government from drafting them. The Mohawks of the St. Regis Reservation in Honansburg, New York, made a year-long concerted effort to avoid the draft by contending that the Six Nations constituted an independent sovereignty and had not come under the jurisdiction of the Snyder Act. Herrick and Hershey hastened to inform the Mohawks that they were indeed citizens. Chiefs Thomas Lazore and Louis Terrance found this decision to be unsatisfactory and asked for further consideration from President Roosevelt. Events proceeded quietly with "undeniable delinquencies" in New York until the summer of July, 1941, when the Honansburg local draft board reported that the Indian tendency to cooperate with registration had disintegrated. Members of the board blamed two college graduates who "openly defied our regulations" for sparking a rebellion which resulted in one army desertion.[17]

Another member of the Six Nations Confederacy, from the Tuscarora Tribe, also protested that seventy-three tribal members had been inducted into the Armed Forces. Collier told this tribe that they would be exempt from service, but not from registration, if the courts sustained their argument. As usual Collier felt torn between his innate sympathy for the unique traditions of Indian tribes and his desire to fully cooperate with Selective Service. "I am well aware," he told the Mohawks, "of the deeply-rooted sentiment, pride, and ideal which is expressed in the position which you have taken . . . nor do I question your American patriotism."[18]

Other tribes followed the example of the Six Nation Confederacy in claiming exemption because of tribal sovereignty and possibly cultural genocide. John Tatapash, Chief of the Sac-Fox-Tama tribe in Iowa, explained that after the War of 1812, President James Madison had promised this tribe that they would never again have to fight. Furthermore, he explained that their tiny tribe of only 480 people had already sent many volunteers into the armed forces, causing hardships in some families. "My people do not object to voluntary enlistment," said Chief Tatapash, "but there are those boys whose parents would be better off if they were allowed to stay home." In Montana, a Creek registrant also claimed that a treaty between the government and his tribe prevented his induction into the armed forces. A bewildered state board officer deferred to national headquarters for advice.[19]

Canadian Indians added a new twist to the question of tribal sovereignty. Many Iroquois Indians, claiming neither American nor Canadian citizenship, traveled freely between the two countries and often resided for several months out of the year in both places. Selective Service appeared unable to arrive at a decision concerning their status. The American government, by rejecting many Canadian Indians who sought to volunteer, created great resentment among the American Iroquois. In other cases, the government insisted that these tribes must register, and when many failed to do so, the United States Attorney General indicted them for draft evasion. In January, 1944, Harry Howard Bomberry, a member of the Canadian Six Nations Reservation, declared he would serve voluntarily only if the courts decided that he was liable for military service. New York United States Attorney George L. Grobe deferred prosecution until the court settled the legal question.[20]

As Collier had predicted, eventually the courts settled the issue of tribal sovereignty. To the Montana State Board, Selective Service officials cited the case of *Totus et al v. United States et al*. This decision held that Congress reserved the right to repeal or to suspend any treaty during an emergency. Furthermore, the Selective Service Act superseded all previous treaties and laws. New York Indians suffered from a similar decision arising from the court case of Warren Eldreth Green. On April 26, 1941, the army drafted Green, an Onondaga Indian from Syracuse, New York. Green immediately appealed for a discharge claiming that he was not a United States citizen. As with previous claimants, he asserted that the government had violated his treaty rights, based on the Canandaigua Treaty of 1794 which stated:

> The United States acknowledge the lands reserved to the Oneida, Onondaga, and Cayuga Nations, in their respective treaties with the State of New York, and called their reservations, to be their property; and the United States will never claim the same, nor disturb them or either of the Six Nations, nor their Indian friends residing thereon and united with them in the free use and enjoyment thereof. . . .[21]

Furthermore, Green contended that he was not a citizen because the Citizenship Act of 1924 and the Nationality Act of 1940 were unconstitutional and violated the treaty rights of the Six Nations. Therefore, he could not be drafted. Jerome Frank, federal judge with the Second Circuit Court of Appeals, however, disagreed, albeit reluctantly. Although conceding that the Six Nations of Indians were an independent nation and that the acts may have violated treaty status, Frank ruled that a domestic act took precedence over an earlier treaty in domestic courts. By this reasoning, Green was a citizen and subject to the draft. Furthermore, other court decisions held that Canadian Indians, like other resident aliens, must register and serve under the Selective Service requirements.[22]

Several Indian tribes resisted the draft because of their traditional distrust and suspicion of the white world. Generally, these non-English-speaking, unassimilated, and less literate tribal Indians strained the sympathy and patience of government officials with their refusal to conform. In December, 1940, Arizona Governor John Miles informed Dykstra that his state had confronted a "peculiar situation" concerning the Navajo. Because of that tribe's nomadic nature, the San Juan and McKinley County Draft Boards encountered difficulties locating draft-age individuals, who also refused to return questionnaires. Miles suggested that Selective Service hire a San Juan County Deputy Sheriff named Charlie Ashcroft to follow the registrants from place to place in their wanderings. Ashcroft could place ringleaders under arrest and bring them to Santa Fe. In addition Ashcroft, fluent in several Indian languages, could be employed to explain the physical examinations and questionnaires. Miles praised Ashcroft highly as a man who had lived among Indians, gained their trust, understood their dispositions, and could act as a "propaganda agent to disseminate the truth." Finally, the governor explained that while most Navajo wished to obey the law, they remained unaware that Congress had passed the draft lottery and believed it to be merely another Indian Bureau regulation.[23]

Because Selective Service powers extended only to informing on delinquents, Dykstra objected to utilizing Ashcroft as a police agent or as anything other than an interpreter. Prosecution of violations fell within the jurisdiction of the FBI, which could solicit the cooperation of local law enforcement officials. "I wish to assure you," Dykstra intoned, "that we thoroughly understand the complexity of the problem." As had many before him, Dykstra definitely erred when he believed he comprehended the Navajo. Coons, who had gained some insight into Native American character in his brief encounters with them, reminded his superiors that they should "continually attempt to convince the Indians that their traditions and beliefs are not incompatible with their duties . . . as citizens." He further suggested that because Major R. R. Sedillo of the Manpower Division had the most interest and experience with Indians, he should handle tribal affairs.[24]

Unlike Dykstra, Sedillo favored hiring Ashcroft to perform special police duties, as did the San Juan County Local Board in Farmington, New Mexico. Three members of this board sent a strong protest to State Director Russell Charlton complaining that Navajo delinquencies caused undue hardship for the local whites. Bemoaning the ineffectiveness of state and local police, they declared that only Ashcroft, briefly employed for one month, had been successful in locating delinquents. "We wish that something might be done to give us the assistance of a special officer," they pleaded, "without which we will be unable to handle the Navajo situation."[25]

Charlton agreed that only Ashcroft could handle the situation, but he vacillated by passing the problem on to Collier. The State Director complained that because National Headquarters had declined to pay Ashcroft's salary in November, the state had temporarily assumed responsibility, but lacked the funds to continue his employment. Since Ashcroft had been relieved of his duties, the counties of San Juan and McKinley could furnish only half their quotas. Charlton requested that Ashcroft "or some person of equal ability" be employed as "special police," and he hoped for financial assistance from National Headquarters or the Indian Bureau. Before the situation completely disintegrated, the New Mexico State Board assumed responsibility for the upcoming July, 1941, registration, set up eighteen registration sites on the Navajo Reservation covering four states, and hired Ashcroft to bring in "recalcitrant Navajos."[26]

A similar situation of "passing the buck" between the Indian Service and Selective Service occurred with the Seminole Tribe. Superintendent Dwight Gardin of the Seminole Indian Agency in Dania, Florida, complained that when he reported draft delinquencies, the FBI and local draft boards took the attitude of "let the other fellow do it." The Superintendent contended that such inaction undermined his credibility when he warned Indians of the penalties for non-registration, because they simply ignored him and left the reservation to avoid the draft. Gardin also believed that local whites exerted negative influences on many of the delinquents. Collier, who considered this "a most embarrassing situation," agreed with Gardin and hastened to urge the Attorney General's office to take legal action "promptly and vigorously."[27]

Unlike the Navajo, the Seminole slipped through the bureaucratic cracks. Two years after Collier recommended vigorous prosecution, many Florida draft boards still believed that the Seminole did not have to register. Furthermore, Selective Service never classified several Florida Indians who did register. Lieutenant Colonel Glenn Parker, Alien Section of the Manpower Division, estimated that of the 150 to 175 eligible Seminole males who lived in Florida, only a hundred had already registered. Because so few of them had been found "fit for service," he considered "it probably is not worthwhile to take any positive action." The Florida Selective Service Board concurred that prosecution of delinquencies would serve little purpose. "It is believed that enforcement of registration," said State Director Vivian Collins, "would only serve to produce further distrust of and animosity toward the white man."[28]

The Seminole furnished classic examples of Native American forms of and reasons for resistance. First, like the Navajo, the Seminole could simply disappear at will. "It is a known fact," stated Collins, accepting the obvious, "that these Seminole Indians are well acquainted with the Florida Everglades, a wilderness through which white men cannot attempt to travel without the assistance of an Indian guide." Second, many whites, like Superintendent Gardin, often mistook Native American uncooperativeness for lack of patriotism or willfulness. Despite their open reluctance and antagonism, the new Seminole superintendent, William Hill, protested that his charges were not unpatriotic or "slackers," but merely timid, bewildered, and self-conscious about being forced into white society where they felt incapable of competing. "I honestly feel they would fight for us in their way," he assured Collier.[29]

On a more sophisticated level, both the Hopi and the Zuni claimed status as conscientious objectors and opposed fighting in any form. Throughout the war, the New Mexico Zuni made continuous efforts to keep their young men from being drafted. This clannish Pueblo tribe exhibited an historical suspicion of the white world, and many believed the war to be none of their concern. Despite this attitude, from February, 1941 to March, 1946, the Zuni contributed 213 men, ten percent of their population of 2,205, to the armed forces. When the military tried to draft more men, the Pueblo governor, the civil council, and the high priest council requested deferments for men who held both short and lifetime religious offices.[30]

At first the United Pueblo Agency in Albuquerque complied with these requests by recommending that the local draft board give these men 4-D classification, which exempted regular ordained religious ministers or students preparing for the ministry. As the Zuni tribe made increasing requests for deferment, however, the local board decided to exempt only those priests serving for life. Hoping to achieve a compromise, the board suggested that the tribe choose lifetime priests from men either too old or too young to serve in the armed forces. In response, the Zuni chose draft-age men to fill life term positions. It appears that the tribe experienced an increased religious fervor during the war.[31]

With cultural misunderstandings rampant on both sides, the government generally advised patience in handling delinquencies, but patience expired when dealing with the Hopi, destined to be the only tribe persecuted for draft evasion. In 1940 six Arizona Hopi refused to register for Selective Service. These young men came from families who followed James Chanhongva and Dan Katchongva, leaders of a group known as the "hostiles." Fiercely opposed to any government authority, the members of the group refused to conform to regulations, even to the extent of not sending their children to school. Acknowledging that enforcement of the rules meant imprisonment for these "hostiles," the reservation superintendent had never exercised strict authority, and these tribal members simply ignored the new draft law as another meaningless Indian Bureau regulation. When confronted by Selective Service officials who demanded that they register, these Hopi claimed their Bear Clan traditions forbade subservience to outside authority.[32]

Collier immediately tried to defuse the situation by explaining to Coons that the Hopi refusal "grows out of a religious tradition even though it may not be a conscientious objection against warfare . . . in the way that the white men construe it." Superintendent Wilson, however, disagreed with his superior, stating that several Hopi ceremonial chiefs had announced that nothing in their religious traditions prevented participation in defense measures. In addition, he said, the recalcitrant men had testified that their refusal did not "result from a ceremonial instruction, and for over four hours, the draft board and Indian Service employees had patiently explained the registration requirements to the young men, all educated, literate and English speaking."[33]

The Hopi situation embarrassed the draft board, the Indian Bureau, and the Hopi ceremonial leaders—indeed, everyone except the draft evaders. In December, 1940, the board recommended leniency regarding the young men, but then claimed that the boys' attitude prejudiced their case. "The boys have on several occasions been insolent in their attitude," Superintendent Wilson told Collier. "They have stated that no one is powerful enough to make them do something they don't want to do." Convinced that conscientious objection on religious or any other grounds could not be proven, Wilson reluctantly planned to testify in court and plead "the peculiar psychology of the Hopi toward law and order."[34]

In 1942, despite Wilson's good intentions, five of the young men still refused to register. After serving prison sentences, they returned to their tribe and boasted to their friends that "prison is a cinch." Encouraged by this negative example, fifteen more Hopi refused to register. Clearly out of patience and unconvinced by cultural or traditional arguments, the Department of Justice planned to again prosecute those five recently released from prison. The justification for prosecution stemmed from their charges that these Hopi were influencing others to refuse to answer questionnaires and to evade the draft. Justice Department officials also targeted two elderly Hopi leaders who were committing the same offense.[35]

The Department of Justice might have prosecuted other tribes as vigorously as the Hopi had the government clearly delineated areas of jurisdiction during the war. Issues such as wardship, citizenship, and tribal sovereignty confused officials, who hesitated to encroach on other department domains. Such caution added to Native American doubts concerning their role in the war, discomposed superintendents who often received conflicting orders from different agencies, and irritated local boards, who blamed regional tribes when they were unable to fill draft quotas. Superintendent Charles Berry expressed an often repeated regret to Lieutenant Francis Roddy, Director of the New York State Selective Service, that he could do so little about the violations at his New York Indian Agency. He added, however, that the Indian Bureau had informed him that the Justice Department retained responsibility for prosecutions.[36]

Many state directors reported to National Headquarters that Indians violated the draft law more than non-Indians simply out of confusion. "However, I believe that was mostly due to the fact that the Department of Justice and the Indian Service passed the buck back and forth for months before they got down to business," charged A. M. Tuthill, Arizona State Director for Selective Service. "Had they been ready to clean up on these cases the first day, there would have been no subsequent trouble." Collier strongly objected to such allegations and maintained that he always cooperated. When he heard that the Mississippi Choctaw had been advised they did not have to register, he instantly contacted the Choctaw Superintendent, A. H. McMullen. Ickes too, in this and every other case, supported his employees and related to Hershey that "unauthorized sources" had misinformed the Indians.[37]

When other officials attempted to take charge of any situation, agencies jealously guarded their prerogatives. As in the case of the Navajo, Dykstra frustrated Miles's attempt to employ a private citizen to enroll the tribe and instead insisted that the FBI agents could adequately cope with the enrollment. Only when these agents failed to handle the issue did local authorities rebel and assume responsibility.[38] Further aggravating the situation, Indian tribes expressed resentment when so many of the potential draftees finally came into register, only to be rejected by the military. Because the primary reasons for rejection stemmed from health problems, lack of English skills, and illiteracy, the Navajo and Seminole constituted the majority of rejectees. In Arizona, forty-five percent of Indian men failed to pass military standards. The largest number of rejections, forty-eight and a half percent, stemmed from educational deficiencies, as compared with twelve percent for the white population. Among the Navajo, the illiteracy rate stood at a whopping eighty percent, and fifty-seven percent spoke only their native language.[39]

The high Navajo rejection rate caused an outcry in Arizona from Superintendent Reeseman Fryer, Governor John Miles, the local draft boards, and the Navajo Tribal Council. Miles pointed out to Dykstra that Navajo men equaled white men in the counties of McKinley and San Juan for the number of registrants, but the military had classified only five percent of Class 1-A Indians to be eligible. Although these Class 1-A registrants passed the physical and mental requirements, they failed the tests for language ability or literacy. Concerned for a further burden imposed on the white community, Miles implored Dykstra to use his influence with the War Department to lift these literacy requirements. Discounting past difficulties, Miles asserted, "The Navajo people in general desire that they shall assume their duties as citizens and serve in the armed forces." He described Navajos as "natively intelligent" people who learned readily "when given the opportunity."[40]

Navajo Superintendent Fryer, joined by General Charlton, also urged that Collier pressure Dykstra "to secure special consideration [for] southwestern Indians." Fryer relayed that the Navajo, who strongly believed the disqualifications to be unfair, were apt to say "the government is fooling us again." He suggested that Navajo recruits be sent to Fort Bliss, Texas, under the supervision of English-speaking non-commissioned Navajo officers. Collier lost no time in leaping to the attack, claiming that these rejections ranked as "distinct discrimination." While acknowledging that the lack of English speaking skills presented difficulties, he doubted that language alone should be the basis to declare the majority of Navajo ineligible. In a tone similar to Governor Miles, Collier highly praised the tribe's loyalty, stating, "Our Indians displayed their patriotism in the highest degree in the World War, and as our 'First Americans,' they certainly wish to have a part in our defense program by serving their country."[41]

By January 7, 1941, obviously convinced that he had made some headway with the problem, Collier told Fryer that the Selective Service had promised him that the non-English speaking Navajo would not face rejection much longer, but would be placed in a deferred status pending the establishment of a special training battalion. The Commissioner intended to urge authorities to create these battalions in order that the Navajo and other Indians would "have equal opportunity to render service." Other Native Americans rejected for language reasons included the Tohono O'Odham, who often memorized a few English phrases or learned to write their names when called to the induction center in order to be accepted.[42]

Although Collier found sympathetic allies in Coons and Sedillo—who presented the Navajo case to their superior, Major Gareth Brainerd, and argued for special programs—a year later the government had still failed to act. When the army finally instituted special courses for non-English-speaking illiterates, the military unsuccessfully attempted to train them. As a result, the army discharged many potential Indian recruits. Finally prevailed upon by the Indian Service, the War Department agreed to locate former Indian Service personnel serving in field duties and assign them to literacy training of Navajo in basic training centers. This method met with more positive results but took too long to institute. Frustrated by this inexplicible bureaucracy, the Navajo Tribal Council requested that their young men be trained and taught English on the reservation utilizing Navajo interpreters. Despite promises from a government representative that the government would build a military post on the reservation, none materialized. Instead the Indian Service established a pre-induction course for possible draftees at the Wingate Vocational School on the Navajo Reservation, where they taught military English and courtesy, first aid, self-defense, marksmanship, and map-reading.[43]

The Army Air Force, however, could claim the greatest accomplishment when they instituted a literacy program from 1942–1943 in Atlantic City, New Jersey. Given command of the school, Frank Becker, a former schoolteacher, discovered to his great surprise that he had inherited several Indian tribes, including Tohono O'Odham, Pima, and Navajo. With an unusual amount of compassion, patience and interest, Becker instructed his charges so well that they all graduated to military duty. Often expressing anger at the past treatment of the Navajo which he described as "passing along the proverbial buck," the private felt justified at their eventual military record. "It was with great satisfaction that I learned in spite of everything," he glowed, "my Navajo friends still fought a good war."[44]

As with the Navajo, the Seminole faced rejection for illiteracy and non-English speaking skills. Describing the Seminole as uneducated, General Collins stated that attempts at English conversations produced either negative replies or hard stares. Lieutenant Colonel Parker concurred, stating, "It appears that all of these Indians are uneducated, distrustful, and obviously unfit for any service unless it would be of a specialized type, such as might be employed in giving aid to grounding planes in the Everglades." Because of this attitude and the small tribal population of 341 men and 349 women, the army never actively pursued the Seminole.[45]

After educational reasons, the military rejected the largest amount of Indians for health reasons. Nationally, thirty-seven and a half percent of Native Americans failed to pass the physical examination, as compared to thirty-two percent for the white population. Doctors disqualified Indians primarily for trachoma (almost eight percent) and tuberculosis (five percent). Rampant on Indian reservations, these diseases had virtually disappeared among the white population, with its national average of less than four percent and one percent respectively. Arizona Indians specifically, including a large proportion of the Navajo, suffered an eleven percent rejection rate for trachoma and a forty-one percent rejection rate for tuberculosis.[46]

Other reasons for national rejection ranged from age to weight to gender. Among Arizona tribes, elderly Indians faced disappointment when they unsuccessfully attempted to enlist. "I rejected seven times on account of having old," a Pima Indian declared plaintively, "yet I am only thirty-seven years. My chance will come." Classified as overweight, another Arizona tribesman insisted, "Don't want to run. Want to fight." On other reservations, when Native American women endeavored to register in the male fighting branches, the Selective Service referred them to the female auxiliaries. Draft officials in Alaska experienced one of the most unusual incidents for a rejection. When the Alaskan draft registration occurred, Eskimos from the Big Diomede Island, which belonged to the Soviet Union, accompanied their American cousins from Little Diomede Island and insisted on being enrolled in the American Army. Selective Service officials tactfully explained to them that they must instead enlist in the Russian Army.[47]

Because of these rejections, Native Americans suffered embarrasment and disappointment. In contrast to the minority who resisted registration as unnecessary and a violation of their sovereign rights, the majority believed the war to be a personal issue. Native Americans had held a long tradition of military service with white armies, dating from the American Revolution when the Creeks and Cherokees aided the colonials in defeating the English army. From the 1860s to the 1880s, the United States military used Crow, Pawnee, and later Apache Indians as scouts and in battles against the Plains tribes. In 1898 Native Americans fought in the Spanish-American War, and 12,000 Indians—fully eighty-five percent of them volunteers—served in the first World War. During World War I, 600 Indian volunteers dominated the 36th Infantry Division, composed of Texas and National Guard units.[48]

Numerous witnesses attested to the bravery of the American Indian in World War I. Congressman Jed Joseph Johnson, Democratic Representative from Oklahoma from 1927 to 1947, served with Indians in World War I in the 36th Division, Company L, as a private. "I served with many full-blood Indians and part-Indians during World War I in France," he said. "I saw them in action in the front lines, and I was deeply impressed with their valor and courage. There were no better or braver soldiers than were the American Indians." During the twenties and thirties, Indians continued to enlist in all branches of military service. Prior to Pearl Harbor, 5,000 Indians had enrolled in the Army, the Navy, the Coast Guard, and the National Guard.[49]

Immediately after the war declaration, many Indians rushed to enlist in the armed forces. At some reservations half the male inhabitants volunteered for army duty, and many tribes held special war councils to prepare for the event. On January 12 and 13, 1942, the Navajo Tribal Council called a special convention to dramatize their support for the war and adopt a military plan of support for the country's war effort. At this event, attended by 50,000 tribal members, the Council promised to aid Selective Service, requested reservation training for non-English speakers, and announced their full patriotism by stating:

> We . . . the Navajo people . . . reaffirm our allegiance to the United States of America, to the President of the United States . . . to give our assistance where requested and at the times and in the manner deemed most necessary . . . until this nation shall achieve final, complete, and lasting victory.[50]

Although the Navajo claimed a large rejection rate of forty-five percent, they responded to the nation's need by sending 3,000 people, six percent of their population, into military service. Observers passed around stories of Navajo and other tribes so eager to instantly enter battle that they carried their rifles to registration centers. Navajo at Fort Defiance, Arizona, reportedly stood in the snow for hours to sign their draft cards. Among the Ramah Navajo, 800 men out of a population of 3,600 enlisted the day after war was declared. Other tribes quickly followed suit, leaving many reservations with a severe manpower shortage. Unwilling to wait for their draft numbers, one-fourth of the Mescalero Apache in New Mexico enlisted. This cut their herd-rider number in half, and the tribe faced difficulties driving their $75,000 worth of livestock to market that year.[51]

Throughout the United States, tribes exhibited the same war fervor as those in the Southwest. Wisconsin Chippewa at the Lac Oreilles Reservation contributed one hundred men from a population of 1,700. Nearly all the able-bodied Chippewa at the Grand

Portage Reservation enlisted. At the Montana Fort Peck Reservation, 131 Blackfeet volunteered. It was reported that many Native Americans misunderstood the need for a draft lottery and felt that everyone who signed up should automatically be sent to the front lines. In an apocryphal story that has been attributed to almost every other American Indian tribe, the Blackfeet supposedly mocked the need for a conscription bill. "Since when," one incredulous tribal member supposedly sneered, "has it been necessary for the Blackfeet to draw lots to fight?" Canadian Indians proved as zealous as American Indians. When a band of Cree tribesmen traveled 400 miles to enlist in the Canadian Army, they explained to officials that they would enjoy army life since they customarily fished in fifty-degree-below-zero weather. "Many Indians volunteering in both the Canadian and American armies are young men who have not been out of their forest and mountain fastnesses for several years," reported one satisfied congressman.[52]

The actual enlistment figures for Native Americans in military service jumped from a low of 7,500 in the summer of 1942 to a high of 22,000 at the beginning of 1945. According to the Selective Service in 1942, at least ninety-nine percent of all eligible American Indians, healthy males aged twenty-one to forty-four, had registered for the draft. Army officials maintained that if the entire population had enlisted in the same proportion as Indians, they would have rendered Selective Service unnecessary. By the end of the war, Indian Bureau officials estimated that 24,521 American Indians, exclusive of officers, had served, and another 20,000 off-reservation Indians had also enlisted. The combined total figure of 44,500 comprised more than ten percent of the Native American population of approximately 400,000.[53]

Native Americans exhibited various reasons for their high enlistment rate. As was the case for the rest of the population, military pay offered a welcome relief to many families devastated by a ten-year depression. Because the depression years affected reservations even more drastically than they did the mainstream population, these monetary supplements greatly aided most servicemen's relatives. Furthermore, most tribes viewed military service and training as honorable endeavors. Tribal members offered departing and returning servicemen and women all the traditional ceremonies and honors due to warriors. All these rituals sanctioned the tribal members' military participation, fulfilled religious criteria for battle, and added status and prestige to his or her tribal standing.[54]

When pressed by whites to explain their reasons for enlistment, however, the majority of Native Americans cited patriotism as their primary motive. In spite of past rejection and discrimination, American Indians joined the rest of the country to defend their nation. On a secondary level, Indians expressed a general distaste for the Nazi concept of racial superiority, and saw this as a threat to their own minority status. The Utah Shoshoni, for example, demonstrated their awareness of the German threat and an antagonism to Nazi propaganda in a tribal resolution. Although they sincerely hoped that America would avoid war, they promised to defend their country, but not Europe, "in the event of any foreign power invading our land." With a confidence bred through centuries of survival, the Northwest Band of Shoshoni boasted that "the Indian tribesmen of Utah, whose forebears made up a great American Nation centuries before there were such things as Nazism and Fascism, stand ready to do battle against invasion." Two years later an Indian member of the Celilo Tribe reiterated this antagonism as he described his reason for enlisting by comparing historical precedent with future possibilities:

> My grandparents fought against the white man. They were defending their homes. In many respects we have been treated badly. In this land which once was ours, we are poor. Many people treat us as outcasts and inferiors. Yet our conditions have slowly been improved. The reservation schools are good. We are trained for trades and farming. The government defends our rights. We know that under Nazism we should have no rights

> at all. We are not Aryans and we [w]ould be used as slaves.[55]

The Navajo also expressed their hostility to the Third Reich and evinced enthusiasm for defending their country. In 1934 this tribe had rejected overtures from the American Indian Federation, which had close ties to the German-American Bund and American Fascist sympathizers. Furthermore the Navajo Tribal Council had criticized one of its members, J. C. Morgan, whom they called a "tool and associate of unscrupulous white parasites," for becoming the association's vice-president. Much to Collier's delight, they continued to snub this group and another closely-associated group, the Silver Shirts. Because the Navajo language constituted one of the world's "hidden" languages, Germany correctly assumed that this tribe would be used as radio operators in the coming war. Despite their differences with the present administration, the tribe refused to accept the advances of German agents who attempted to enter the reservation posing as anthropologists in order to learn the language. Furthermore, the tribe rejected another newly-formed organization, the Navajo Rights Association, because they claimed it was "sowing seeds of discontent and confusion in the minds of the Navajo people." In June, 1940, the tribal council announced that they recognized "the threat of foreign invasion" and seized the opportunity to "serve notice that any un-American movement among our people will be resented and dealt with severely." Furthermore, the resolution added:

> We resolve that Navajo Indians stand ready as they did in 1918 to aid and defend our government and its institutions against all subversive and armed conflict and pledge our loyalty to the system which recognizes minority rights and a way of life that has placed us among the greatest people of our race.[56]

Forty years later Raymond Nakai, former Navajo Codetalker, stated his belief about Indian participation in World War II. "Many people ask why we fight the white man's war," he mused. "Our answer is that we are proud to be American. We're proud to be American Indians. We always stand ready when our country needs us."[57]

Native Americans certainly stood ready to "fight the white man's war," but they went to war on their own terms. Nationwide, tribes delivered war messages and prepared military ceremonies for departing servicemen. Zuni medicine men gave their draftees the "eutakya," a brief blessing ceremony for the protection of warriors. Using corn pollen and holy water, the Navajo performed the "Blessing Ceremony" for their inductees. In Wisconsin the Chippewa held "Going Away" and "Chief" dances to honor their enlistees and to ask the guardian spirits to aid and protect them overseas. Cheyenne and Arapajo women wove servicemen's names and insignias into blankets. Tribes honored women entering the military as well as men. When a young Sioux woman joined the Women's Army Auxiliary Corps, her family arranged a "Give-Away," a ceremony in which the family gives presents to other tribal members to show their gratitude for her new stature. Such ceremonies fulfilled both religious and social functions in addition to granting communal recognition of a newly-acquired status for the warrior. Although tribesmen publicly declared patriotism to be their prime motivation for entering the armed forces, privately they reaped far greater psychological and social benefits within their own communities.[58]

As Native Americans went to war on their own terms, they offered special gifts to a country only too delighted to receive them. Tribesmen exonerated their less fortunate members by making a virtue of language, that very skill for which so many had previously suffered rejection. In World War I the military had discovered the unique value of Native American languages when a front-line artillery unit experienced difficulty in transmitting messages, the enemy having continually decoded all transmissions. Because he had two Native Americans from the same tribe in his unit, an officer decided to test them as telephone operators. Speaking in their tribal language, "they completely baffled the enemy, who never succeeded in decoding the mysterious and unintelligible sounds that came across the wires."[59]

Encouraged by the success in World War I, the military made plans to utilize native languages early in the second world war. In January, 1941, the Fourth Signal Company recruited thirty Oklahoma Cherokee Indians to be part of a special Signal Corps Detachment. And the Thirty-Second Division of the Third Army in western Louisiana employed seventeen Michigan and Wisconsin Indians to work with microphones and transmit messages.[60] In a strange twist of fate, the Navajo Codetalkers became the most celebrated and publicized of all the radio units. The project was a joint effort between Navajo recruits and Philip Johnston, the son of white missionaries who grew up on the reservation and became one of the few whites who could speak fluent Navajo. A World War I veteran, in 1942 Johnston approached the marines with the idea of recruiting Navajo Indians as radio operators using a special code based on their language. Because Indian vocabularies lacked modern military terms, the Navajo recruits invented names, such as turtle for tank and insect for airplane, creating a code which became impossible for the Japanese to break. After several months training, the Marine Corps placed the Navajo recruits, who eventually numbered over four hundred, by pairs in separate units. Displaying justifiable pride in the Codetalker graduates, Johnston declared, "From Guadalcanal to the last bitter, bloody days on Okinawa, they played a crucial role."[61]

Another all-Indian unit, Company F of the 158th Infantry Regiment, 40th Division in the Arizona National Guard, "drew its members entirely from Phoenix Indian School and its alumni." When the Arizona National Guard had been reorganized in 1924, the guard allowed Company F to drill at the Phoenix Indian School, maintain an armory, and conduct inspections. In September, 1940, the Arizona National Guard was reactivated for federal service, and sixty-one students were recruited from the Phoenix

Indian School and from Company F reserves. On December 8, 1941, the military sent these men to Panama as part of the 158th Regimental Combat Team. Ultimately this elite fighting unit, trained in hand-to-hand combat, knives, and assault weapons, would gain distinction in the Pacific Theatre and earn the name "The Bushmasters." In one significant battle at Arawe Island, the Bushmasters, composed of both whites and Native Americans from twenty different tribes, rescued the Texas Cavalry.[62]

Of equal significance to the role of rituals and language usage, Native Americans again expressed their tribal sovereignty in electing to separately declare war on the nation's enemies. In July, 1942, even as they battled in court the government's right to draft their young men, the Six Nations formally declared war on Italy, Japan, and Germany. Several other tribes, including the Oklahoma Osage, the South Dakota Sioux, and the Oklahoma Ponca tribes, also made their own declarations of war on the Axis powers. Through these war declarations, Native American tribes proved that they viewed the war from their own personal perspective, both on the battlefield and in the courts. Influenced by their servicemen, American Indians would continue after the war to express this resurgence of tribal sovereignty by other means and for other purposes. Furthermore the idea of tribal sovereignty, coupled with a strong American Indian war participation, caught the attention of the nation. Intrigued by the concept of patriotism and sovereignty, Americans read about the activities of Indians with great interest. Eventually, as the War Department and the Department of the Interior realized the potential propaganda value of Native Americans, they launched full-scale publicity campaigns in journals, newspapers, radio, and film to exploit the Indian record. In essence, after "bringing them in alive," America discovered that the Indian had become one of America's greatest weapons.[63]

[1] Congressional Record, 77th Cong., 2d sess., A4386, December 16, 1942.

[2] J. R. McGibony, "Indians and Selective Service," *Public Health Reports*, No. 1 (January 2, 1942): 57:1.

[3] Brian Dippie, *The Vanishing American: White Attitudes and United States Indian Policy* (Connecticut: Wesleyan U P, 1982): 276; *Newsweek*, April 26, 1943, 21:80–81.

[4] 1938 Document on Indian Reservations; January 1, 1939 Document on Estimated Indian Male Population, July 9, 1940; July 9, 1940, Captain W. B. Palmer to John Collier; July 10, 1940, Collier to Palmer; August 6, 1940 Memorandum in Connection with Indian Reservations, Record Group 147, entry 1, box 33, folder "105.1 Indians—General," National Archives, Suitland, Maryland.

[5] Plan of the Pueblos, October 1, 1940; William Zimmerman, August 13, 1940; Record Group 147, entry 1, box 33, folder "105.1 Indians—General."

[6] Zimmerman to Hershey, August 13, 1940; Hershey to Zimmerman, August 22, 1940; Record Group 147, entry 1, box 33, folder "105.1 Indians—General."

[7] Daiker to Hershey, September 13, 1940, September 23, 1940; Collier to All Superintendents, October 7, 1940; Captain Robert Coons to R. V. Venning, Division of Indian Affairs, October 8, 1940; Record Group 147, entry 1, box 33, folder "105.1 Indians—General"; "Selective Service Act," Public Law 720, 76th Cong., 3d sess., *United States Laws and Statutes* (Washington, D. C.: Government Printing Office, 1971): September 16, 1940, 885–88.

[8] American Association on Indian Affairs, Inc. *Newsletter*, November 20, 1940, Record Group 75, entry 178, box A–B, folder "American Association on Indian Affairs," National Archives, Washington, D. C.

[9] Cherokee Council House Resolution on November 5, 1940; Zimmerman to C. M. Blair, Superintendent of Cherokee Agency, December 14, 1940; Record Group 147, entry 1, box 33, folder "105.1 Indians—General."

[10] Seth Wilson, Chairman, Navajo Country Local Board No. 2, to William R. Bourdon, Chairman, Navajo Country Local Board, June 3, 1941; Major Harry S. Bowman, Acting State Director, New Mexico, to National Headquarters, Washington, D. C., June 7, 1941, Record Group 147, entry 1, box 33, folder "105.1 Indians—General"; *Navajo Tribal Council Resolutions 1922–1951* (Washington, D. C.: Government Printing Office, 1952): 469.

[11] Collier to Hershey, June 22, 1942; Collier to Hershey, March 29, 1942; Colonel C. G. Parker, Jr., U.S. Marines Corp to Collier, September 30, 1942; Record Group 147, entry 1, box 421, folder "214. Indian Reservations, Alabama to Wyoming, 1942."

[12] McGibony, "Indians and Selective Service," 1; Collier to Bernard Gorrow, Governor, New York, January 16, 1941; Record Group 147, entry 1, box 136, folder "214. Indians Reservations—General"; 54th Statute, 76th Cong., 3d sess., October 14, 1940.

[13]Memorandum for the Press, October 30, 1940; Zimmerman to Dr. Clarence A. Dykstra, November 27, 1940; E. K. Burlew to John Rogge, November 15, 1940; Record Group 75, entry 178, box 1, folder "American Indian Federation, 1938–1940," National Archives, Washington, D. C.

[14]Purl Willis to Collier, October 5, 1940; Collier to Willis, October 18, 1940; Record Group 147, entry 1, box 136, folder "214. Indian Reservations, Alabama to Wyoming, 1941."

[15]Collier to William Palmer, January 3, 1941; Record Group 147, entry 1, box 136, folder "214. Indian Reservations—General, 1941."

[16]John Hamilton, President, National American Indian Defense Association, Inc., April 3, 1941; Record Group 147, entry 1, box 136, folder "214. Indian Reservations—General, 1941."

[17]John Herrick to Thomas Lazore, Alex Solomon and Louis Terrance, October 12, 1940; Lazore, Solomon and Terrance to Franklin Delano Roosevelt, March 11, 1941; Lieutenant Colonel Francis G. Roddy to Lieutenant Colonel Cariton S. Dargusch, Selective Service National Headquarters, June 10, 1941; Dr. Aloney L. Rust, Chairman, Malone, New York Local Board to Roddy, July 9, 1941; Record Group 147, entry 1, box 136, folder "214. Indian Reservations—General, 1941."

[18]C. H. Berry to Roddy, January 14, 1941, Record Group 147, entry 1, box 36, folder "214. Indian Reservations, Alabama to Wyoming, 1941."

[19]Bertha Wasesku, Milwaukee, Wisconsin, to Representative John Gwynne, Washington, D. C., November 25, 1942; Gwynne to Hershey, December 1, 1942; Record Group 147, entry 1, box 427, folder "214. Indian Reservations, Alabama to Wyoming, 1942"; Adrian Williams, Montana Advisor on Occupational Deferments to National Director of Selective Service, September 13, 1941, Record Group 147, entry 1, box 136, folder "214. Indian Reservations—General, 1941."

[20]"Selective Service Act," Section 3A; Memorandum from Lieutenant Colonel Glenn Parker, Manpower Division, January 5, 1944; George L. Grobe, United States Attorney, Buffalo, New York, to Attorney General, Washington, D. C., January 16, 1944; Record Group 147, entry 1, box 1278, folder "214. Indian Reservations—General, 1944"; Major William Brewer, Foreign Liaison Section, Manpower Division, to Lieutenant Colonel Charles Bartlett, Acting State Director, Maine, March 11, 1944; Bartlett to National Headquarters, February 24, 1944; Parker to General Pearson, Michigan State Director of Selective Service, March 27, 1944; Record Group 147, entry 1, box 1278, folder "214. Indian Reservations, Alabama to Wyoming, 1944."

[21]Dargusch to Colonel Bixley, Montana State Director of Selective Service, September 22, 1941, Record Group 147, entry 1, box 136, folder "214. Indian Reservations—General, 1941"; "Ex parte Green," 123 Federal Reporter 2d, 862, November 24, 1941; "Treaty with the Six Nations, 1794," from *U. S. Laws and*

Statutes, Indian Affairs, Laws and Treaties, Vol. II ed. Charles J. Kappler (Washington, D. C.: Government Printing Office, 1971): 34–35.

[22]Ibid.

[23]John Miles to Clarence Dykstra, December 24, 1940, Record Group 147, entry 1, box 136, folder "214. Indian Reservations—General, 1941."

[24]Dykstra to Miles, January 3, 1941; Coons to Major Gareth Brainerd, January 7, 1941; Record Group 147, entry 1, box 136, folder "214. Indian Reservations—General, 1941."

[25]Dykstra to Miles, January 3, 1941; Coons to Brainerd, January 7, 1941; Record Group 147, entry 1, box 136, folder "214. Indian Reservations—General, 1941.

[26]Charlton to Collier, April 1 , 1941; Bowman to Selective Service, National Headquarters, January 7, 1941; Record Group 147, entry 1, box 136, folder "214. Indian Reservations—General, 1941."

[27]Dwight R. Gardin to Collier, February 10, 1941; Collier to James McInerney, Special Assistant to the Attorney General, Department of Justice, February 20, 1941; Record Group 147, entry 1, box 136, folder "214. Indian Reservations—General, 1941."

[28]Parker to General Vivian Collins, Florida State Director of Selective Service, August 30, 1943; Parker Desk Memorandum on Seminole Indians, September 23, 1943; Wendell Berges, Assistant Attorney General, Department of Justice, to Herbert S. Phillips, United States Attorney, Miami, Florida, August 13, 1943; Phillips to Attorney General, August 12, 1943; Record Group 147, entry 1, box 817, "214. Indian Reservations, Alabama to Wyoming, 1943."

[29]Ibid.

[30]John Adair and Evon Vogt, "Navajo and Zuni Veterans: A Study of Contrasting Modes of Cultural Change," *American Anthropologist*, 51 (October–December, 1949): 548.

[31]Adair and Vogt, 548; "Selective Service Act," 888.

[32]Collier to Coons, December 10, 1940; Seth Wilson, Superintendent of Hopi Indian Agency, to Collier, December 24, 1940; Record Group 147, entry 1, box 136, folder "214. Indian Reservations, Alabama to Wyoming, 1941."

[33]Ibid.

[34]Ibid.

[35]July 18, 1942, Major William S. Iliff, Jr., Memorandum to Colonel Baker and Colonel Shattuck, Record Group 147, entry 1, folder "214. Indian Reservations, Alabama to Wyoming, 1942."

[36]Berry to Roddy, August 8, 1941; Record Group 147, entry 1, box 136, folder "214. Indian Reservations—General, 1941."

[37]A. M. Tuthill, State Director for Selective Service, to Dargusch, June 11, 1941; Record Group 147, entry 1, box 136, "214. Indian Reservations, Alabama to Wyoming, 1941"; Collier to Hershey, July 2, 1942; Ickes to Hershey, July 31, 1942;

Mable Stennis, Clerk, to Colonel H. J. Dolton, State Director Selective Service, Mississippi, June 15, 1942; Record Group 147, entry 1, box 426, folder "214. Indian Reservations, Alabama to Wyoming, 1942."

[38]Miles to Dykstra, January 13, 1941; Record Group 147, entry 1, box 136, folder "214. Indian Reservations—General, 1941."

[39]*Time*, August 12, 1946; Carling Malouf, "Observations on the Participation of Arizona's Racial and Cultural Groups in World War II," *The American Journal of Physical Anthropology*, Vol. 5, No. 4 (December, 1947): 493.

[40]Miles to Dykstra, December 24, 1940; Record Group 147, entry 1, box 136, folder "214. Indian Reservations—General, 1941."

[41]Superintendent Fryer, Windowrock, Arizona, to Collier, December 30, 1940; Fryer to Collier, January 2, 1941; Record Group 147, entry 1, box 136, folder "214. Indian Reservations—General, 1941"; Collier to Dykstra, January 3, 1941; Record Group 147, entry 1, box 136, folder "214. Indian Reservations, Alabama to Wyoming, 1941."

[42]Collier to Fryer, January 7, 1941; Record Group 75, entry 195, box 3, folder "National Defense"; *Indians at Work* Vol. X, Nos. 2–6 (Washington, D. C.: United States Department of the Interior, Bureau of Indian Affairs, February, 1943): 49.

[43]Coons to Brainerd, January 14, 1941; Sedillo to Brainerd, January 7, 1941; Record Group 147, entry 1, box 136, folder "214. Indian Reservations—General, 1941"; E. W. Thomas, "America's First Families on the Warpath," *Common Ground* 2, No. 4 (1942): 99; Thomas E. Becker, *Navajo Way* (New York: The Indian Association of America, Inc., 1956): 22.

[44]Indian Office History, 93, Record Group 48, entry 858, box 7, folder "Indian Office History," National Archives, Washington, D.C.; Becker, *Navajo Way*, 22; *Indians at Work* Vol. X, Nos. 2–6 (October, 1942–January, 1943): 17.

[45]General Vivian Collins, Florida Selective Service Director, to National Selective Service Director, September 13, 1943; Parker Desk Memorandum, September 23, 1943; Record Group 147, entry 1, box 816, folder "214. Indian Reservations, Alabama to Wyoming, 1943."

[46]McGibony, "Indians and Selective Service," 1–7; Malouf, "Arizona's Racial and Cultural Groups," 493.

[47]*Congressional Record*, 77th Cong., 2d sess., 4125, November 30, 1942, A4386; John Collier, "Indians in a Wartime Nation," *Annals of the American Academy of Political and Social Science*, 223 (September, 1942): 29; New York *Times*, January 7, 1942, 4:5.

[48]Lonnie White, "Indian Soldiers of the 36th Division," *Military History of the Texas Southwest* 15, No. 1 (1979): 8; *Annual Report of the Commissioner of Indian Affairs*, 1941, 410.

[49]Collier, "Wartime Nation," 223; New York *Times*, September 21, 1942, 15:2; Elizabeth Shipley Sergeant, "The Indian Goes to War," *New Republic*, 107 (November 30, 1942): 708–709.

[50]Navajo Tribal Council Resolutions, 22; *Congressional Record,* 78th Cong., 2d sess., A4385, December, 16, 1942; New York *Times,* May 10, 1942, 20:8; *Indians at Work,* Vol. IX, No. 7, 17.

[51]New York *Times,* May 10, 1942, IX, 2:5, October 23, 1942, 20:3, August 30, 1942, IV, 7:6; "Establishment of Joint Committee to Investigate Claims Against the United States," Congressional Committee Hearings, Senate Committee on Indian Affairs, Senate Joint Resolution 79, 79th Cong., 2d sess., May 14, 1946; *Congressional Record,* 77th Cong., 2d sess., A4385; *Annual Report of the Commissioner of Indian Affairs 1942,* 237; Adair and Vogt, "Navajo and Zuni Veterans," 551.

[52]Robert Ritzenhaler, "The Impact of War on an Indian Community," *American Anthropologist* 45 (April–June, 1943): 325; Richard Neuberger, "On the Warpath," *Saturday Evening Post,* 215 (October 24, 1942): 79; *Congressional Record,* 77th Cong., 2d sess., A3160, A4385, December 16, 1942.

[53]Collier, "Wartime Nation," 29; New York *Times,* January 23, 1945, 6:1; August 30, 1942, IV, 7:6; Neuberger, "On the Warpath," 628; McGibony, "Selective Service," 1.

[54]Becker, "Navajo Way," 1, 21–22; Thomas, "First Families," 95; O. K. Armstrong, "Set the American Indians Free!" *The Reader's Digest* (August, 1945): 47:51; Stanley Vestal, "The Plains Indian and the War," *Saturday Review of Literature,* 25 (May 16, 1942): 10.

[55]*Congressional Record,* 77th Cong., 2d sess., A4385; *Indians at Work,* Vol. VIII, No. 4 (December, 1940): 24.

[56]New York *Times,* April 25, 1942, 6:5; *Navajo Tribal Council Resolutions,* June 23, 1942; June 4, 1940; Chee Dodge, Navajo Tribal Chairman, to Collier, February 6, 1935, Record Group 75, entry 178, box 8, folder "J. C. Morgan Activities."

[57]Dan B. McCarthy, "Samuel Smith and Son Michael . . . Plus 52 Other Navajo U.S. Marines!" *VFW Magazine* (January, 1982): 26.

[58]Robert Ritzenhaler, "The Impact of War on an Indian Community," *American Anthropologist,* 45 (April–June, 1943): 326; Adair and Vogt, "Navajo and Zuni Veterans," 548, 552; Thomas, "First Families," 993, New York *Times,* April 10, 1944, 13:2.

[59]*Indians at Work,* Vol. VIII, No. 7 (March, 1941): 10.

[60]*Fourth Signal Company* (Baton Rouge, Louisiana: Army and Navy Publishing Company, 1946): 1; *Indians at Work,* Vol. IX, No. 2 (October, 1941): 13.

[61]Philip Johnston, "Indian Jargon Won Our Battles," *The Masterkey,* 130–37; New York *Times,* September 19, 1945, 9:1, July 5, 1942, 13:5.

[62]Dorothy R. Parker, *Phoenix Indian School: The Second Half-Century* (Tucson: The U of Arizona P, 1996): 26–27, New York *Times,* January 19, 1944, 3:1.

[63]New York *Times,* June 13, 1942, 17:5, September 9, 1945, 18:4, August 6, 1945, 17:6.

Three Marine Corps women reservists, Camp Lejeune, North Carolina. L-R: Minnie Spotted Wolf (Blackfoot), Cecelia Mix (Potawatomi), and Viola Eastman (Chippewa). U. S. Marine Corps photograph, October 16, 1943. National Archives 208-NS-4350-2.

PFC Ira H. Hayes, a Pima, at age nineteen, ready to jump, Marine Corps Paratroop School. U. S. Marine Corps photograph, 1943. National Archives 75-N-PIM-33.

Lt. Woody J. Cochran, holding a Japanese flag in New Guinea. A Cherokee from Skedee, Oklahoma, and a bomber pilot, Cochran earned the Air Medal, the Distinguished Flying Cross, the Silver Star, and the Purple Heart. On April 1, 1943, when this picture was made, he had just been released from a hospital where he had been recovering from a neck wound received on a mission over Gosmata. After further convalescence in Australia, he returned to active duty. National Archives 075-N-FIVE-148.

Cpl. Henry Bake, Jr. (l) and PFC George H. Kirk (r), Navajo Indians serving with a Marine signal unit, operate a portable radio set in a clearing they've hacked in the dense jungle close behind the front lines. U. S. Marine Corps photograph, USMC 69889-A, Bougainville, December 1943. National Archives 127-GR-137-69889-A.

PFC Carl Gorman of Chinle, Arizona, an Indian Marine who manned an observation post on a hill overlooking the city of Garapan while the Marines were consolidating their positions on the island of Saipan, Marianas. Defense Department photograph, Marine Corps, Saipan, 27 June 1944. National Archives 127-GR-137-83734.

These New Mexican Indians, serving with the veteran First Marine Division, played an important part in maintaining communications during the Peleliu campaign. Front row, l to r: PFC James T. Nakai of Ship Rock; PFC John H. Bowman of Tohatchi; PFC Ira Manuelito of Tohatchi; PFC Jimmy King of Ship Rock; PFC Andrew Calleditto of Crownpoint; PFC Lloyd Betone of Crownpoint; Cpl. Lloyd Oliver of Ship Rock. Back row, l-r: PFC Preston Toledo of Crownpoint; Cpl. John Chee of Ship Rock; PFC Sandy Burr of Ship Rock; PFC Ben Manuelito of Tehatchi; PFC Dan [unreadable] of Gallup; PFC Edward Lueppe of Tohatchi; PFC Del Calleditto of Crownpoint; and PFC Ralph Calleditto of Crownpoint. In the foreground, commending them for their work, is Lieutenant Colonel James G. Smith, signal officer for the First Marine Division. Defense Department photograph, Marine Corps. National Archives 127-GR-137-101511.

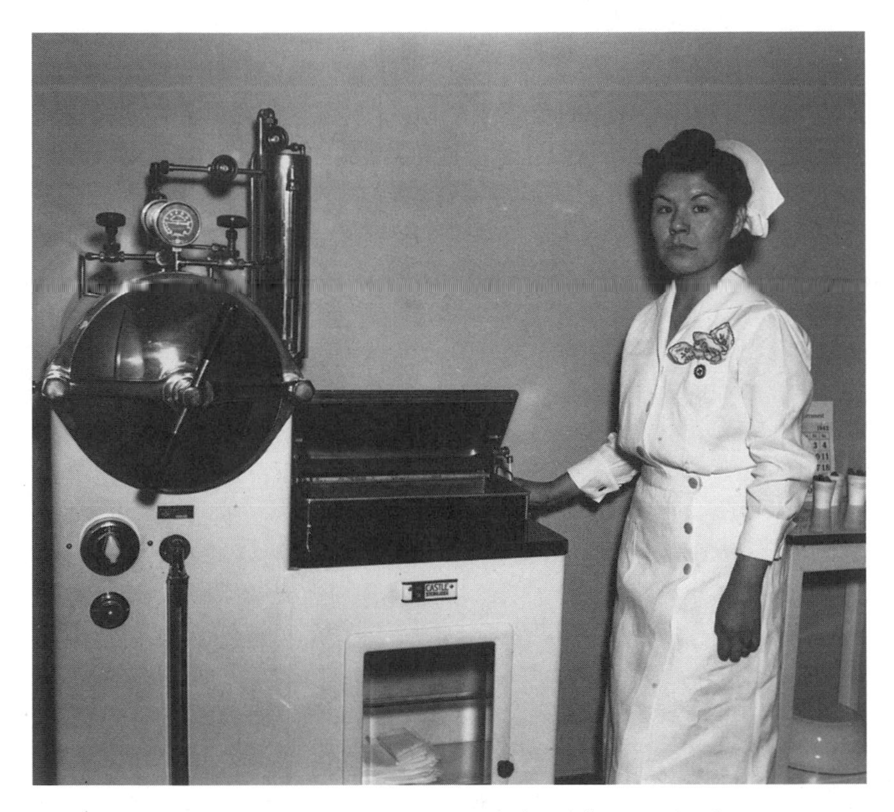

Second Lieutenant Mabel Aungie, a Sioux from the Rosebud Reservation, South Dakota, graduated from the Protestant Episcopal Hospital in Philadelphia in 1941, after which she was employed for several months in the Office of Indian Affairs, Washington, D. C. She volunteered for duty in the Army and was assigned to Camp Pickett, Virginia, July 31, 1942. National Archives 075-N-W0-55.

The Return of the Native: American Indian Laborers

During the 1940s, for the first time, Native Americans found themselves being pursued by businesses to the point of full tribal employment. Maximum utilization of tribal members appeared to many observers to portend two significant changes. First, opponents of the Indian Reorganization Act maintained that American Indians had rejected their reservation wardship status and would willingly assimilate into mainstream society during the war's aftermath. Second, these same critics asserted that wartime work experience would make this acculturation process an attainable goal. Neither of these assumptions would prove correct, as thousands of workers, along with veterans, returned to the reservation at the end of the war.[1]

The sheer number of workers seemed to validate the argument that Native Americans desired to acculturate into white society. From 1942 to 1945, as part of a larger national relocation ranging from the Rocky Mountain states to the coastlines of California and the eastern United States, forty thousand Indian men and women, aged eighteen to fifty, left reservations for jobs in the defense industry. Assistance from the Indian Bureau in the 1930s and 40s, in the forms of technical training, help in securing jobs, and on-the-job-counseling, accounted for this employability. Furthermore, the government offered many courses such as automobile mechanics, welding, and radio work in conjunction with the Civilian Conservation Corps (CCC).[2]

The Indian Division of the CCC played a major role in preparing Indians for their vital war work by eventually employing a total of 85,200 Native Americans. Although initially established in 1933 "to relieve the acute condition of widespread distress and unemployment," the Corps, which existed until July 10, 1942, actually revitalized many areas of Indian life. Not only did Indians earn needed wages and improve reservations by constructing truck trails, lookout towers, and telephone lines, but they also aided in soil conservation by protecting timber stands, implementing reforestation, and introducing insect pest control.[3]

Job-connected skills, an important auxiliary of the Corps, benefited Indians during the Depression and through the war years. Health and education conditions also improved, because the Corps promoted sanitary measures, Red Cross first-aid training and Indian Health Division instruction for enrollees. Furthermore, during the program, 126 men, ranging in age from seventeen to sixty-nine, completed the eighth grade. Educational interest stimulated further instruction, and officials designated Friday afternoons as study sessions. Attended by an average of 3,546 persons, these sessions included lectures, visual presentations, demonstration projects, and training in forest fire fighting, truck driving, tractor operation, and mechanics. These skills naturally directed graduates toward defense work, and a total of 932 men enrolled in National Defense training courses. War industries eventually hired seventy-five percent of these graduates.[4]

In July, 1941, realizing that a majority of Native Americans wished to enter National Defense work, the Indian Office queried all reservation superintendents, employment officers, and the Indian Division of the CCC in order to secure information on the workers engaged in National Defense trades courses and employment. The officials particularly worried that many tribes lacked sufficient funds to train their prospective workers and also that Native Americans might encounter discrimination from labor unions or employers. Additional funding for National Defense employment presented another controversial issue, as many tribes felt the government should assume the financial obligation. Other tribes eagerly jumped at the chance to provide better opportunities for tribal members. The Montana Blackfeet, for example, appropriated three thousand dollars for "financing laborers to fit themselves for National Defense jobs." In other cases, individuals—including women—paid for their own technical training.[5]

In the labor vacuum created by the male exodus from the reservation, Indian women assumed many traditional male roles as they cared for livestock, drove schoolbuses, and worked as mechanics and chemists. Navajo women in New Mexico became silversmiths, and in North Carolina, Cherokee women drove tractors and planted crops. On the Colville, Klamath, and Quinielt Reservations in Oregon and Washington, tribeswomen manned fire lookout stations and operated radios, while in the Red Lake Forest of Minnesota, Ojibwa women planted 90,700 trees on 238 acres.[6] Off-reservation employers also recruited heavily among Native American women. It was estimated that in 1943, fifty percent of all off-reservation Navajo farm laborers were women. Large produce farmers claimed that they preferred Navajo women, because they were hardworking. By 1943 at least 12,000 women had left the reservations to work in factories and in the nurses corps. Native American women worked as riveters, inspectors, sheet metalworkers and machinists. One Indian woman had such an outstanding record as a welder in a solar aircraft company that she earned the Army-Navy "E" award.[7]

Agnes Begay was one of hundreds of Navajo employed at an ordnance depot near Flagstaff, Arizona. In 1943 the Bellmont Corporation hired her as an interpreter, clerk and guard while her husband worked as a truck driver. Begay remained with her family while enjoying the benefits of two-bedroom modern housing, child care, and transportation for shopping. In her non-traditional role of guard, she carried a pistol and searched incoming people on buses. Although she admitted she hated this part of the job, Begay added that she never had trouble, because people "were good and cooperative."[8]

By December, 1941, Indians from all parts of the country had entered National Defense work, and the Indian Service, feeling justifiably proud of its charges, maintained that they possessed "natural gifts of precision, endurance, poise, and high intelligence." In addition, the Indian Service reported that Indians exhibited great patriotism in their defense work. In 1940, after President Roosevelt had embargoed arms to Japan, several Indians working on railroad construction in the high Cascades refused to dismantle an abandoned logging railroad when they discovered the parts were destined for Japan.[9]

After the Japanese attacked Pearl Harbor, the Indian Bureau intensified and amplified its tuition-free courses, which made it possible for 2,500 Indians to find employment in 1942. By the end of 1943, 5,000 Native Americans worked in war industries, and by the next year, this figure jumped to 23,000. In New York alone, approximately 1,600 American Indians from different tribes filled defense jobs. Twelve members of the Tuscarora tribes from the Iroquois Confederacy in northern New York worked in airplane construction in the Buffalo plant of the Curtiss-Wright Corporation, and a number of Mohawks worked as skilled ironworkers in the New York City Navy Yard.[10]

Of all the Indian tribes, the Navajo constituted the largest labor force in defense work, as approximately twenty percent of the tribe entered industrial occupations. In 1942, 2,500 Navajo worked on the construction of a large ordnance depot in Fort Wingate, New Mexico, where they operated jackhammers and welded. Others labored in airplane plants, tank factories, and shipyards. Cooperating with the United States Employment Service, James A. Tadlock, Acting Field Supervisor in the War Manpower Commission for Region X, stationed in Albuquerque, New Mexico, arranged to have many Navajo employed in the Gallup area. Under this joint supervision, he asserted, the Navajo found suitable employment, adequate wages, sanitary living conditions, and transportation. Tadlock insisted, however, that most Navajo preferred a hard, rugged outdoor lifestyle, and he placed them on railroad construction and at the ordnance depot. Thus many Navajo with highly-trained technical skills often worked as unskilled labor at possibly lower wages.[11]

Similarly the Pueblo Indians of New Mexico also rendered great contributions to the nation's industrial needs, most notably at the Naval Supply Depot in Clearfield, Utah. Established in 1943, this depot acted as a general service to the naval fleet by sending a lifeline of essential war supplies to the Pacific. When the Pueblos learned that the nation suffered a labor shortage, they advertised in local newspapers volunteering to work temporarily in defense factories. Having already sent ten percent of their population into the military, the Pueblos themselves experienced a labor shortage. With this in mind, in 1943 a Denver Civil Service Commission representative negotiated with John Bird, Santo Domingo Pueblo leader, to recruit Pueblo men to work in Utah at the Naval Supply Depot on the condition that they be allowed to return home in summer in order to plant and harvest crops.[12] Bird, who agreed to recruit men from other pueblos to work at the Depot, experienced the most success at Santa Clara, Jemez, and Santo Domingo Pueblos. After being examined by Indian Service physicians, 150 men left for Clearfield. Bird's leadership ability and intelligence so impressed the military that Lieutenant Frederick W. Sleight, United States Naval Reserve Officer in charge of the Naval Supply Depot, made him a supervisor. Under Bird's leadership, some Indians worked in the transportation division while others loaded supplies onto sea-bound ships. Joined by the Shoshone, Apache, Sioux, Navajo and Ute, the Pueblo Indians gained a reputation as outstanding workers. Employers asserted that they followed instructions well, worked hard, kept out of trouble, and never missed work. In addition to all these attributes, the tribesmen kept their promise and at the end of summer, 1943, they returned to Utah bringing new recruits. "I know that these fine people are doing a splendid job," praised Rear Admiral Arthur

H. Mayo when speaking at the second annual Commemoration Ceremonies in April, 1945.[13]

Sleight had no cause for regret over his recruitment of the Pueblo Indians and, in particular, of John Bird. He also displayed more insight and empathy for Native Americans than the average white employer. After working with them for more than a year, he claimed:

> High credit should go to the Indian for an outstanding part in our victory. He has sacrificed more than most men who are doing this work. He has left the land he has known all his life and has had to travel to strange places where people do not understand him and his way of living. In most cases he has left his family behind. He has had to forego attending the dances and other religious ceremonies that are so much a part of his life. He has had to work under foremen and supervisors, in a way that is new to him. It is an adjustment more difficult for him than for the white men who have known these conditions before.

Sleight concluded by praising Bird for his leadership of the Native American workers. Under Bird, he felt, the tribesmen had acquired new skills and confidence which would help them in peacetime.[14]

Unlike the Navajo or Pueblo tribes, Alaska natives entered defense work without leaving their villages or abandoning traditional pursuits. As early as 1940, the Army's experimental project at Fort Richardson, Alaska, awarded a contract to the Nome Skin Sewers Cooperative Association, incorporated under the Indian Reorganization Act, to provide mukluks, parkas, sealskin trousers, and moose-hide moccasins. Eskimos, supervised by the Educational Division of the Alaska Indian Service, generated an annual income of more than $100,000. Other contributions by Alaska natives remained, for military reasons, undisclosed. The Indian Office, however, intimated that these natives possessed uniquely desired talents for "territorial defense." These talents included the ability to "travel all day by snowshoe" and the use of rifles and guns, as well as an intimate knowledge of geographic and climatic conditions.[15]

While these varied talents elicited high praise from employers, the increasing demand for Native American workers also created extreme labor shortages on the reservations. As early as 1943, reservation superintendents, "combing the reservations for workers," discovered they could not fulfill employment demands. On some reservations school absenteeism increased from twenty-five percent to seventy-five percent, signifying the large numbers of families leaving for defense work and military service. Because of their agricultural experience, Arizona tribes were particularly recruited. At the Pima Agency, 900 out of 5,095 tribal members worked off-reservation, primarily in agriculture, the armed forces, railroad construction, and war industries. On the Tohono O'Odham Reservation in Arizona, two-thirds of the population of 6,200 relocated for military service, war industries, copper mining, or to work in the cotton fields. Only fifty unemployed people remained behind, asserted Superintendent Head, and all those were too old to work. These families combated the labor shortage by assigning one person to care for the livestock and gardens of as many as five families.[16]

School attendance statistics reveal the devastating effects of the war on reservation populations. From 1942 to 1945 attendance in boarding schools and day schools progressively declined:

School	*1942*	*1943*	*1944*	*1945*
Non-reservation boarding schools	6,513	5,680	5,363	5,550
Reservation boarding schools	5,609	5,268	5,162	5,730
Boarding school day pupils	1,697	1,296	1,348	1,531
Consolidated schools	4,150	3,409	3,609	3,605
Day schools	7,870	6,554	6,346	6,086
	25,839	22,207	21,828	22,502[17]

Despite much well-deserved praise for their sacrifices and hard work, Native Americans encountered many problems in this sometimes alien work force. They were in a situation, according to John Collier, of being the last hired, first fired. Facing job discrimination on the one hand and cultural shock on the other, Indians also discovered that their traditional tribal customs often conflicted with white values. Some employers claimed that many American Indians were inferior workers and criticized them for drinking on the job. Other employers objected when Native Americans, who often misunderstood the impersonal Anglo-Saxon workplace, took complaints directly to their bosses in the mistaken belief that, like Indian leaders, these men would care for their charges. When a supervisor lost credibility with Native American workers, the Indians simply refused to follow him. At the Wingate Ordnance Depot, the Navajo generally maintained good relations with their co-workers, but if they considered a foreman to be incompetent or too tough, they often left his supervision without permission to work for a more popular foreman. Rather than seeking to understand the reasons why Navajo quit work without giving notice, employers often stereotyped this practice as a traditional characteristic of living for the present rather than for the future.[18]

Many white employers, unfamiliar with American Indian customs and impatient with what they deemed to be superstitions, viewed Indians as primitive and unskilled. Taos Indians, for example, worried that National Defense conscription might mean losing their long braids, an essential part of their religions, and hoped for a special dispensation from this rule. Many Navajo workers, who held a fear of cameras which they believed stole their souls, often balked at being photographed for work cards. Officials confronted another problem when these workers also resisted naming their dead parents for Social security purposes because mentioning the deceased constituted another Navajo taboo.[19]

Tadlock also asserted that traditional Indian attitudes regarding work also retarded career advancement. He claimed that, because the Navajo particularly disliked indoor work, commission payments, and piecework, they often passed up better-paying jobs in coal mines to work outdoors. Furthermore he criticized the Navajo for failing to join unions and pay initiation fees, which resulted in their being offered work as common laborers rather than being able to use their technical skills for higher pay. Indian Service officials often expressed surprise when they discovered skilled mechanics and precision workers laboring with jackhammers and bulldozers. Neither Tadlock nor the Indian Service questioned whether the Navajo were given a choice of higher-paying jobs or simply relegated to the lesser-skilled, lower-paying jobs.[20]

In addition, traditional prejudices played a part in an area's attitude concerning American Indians. Towns located close to a reservation usually evinced the most hostility toward them. For this reason, Indians often preferred to travel to more distant towns, where less bias existed. Ripe for exploitation, tribesmen readily accepted employment from private labor recruiters for large salaries at distant locations, then on their arrival, often discovered that in reality their new jobs paid substandard wages, and their new communities offered little in the way of resources or aid for Native Americans. Furthermore these Indians lacked access to the acculturation process because of nonexistent mentor relationships. In 1942, the Rosebud Sioux, lured to distant industrial centers, earned less than the going wage, possessed meager personal resources, and confronted a lack of social aid. Until they received their first paychecks, families often could barely pay for transportation to their new jobs, clothes, and housing. When they turned to social institutions for help during emergencies, these agencies denied them aid, because public officials incorrectly believed that the federal government completely cared for off-reservation Indians. In many cities the hospitals even refused health care to Native Americans, and public agencies offered only enough assistance to enable an Indian to return to his reservation.[21]

The contrasting experiences of Thomas Segundo, an engineer from the Tohono O'Odham Reservation, and Harvey Allison, a laborer from the Pima Reservation, proved that distance could affect employer attitudes toward Indians. Segundo, who would be elected tribal chairman in the postwar era, applied for army duty three times and was rejected each time. Failing to secure military duty, he traveled to San Francisco to work for the Pacific Bridge Company building dry docks and land craft. During his employment, he was assigned to engineering jobs such as sketching and drafting. When speaking of his experience, Segundo said:

> I learned to get along with every other kind of people besides my own tribe. I got along fine with everybody. I found a lot of racial prejudice in San Francisco. The racial feeling was very strong, but there was no indication of any feeling toward me as an Indian. . . . I was never intimidated or belittled.

Furthermore, Segundo pointed with pride to the fact that he was the first and only Indian to join the American Technical Engineers, Architects, and Draftsmen Union in Oakland.[22]

In contrast to Segundo's positive wartime experience, Harvey Allison confronted racism at both local and national levels. Ironically, the discrimination originated within the Department of the Interior and reached into the office of the Secretary of the Interior Harold Ickes. On June 11, 1942, the United States Department of the Interior in Phoenix, Arizona, advertised job openings for five axmen. The United States Employment Service (USES) in Phoenix sent the "husky and capable" Allison, who was classified as a gardener and maintenance man, for an interview. Ty White, assistant industrial engineer, rejected him as unqualified. The representative then informed the head of the Arizona USES that "he wanted a white man for this job and would not hire either Indian, Mexican or Negro."[23]

In response to this demand, the USES immediately canceled the work order, and the manager, Mr. Carlisle, visited the Interior Department to speak with Mr. Fisk (office head), and Mr. Kinsey (engineer). Fisk and Kinsey reported that Ty White and Mr. Warren, the engineers who had conducted the interview, were away in the field. He added, moreover, that while "they had no part in this particular deal . . . they agreed that whites only were desired for their survey parties."[24]

Carlisle reported the conversation to the director of the Arizona USES, Henry Arneson, who notifed his regional director and then filed a complaint with Barron Beshoar of the War Manpower Commission Minority Groups Branch in Denver. Beshoar transmitted the report to Dr. Will Alexander, his superior in Washington, stating that "in view of the Department of the Interior's past statement in regard to Indians and other racial groups, it occurred to me that this complaint might best be taken up directly with Mr. Ickes." He added that the southwestern USES officials would appreciate receiving "a clear statement of policy from the Department of the Interior on hiring practices."[25] Dr. Alexander wasted little time in reporting the incident to Lawrence Cramer, Executive Secretary of the President's Committee on Fair Employment Practices. Having previously dealt with Ickes while Cramer was governor of the Virgin Islands, Cramer felt little regard for the secretary, whom he believed had undermined his authority. According to Cramer, Ickes employed Blacks on the island only at the governor's insistence, and then took full credit for the hirings. In one instance, the secretary blocked the appointment of a local man whom Cramer had recommended. Cramer further alienated Ickes by going over his head and personally appealing to President Roosevelt during a presidential visit to the islands. "Ickes reproached me bitterly and avowed to me that he would not agree to the appointment in question," recalled Cramer, "because he had reason to believe that the prospective appointee was a colored man."[26]

When the Allison issue surfaced, the executive secretary seized on the complaint as a violation of Executive Order 8802 forbidding discrimination in the workplace. He requested that Ickes investigate the matter, take appropriate disciplinary action, and advise the FEPC of any subsequent results. Two and a half months later, Assistant Secretary of the Interior Oscar Chapman informed Cramer that during his investigation, he was told that Ty White had rejected Allison on the basis of his small stature and the specific work in "the dense pine, timbered country near Williams, Arizona where an axman's work is very difficult." Chapman added that White now had "two American Indians working on his survey party" and concluded that there appeared to be no grounds for disciplinary action.[27]

Neither Cramer nor Malcom MacLean, Chairman of the FEPC, accepted this investigation as thorough or unbiased. They continued to press the complaint along with other complaints of discrimination, including those involving Blacks in the Virgin Islands. MacLean particularly took issue with Ickes's position that the FEPC had no jurisdiction over United States government employees stationed in the Virgin Islands. "The Committee holds," MacLean warned Ickes, "that it has a duty to investigate any complaint of discrimination in the Government service." Drawing attention to the fact that only 1.6 percent of all Interior Department employees were Black, the FEPC Chairman pointedly noted that of this small percentage, only 2.3 percent held noncustodial jobs.[28]

Cramer responded to Chapman's noninterventionist policy by forwarding the assistant secretary's letter to Paul McNitt, Chairman of the War Manpower Commission, to Barron Beshoar, to Henry Arneson, and finally to President Roosevelt. He then forcefully requested additional information from Chapman concerning the Allison case. Specifically Cramer demanded an explanation for the differences between Chapman's and Beshoar's reports. Pointing to discrepancies in the physical description of Allison, the executive secretary also requested that he be advised whether Kinsey and Fiske denied that they had also stated that they preferred whites only in the survey parties. Furthermore, Cramer once again asked for a formal statement from the Interior Department to the Arizona Director of USES which would insist that agencies hire on the basis of qualifications "without regard to race, creed, color or national origin." Finally, Cramer questioned Ty White's assertion that he had previously hired American Indians and wanted to know the exact dates of their employment.[29] Only a few days later, a rather chastened Oscar Chapman replied to Cramer that "in order to answer fully your inquiry, it will be necessary for the Department to investigate the matter further. As soon as a report of the inquiry has been received, I shall advise you of the findings."[30]

Although the final outcome of the Allison complaint remains unclear, the experiences of Joseph Medicine Crow from the Montana Crow Tribe revealed that no matter how well educated a Native American was in this time period, he still faced discrimination in his home town. In 1938, Medicine Crow, whose philosophy was always to work twice as hard as the white man, gained the distinction of being the first male Crow tribesman to receive a college degree (two Crow women had received degrees prior to him). When he returned to the Crow Reservation wearing a necktie and sports jacket, he claimed, "I thought I was it." Applying for his first job at Willow Creek Dam as a bookkeeper, he never received a call from the employer and learned later that the job had been given to a white man with less education. "That was my first experience of the disadvantage of being an Indian," he recalled.[31]

Unable to find employment near the Crow Reservation, Medicine Crow entered the University of Southern California on a scholarship where he eventually received his Ph.D. in 1940. In the university, far from his reservation, the people "respected him and treated him kindly." After serving in the army, he returned to civilian life and obtained a teaching job at the Fort Wingate School in Arizona. In 1942 the Indian Service transferred him to Chimayo Indian School, also in Arizona. Although the other teachers (all white) had less education than he did, the government still paid him lower wages. "There was discrimination," he admitted, "but those kind of things became a challenge to do better."[32]

The experiences of Harvey Allison and Joseph Medicine Crow highlight the segregationist attitudes of the time period. In the 1930s and 1940s local racism frequently occurred, particularly in the area of job competition where whites were generally granted preference. The discrimination uncovered in the government hierarchy from Indian Service schools to the Department of the Interior, however, reveals a peculiar dimension to Harold Ickes's public record as a Progressive Liberal and as the former president of the NAACP. Long acclaimed by historians as the primary motivator behind the New Deal civil rights efforts, he was lauded by Arthur Schlesinger, who asserted that Ickes was an "ardent libertarian," and Richard Morris, who declared him to be "the staunchest advocate of civil rights within the New Deal." Ickes's civil rights achievements included hiring Blacks in New Deal Programs and integrating the Interior Department cafeteria. In his most publicized event, Ickes arranged with Eleanor Roosevelt to have Black opera singer Marian Anderson perform before the steps of the Lincoln Memorial when she was denied the use of Constitution Hall by the Daughters of the American Revolution. Furthermore Ickes openly praised American Indian war efforts in newspaper and magazine articles and boasted of their advancements under the Indian Bureau and Interior Department.[33]

While his responses to the Allison complaint and the Virgin Islands situation may have arisen from the personal animosity between Ickes and himself, Cramer certainly suspected the secretary of less than honorable intentions. In late December the executive secretary disclosed the entire situation to Michael Strauss, the former publicity director of the Interior Department who had just arranged for Ms. Anderson's concert. Strauss supposedly dismissed the issue by countering that he would have to schedule Ms. Anderson "to sing for the secretary again."[34]

During World War II, America's ambivalent attitudes toward Native Americans were clearly revealed in their relationships with working-class Indians. On the one hand, government officials and employees encouraged the use of these people as a necessary work force in a time of extreme labor needs. On the other hand, personal attitudes and biases dictated the level of acceptance which Native Americans could expect. Tribal members employed close to their reservations often encountered whites who possessed locally accepted stereotypes and often prejudices against the nearest tribes. Conversely, tribal members employed at distant locations confronted less deeply-held convictions but had very little access to social aid, and as exemplified in the case of Medicine Crow, very little room for advancement.[35]

Although Native Americans had proven they could function in the off-reservation environment, their wartime experiences failed to generate a massive voluntary removal process. In 1940 the Indian Bureau claimed the Native American population under its supervision numbered approximately 333,969; by the beginning of 1945, the Native American population on the reservations had risen to 401,819. "The Return of the Native" had become a reality. Rather than reducing the numbers on the reservation, the war had actually increased tribal ties. Not until the Termination Acts of the 1950s and the forced relocation to the cities would the population trend reverse and create another "reservation exodus."[36]

---

[1]The majority of these observers and critics were Republicans, although a significant number of Democratic congressmen advocated assimilation.

[2]New York *Times*, February 6, 1943, 16:3; *Annual Report of the Commissioner of Indian Affairs* (Washington, D.C.: Government Printing Office, 1941): 412–13; *Annual Report of the Commissioner of Indian Affairs* (1944): 237; Elizabeth Shepley Sergeant, "The Indian Goes to War," *New Republic* 107 (November 30, 1942): 711; John Collier, "The Indian in a Wartime Nation," *Annals of the American Academy of Political and Social Science* 223 (September, 1942): 31; John Useem, Gordon MacGregor and Ruth Hill Useem, "Wartime Employment and Cultural Adjustments of the Rosebud Sioux," *Applied Anthropology* 2 (January–March, 1943): 4.

[3]Indian Office History, Record Group 48, entry 858, box 6, folder "Indian Office History," 87–89, National Archives, Washington, D. C.

[4]Indian Office History, 89–90; J. W. Studebaker, Commissioner of Education to Executive Officers for Vocational Training, January 28, 1941, Record Group 75, entry 195, box 3, folder "National Defense," National Archives, Washington, D. C.

[5]United States Department of the Interior Circular Letter, July 2, 1941; Minutes of Blackfeet Tribal Business Council, February 1, 1941, 5, Record Group 75, entry 195, box 3, folder "National Defense."

[6]*Annual Report of the Commissioner of Indian Affairs,* 1944, 237; 1943, 279; New York *Times,* February 6, 1943, 16:3, December 22, 1942, 17:4; *Indians at Work* Vol. X, No. 2–6 (Washington, D. C.: Department of the Interior, Bureau of Indian Affairs, October, 1942 to January, 1943): 26; *Indians in the War* (Haskell, Kansas: Department of the Interior, Bureau of Indian Affairs, 1945): 49.

[7]J. A. Tadlock, "Navajos Respond to Nation's Need," *Manpower Report* (April, 1943): 8; New York *Times,* February 6, 1943, 16:3, February 9, 1943, 5:5; *Indians in the War,* 49; *Annual Report of the Commissioner of Indian Affairs,* 1943, 235; *Indians at Work,* Vol. X, No. 2–6 (October, 1942–January, 1943): 25.

[8]"Interview with Agnes R. Begay," *Navajos in World War II* (Navajo Community College Press: 1977): 48–49.

[9]*Indians at Work,* Vol. IX, No. 8, 5; New York *Times,* February 6, 1943, 16:3; Annual Report of the Commissioner of Indian Affairs, 1944, 237; "Revision of Laws and Legal Status," Congressional Committee Hearings, House Committee on Indian Affairs, House Resolution 166, 78 Cong., 1 sess., December 4–8, 13, 1944; February 2–25, 1944, 59; Sergeant, "The Indian Goes to War," 711; Collier, "The Indian in a Wartime Nation," 31; Useem et al., "Wartime Employment," 4; *Congressional Record* 77 Cong., 2 sess., A4386.

[10]Sergeant, "The Indian Goes to War," 711; *Indians at Work,* Vol. IX, No. 8, 26, 29; House Resolution 166, 59; New York *Times,* February 21, 1942, 21:8.

[11]Senate Joint Resolution 79, 79th Cong., 2 sess., May 14, 1946, 15; Collier, "Indians in a Wartime Nation," 31; *Annual Report of the Commissioner of Indian Affairs,* 1942, 24; *Indians at Work,* IX, No. 7, 17; Tadlock, "Navajos Respond," 8.

[12]*Indians in the War,* 42.

[13]*Indians in the War,* 43.

[14] Ibid.

[15]*Indians at Work,* Vol. X, No. 5, 23–24; Vol. IX, No. 8, 9; Vol. IX, No. 9–10, 9.

[16]*Indians at Work,* Vol. X, No. 2–6 (February, 1943): 9, 49–50; New York *Times,* February 6, 1943, 16:3; *Annual Report of the Commissioner of Indian Affairs,* 1944, 246.

[17]*Indians in the War,* 91–92, 93–95.

[18]Useem et al., "Wartime Employment," 4; Collier, "The Indian in a Wartime Nation," 31.

[19]Tadlock, "Navajos Respond," 8; Useem et al., "Wartime Employment," 4–5; *House Resolution* 166, 243, December 8, 1944; *Annual Report of the Commissioner of Indian Affairs,* 1943, 285.

[20]Sergeant, "The Indian Goes to War," 709; Tadlock, "Navajos Respond," 8; *Senate Joint Resolution* 79, May 14, 1946, 15.

[21]Useem et al., "Wartime Employment," 4; Collier, "The Indian in a Wartime Nation," 31.

[22]Interview with Thomas Segundo, June 22, 1949, Henry Dobyns Fieldnotes, Manuscript A478–A, Arizona State Museum, Tucson, Arizona.

[23]Arneson to Gross, August 24, 1942, Record Group 228, Federal Employment Practices Commission, Region XII–SF, box 13, folder T–Z, National Archives, Pacific Sierra Region.

[24]Ibid.

[25]Beshoar to Alexander, August 31, 1942, Record Group 228, FEPC, Region XII–SF, box 13, folder T–Z.

[26]Alexander to Cramer, September 21, 1942, Cramer to Harper, January 1, 1943, Record Group 228, FEPC, Region XII–SF, box 13, folder T–Z.

[27]Cramer to Ickes, September 21, 1942, Chapman to Cramer, December 3, 1942, Record Group 228, FEPC, Region XII–SF, box 13, folder T–Z.

[28]MacLean to Ickes, December 7, 1942, Record Group 228, FEPC, Region XII–SF, box 13, folder T–Z.

[29]Cramer to Chapman, Beshoar, Arneson and McNitt, December 14, 1942, Record Group 228, FEPC, Region XII–SF, box 13, folder T–Z.

[30]Chapman to Cramer, December 18, 1942, Record Group 228, FEPC, Region XII–SF, box 13, folder T–Z.

[31]Interview with Joseph Medicine Crow, Native American Educators Oral History Project, Montana State Historical Society, Billings, Montana, January 30, 1989, Tape OH1226.

[32]Ibid.

[33]Richard Morris, ed., *An Encyclopedia of American History* (New York: Harper and Row, 1976): 1066; Arthur Schlesinger, ed. *The Almanac of American History* (New York: G. P. Putnam's Sons, 1983): 467.

[34]Cramer to Harper, January 1, 1943, Record Group 228, FEPC, Region XII–SF, box 13, folder T–Z.

[35]Useem, et al, "Wartime Employment."

[36]House Report 2091, 78 Cong., 2 sess. (10848), December 23, 1944, Pursuant to House Resolution 166, 11; *Sixteenth Census of the United States, 1940, Population* (Washington, D.C.: United States Government Printing Office, 1943).

José Ignacio, of Sells, Arizona, Papago Indian welder for the General Services Administration motorpool. Arizona Historical Society / Tucson AHS#52168.

A Tohono O'Odham worker. Arizona Historical Society / Tucson AHS#9970.

The Great Give-Away: Tribal Resources

World War II constituted one of the greatest periods of government bureaucratization and individual sacrifice ever experienced in America's history. Every aspect of the American lifestyle was scrutinized from one viewpoint: its potential contribution to the national war effort. For the majority of Americans, this contribution yielded reciprocal benefits. Workers experienced a full employment economy, agricultural prices quadrupled, and government contracts to private industries created such postwar monoliths as Boeing and Lockheed industries. Native Americans also experienced this government intervention, particularly in the realm of tribal resources, but the results of the benefits varied widely from tribe to tribe.

Decades of experimentation with the Dawes Act and individualized farming units had failed to raise the annual income of Native Americans. As a result, by 1940 it fell far below the national median. After several years of tribal council leadership in the era of the Indian Reorganization Act, Native Americans had identified their resources and clearly recognized the potential worth of tribal enterprises. America's entry into the war in late 1941 prompted a renewed national interest in these resources, an interest not in evidence since the late nineteenth century when reservations were allotted, checkerboarded and sold as surplus land to westerners. By declaring American Indians themselves to be natural resources and transferring authority over reservations from the Department of the Interior to the War Resources Council, the government signified its intention to assume control over tribal commodities deemed necessary for the war effort. Tribes responded to these measures either by voluntarily cooperating, by submitting and negotiating for the best terms, or by resisting the government's demands.[1]

To direct and "formulate a definite war program for the Department of the Interior," Ickes appointed Michael Straus as Director of the War Resources Council. Given the power to requisite personnel and vital resources from all Interior departments, Straus also held authority to designate department functions which he deemed to be vital to the war effort. To assist Straus in these endeavors, Ickes ordered bureau heads to give precedence to the war program in their departments. For Native Americans and the Indian Bureau, this new policy meant not only a departmental revamping, but it also included a cutback in personnel and less funding for vital economic, health, and educational programs. Despite these implications, the government designated Indians, along with Japanese-Americans and conscientious objectors, to be the human element in the nation's natural war resources. Specifically, the government intended to highlight contributions and accomplishments of these minority groups in order to improve national morale and unity.[2]

Prodded by the persuasive exhortations of Ickes and Collier, which deeply influenced Native American patriotic impulses, Indians purchased war bonds and war stamps from tribal funds and individual assets. "Purchase of Treasury Stamps and Bonds by Indian groups and individuals has been considerable," stated one Indian Service writer, who also conceded, "a great many of these transactions do not come officially to the attention of the

Indian Service, because the purchases are made locally with funds not under government jurisdiction."[3] These purchases amounted to several hundred thousand dollars. In 1942 the Euchee and Creek tribes of Oklahoma voted unanimously to purchase $400,000 in defense bonds from tribal funds. The following year the Wind River Shoshoni near Lander, Wyoming, numbering less than 2,000 members, authorized a $500 war bond to be purchased for each member from their oil royalties and Treasury judgment principal fund. When several other tribes requested permission to use interest rates on tribal funds to purchase bonds, the government was forced to refuse, because officials had already appropriated all Treasury interest rates for war purposes. Resource-rich tribes, nevertheless, resorted to sales of land, timber, oil and gas to invest in bonds.[4] In their resolutions requesting that the Secretary of the Interior purchase bonds out of tribal funds, Native Americans invariably resorted to patriotic rhetoric. Referring to the attempt of the United States to "preserve free Governments and the democratic way of life" against totalitarian governments, the Menominee Tribe, in asking that each tribal member be furnished with a $25-dollar defense bond from their fund, began their declaration with the following:

> Whereas the Menominee Tribe of Indians have pledged their loyalty and unqualified support to the vigorous prosecution of that war, over sixty members of that Tribe being in the armed forces of the United States at the time of the declaration of war against Japan, and over eighteen members of the Tribe having voluntarily enlisted in the armed forces of the United States within one day after that declaration of war. . . .[5]

Many tribes earned or raised money specifically to purchase war bonds. Tribal members from the New Mexico Jemez Pueblo appeared eight times in New York City to aid the War Saving Staff. Wearing full-fledged tribal regalia, they danced at the 1942 National

Folk Festival in Madison Square Garden and made several other appearances before touring the rest of the country. By the end of their tour, this award-winning group had helped to raise $300,000 for war bonds. With less artistry but with equal zeal, Canoncito Navajo tribal members gathered tons of scrap metal, only to be frustrated in their attempt to sell the scrap because they did not have access to scales. They solved the problem by placing a woman who knew her weight on one end of a school teeter-totter, with the hunks of scrap metal on the other end. Balancing her weight against each load, they finally weighed five tons of scrap metal. They earned $75, which they spent on war bonds and stamps.[6]

Individual Native American purchases often came from unexpected sources. Six years after a fatal train and school bus collision which claimed the lives of six Navajo school children, a court awarded the families $15,000 as compensation. The families spent $5,500 of this award on defense bonds. John Collier often repeated the story of a destitute Navajo man who trudged miles to an agency to contribute thirty cents—ten cents each for himself, his wife, and his child. A wealthy Kiowa woman from Oklahoma was reputed to have sent a thousand-dollar check to Navy Relief which she signed with a thumbprint. Cherokee women wove and sold traditional Indian baskets to purchase war stamps. The Commissioner considered all these sacrifices to be significant. By 1942 Native American war bond purchases amounted to $2,671,625. Two years later war bond sales to Native Americans had reached fifty million dollars.[7]

In addition to war bond and stamp purchases, Native Americans participated in Red Cross drives by offering not only money but also tribal resources, such as crafts. "We have no record of all the contributions the Indians have made to war relief societies," said Collier, "but such reports as we do get indicate that the Indians are giving all they can. Pueblo and Navajo Indians, in lieu of cash, have given sacks of corn, their staff of life, mutton, silver jewelry, and rugs to the Red Cross." When the New Mexico Zuni Pueblo began a Red Cross drive in 1942, the reservation superintendent praised the families for giving whatever they could afford to give, despite the "blinding snowstorm." One family, he recounted, presented the Red Cross with six dollars and two silver rings, in recognition of a family member who was missing in action. In Oklahoma, Osage women sewed bandages for the Red Cross, and in New Mexico Taos tribeswomen offered to knit. One elderly grandmother who simply could not handle this difficult task, convinced her grandson to perform the knitting, which she then contributed to the Red Cross.[8]

Northern tribes who depended upon herding, trapping or fishing offered the use of these resources. After sending President Roosevelt $10,000 to be used for "guns and bombs," the Montana Crow Indians pledged their nearly-extinct herd of buffalo for the war effort. "No strings are attached to the pledge of resources," promised Robert Yellowtail, Crow Agency Superintendent. The Red River Band of Chippewa pledged muskrat fur, which they still trapped in the forests, the Columbia River and Quilulte tribes pledged a portion of their annual salmon catch, and several Eskimo tribes, whose economic livelihood depended on fishing, offered to sacrifice their fishing boats to the Coast Guard.[9]

As the largest Indian tribe in the United States, the Navajo adopted one of the most comprehensive of the tribal war relief programs when they met on January 12 and 13, 1942, at Window Rock, Arizona. During an entire day dedicated to patriotic demonstrations, the 50,000 tribal members gave "ready assent to the whole war program." After questioning the superintendent about the flag and its meaning, the Indians pledged a Red Cross quota of $3,000 ($1,000 over that requested), set food production goals, and dedicated their entire reservation resources to the war effort. In addition to promising an increase in the wool clip, the use of their sawmill, a packing plant, a flour mill and victory gardens, individual Navajo offered gifts of corn, meat, rugs and money, from pennies to thousands of dollars. Following the example set by Tribal Chairman Chee Dodge, who purchased $20,000 in bonds, some salaried government employees and some wealthy sheep and cattlemen allotted twenty percent of their monthly income for war bonds.[10]

War bond purchases and Red Cross contributions constituted only one aspect of American Indian resources. After reviewing many tribal enterprises, the government prioritized the need for land, minerals, oil and lumber. Remote western lands, with clear year-round weather, sparse populations, and large non-producing areas, appeared particularly attractive for military use as airports, bombing ranges, and aerial gunnery ranges. By the end of the war total utilization of Indian land, through purchase and lease, amounted to 875,000 acres.[11] Several tribes experienced positive results in their transactions with the War Department. On the South Dakota Cheyenne River Indian Reservation, the military leased 288,746 acres of tribal land and 43,546 acres of trust allotments for an aerial gunnery range. Citing leases providing for "concurrent use," the Indian Office maintained that "use by the War Department did not materially interfere with the use of lands for grazing." Similarly, when the War Department leased 850 acres and the War Relocation Authority leased another 19,123 acres on the Arizona Gila River Reservation, the War Relocation Authority agreed to develop and improve the land under lease. At the Nevada Carson Indian Agency, the Navy Department leased fifty tribal acres on the Pyramid Lake Reservation, contingent on the agreement that the lands be returned to the Indians "when no longer needed by the Navy."[12]

While many tribes benefited from such transactions, other tribes suffered losses. In 1942 the War Department leased or purchased a total of 332,445 acres on the Pine Ridge Reservation in South Dakota, forcing 125 Sioux families to "abruptly . . . give up their homes." Although the families received compensation for their homes, crops, and land, the Sioux failed to be reimbursed for "the sudden change in their way of life." Because this "sudden change" involved selling their livestock at a sacrifice, only ten percent of the relocated families managed to reenter the livestock industry at the end of the war. Oklahoma Indians faced a similar dilemma when the War Department acquired 32,000 acres at Camp Gruber. Paid only four and a half dollars per acre, the fifty-five families discovered they could not purchase new lands at that amount and successfully requested the return of their restricted tracts.[13]

Frustrated over similar situations, many tribes resorted to legal action to regain tribal land. In 1942 the Solicitor General's Office of the Indian Service agreed to represent the Montana Blackfeet, who objected to leasing 11,410.45 acres and selling through condemnation proceedings another 575.3 acres to the War Department. Despite these efforts, a year later the War Department acquired the land for use as an airfield. Kenneth Simmons, District Counsel, also attempted to prevent the Washington Tulialip Indians from losing control of 2,203 acres of timber land. Tribal members complained that because the Indian Office took "no action" in the matter, the military gained control of this "potential farm land."[14]

In their confrontations with the War Department, Alaskan natives suffered both economically and psychologically. Military authorities acquired a number of tracts in Alaska, including 12,000 acres at the Metlakatin Reservation for an airport, water supply, and road. Smaller tracts in native villages and settlements served for "undisclosed military purposes." Among the Aleuts, Eskimos, and Athapascan Indians, this military activity transformed "parts of the quiet and peaceful land into tumultuous army camps." Seizing the opportunity to earn cash wages and sell increasingly popular craft items to visiting whites, many natives relinquished their traditional pastimes of hunting and fur trapping for the more lucrative occupations of construction work and craft production. In other ways, charged Indian Bureau officials, military personnel created far more damage on these isolated areas by selling liquor to the villagers, stealing and destroying property, slaughtering local wildlife for sport, and "contributing to the delinquency of native girls." According to local Indian Bureau personnel, the negative results of the military base proximity far outweighed any positive benefits.[15]

Alaskan natives on the island of Attu earned the distinction of becoming the only Native American civilians to serve as prisoners of war with the Japanese. On June 3, 1942, Japanese forces attacked American installations at the island of Unalaska and followed this attack with invasions on the islands of Kiska and Attu. After an elderly American schoolteacher committed suicide on Attu, the Japanese captured the schoolteacher's wife, who had also unsuccessfully attempted suicide, and forty-five Attu natives. Forced to labor in the clay pits of Japan, the Attu population was reduced to twenty-four by the war's end. After the war, the War Department cooperated with the Department of the Interior in repatriating these Alaskan prisoners-of-war to the site of their former village.[16]

In an event which has ironically been compared to Indian Removal of the 1830s, the government negotiated with Arizona tribes for reservation land to be used as concentration camps for Japanese-Americans. Reservations allotted for Japanese evacuees and conscientious objectors included the Colorado River Reservation in southwestern Arizona, the Leupp Indian Plant in Winslow, Arizona, and the Gila River Indian Reservation, also in Arizona. Authorization for these camps came from Executive Order 9102, dated March 18, 1942, which ordered the Director of the War Relocation Authority to relocate, maintain and supervise evacuees to designated areas. This order authorized the Director, initially Milton Eisenhower and later Dillon S. Meyer, to secure cooperation from all government agencies, including the Indian Bureau.[17] By August, 15,000 Japanese-Americans had traveled to the Gila River Reservation, home to the Pima and Maricopa, in southern Arizona. The War Relocation Authority leased 15,000 acres of communal Indian land on which the evacuees cultivated acreage, planted crops, and constructed laterals. Employing Pima tribal members to construct the camps, the government agreed to return this reclaimed land to the Indian Bureau at the end of the war. A year later 1,500 Japanese relocated to the Leupp Indian Plant in Winslow, Arizona, belonging to the Navajo Tribe, where the government remodeled a school and hospital facilities for their wartime purposes. In the postwar years the military transferred these facilities back to the Navajo.[18]

When confronted with the same opportunity to serve as a relocation site, the Colorado River Indian Tribes unanimously opposed the use of their reservation for this purpose. Informing Department of Interior officials that they preferred to produce guayale, a source of rubber, the Tribal Council maintained that this decision would "further the war effort." Despite this argument, Secretary of the Interior Harold Ickes authorized the War Department to take possession of reservation lands "without the knowledge, permission, or approval of (the tribes)."[19] Citing a "Memorandum of Understanding," the Colorado River Indian Tribes claimed that the government had failed to make adequate provision for compensation of their land usage and had also failed to protect the interests of the tribe. Although Ickes and Meyer executed a subsequent memorandum two years later, they still had not received a lease or permit from the tribe for the 25,400 acres or the several buildings erected on the land. These buildings included military barracks, a 250-bed hospital, eighty warehouses, and several water towers. Tribal leaders objected to this appropriation, because the acreage consisted of "irrigable lands already partly developed and suitable for agriculture." Furthermore tribal leaders estimated it would cost $500,000 to restore the land to its prior condition. Even the war's end did not guarantee these tribes restitution. For six years the Colorado River Indian Tribes claimed that the government denied them access to this land, causing them to suspect that the government had actually leased, rented or sold a portion of it. In 1951 the Colorado River Indian Tribes brought suit against the government in the Indian Claims Commission for damages and compensatory payments.[20]

John Collier, who had originally applied for the position of Director of the War Relocation Authority, gave wholehearted cooperation to Dillon S. Meyer, who would eventually replace him as Commissioner of Indian Affairs. After watching hundreds of evacuees arrive at the Poston Center in Arizona, Collier claimed it was a "moving experience" and endeavored to make Poston into a model concentration camp. Eventually the Indian Bureau prepared a manual on Poston's activities including traffic regulations, law and order, and the police department, which the War Relocation Authority distributed to the nine other relocation camps in the United States.[21]

In contrast to the clearly delineated policy between the Indian Service and the War Relocation Authority, the Bureau maintained a vague, ill-defined relationship with the Office of Land Utilization and the Selective Service concerning conscientious objectors. Beginning in March, 1943, these departments exchanged information on the viability of utilizing Indian land for these reluctant draftees. Hoping to alleviate their increasing manpower drain, Superintendent Foster of the Carson Indian Agency School requested that he be allowed to employ conscientious objectors in clerical work, construction work, and as farm laborers. Lee Muck, Assistant to the Secretary in Charge of Land Utilization, informed the Superintendent that he first needed to apply through the United States Employment Service, which would then certify the unavailability of local labor to both the Selective Service and the United States Department of Agriculture.[22]

Shortly after this terse, uncooperative communication, Muck admitted to Collier that the program for conscientious objectors had been "slightly reoriented." Under the new policy, conscientious objectors could be hired for agricultural work "if requested by the United States Employment Service." Fire protection, however, remained a priority, and Collier requested that Civilian Public Service Camps be established for fire protection at the Quinault Indian Reservation, the Colville Indian Agency, and the Flathead Indian Reservation. In each case, Muck declared he could not recommend to the Selective Service camps at these sites.[23] By the summer, Muck had retreated on his position and advised Collier that he would recommend camps be established at the Yakima and Colville Reservations. Only a few days afteward, E. N. Kavanagh replaced Muck as the new commissioner. He cautioned Collier:

> The outlook at present for new CPS camps is not very encouraging. To a considerable extent, men

> who six months ago would have been classified as IV-E (conscientious objectors) now are being deferred for essential work—primarily, farming. With but a single exception, the camps under the jurisdiction of the Department of the Interior are now undermanned.

Because of complicated interdepartmental relationships and a changing climate of opinion regarding conscientious objectors, Collier lost an opportunity to deal with a group of men about whom he must have felt great interest, curiosity, and—considering his experience with Native American draft resistance—even sympathy.[24]

In addition to land utilization for these varied purposes, the government exhibited a marked interest in tribal mineral resources. Clearly the government possessed sufficient knowledge of Indian oil and gas deposits to make tribal leases a top priority. During 1940, oil produced on Indian lands amounted to twenty-two million barrels, coming primarily from the Five Civilized Tribes and the Osage Tribes. In 1941, however, the western tribal lands began to show great promise for future exploration, and the Indian Office intimated that Native Americans would "play an increasingly important role (in national defense) by virtue of the oil deposits on their lands." According to a 1941 survey the following regions possessed the majority of oil lands:

State/Region	*Oil Reserves on Indian Land*	*Percentage of State Reserves*
Montana	15,635	14.3
Wyoming	11,426	2.0
Rocky Mountains	27,942	2.0
New Mexico	880	0.13

State/Region	*Indian Oil-Producing Lands*	*Percentage of State Production*
Montana	1,211	16.1
Wyoming	616	2.0
Rocky Mountains	2,038	2.6
New Mexico	211	0.53[25]

With these statistics in mind, Ickes, who had recently been appointed Petroleum Coordinator for National Defense, chose S. W. Crosthwait, an Assistant to the Commissioner of Indian Affairs, to be the Executive Officer for the Coordinator for National Defense. Crosthwait, an electrical engineering graduate from George Washington University and a naval veteran of World War I, agreed to assume the duties of coordinating federal authority over oil and gas, with the understanding that he be allowed to return to the Indian Service as soon as possible. His request would be deferred until the end of the war, because immediately after Pearl Harbor was bombed, Ickes issued Order Number 1629, which stated that war duties took precedence over all other duties.[26] Ickes clearly intended to exploit Crosthwait's past experience with the Indian Service in order to obtain tribal resources. "Our immediate and primary function is the full mobilization of the nation's natural resources for war," he stated. "The successful conclusion of this war requires that our peacetime and defense jurisdiction over resources . . . be placed upon a basis suited to serve our military and naval forces." The Secretary realized that dealing with Indian tribes and their resources entailed more legal technicalities than dealing with the general public. In previous years, congressional legislation had been deemed necessary whenever transacting business with Indian tribes, but this cumbersome process soon changed after the war declaration, a change Ickes explained was necessary "to adapt the administration of Indian mineral laws and regulations to our wartime tempo." Under the new policy, either the Commissioner of Indian Affairs or any other authorized officials could approve all mineral leases for restricted, allotted Indian lands.[27]

This new streamlined process, combined with a convenient corporate status for some tribes initiated under the Indian Reorganization Act, prompted many Native American tribes to offer their resources to the federal government. During this period, hundreds of Americans wrote to the government concerning copper, coal, or other mineral deposits on their lands, and Native Americans were no exception. Indian agency superintendents, hoping to benefit from the government's increased need for minerals and natural resources, contacted the Bureau of Mines about possible exploration on Indian lands. When Superintendent Ernest McCray requested that the Bureau examine the San Carlos Apache Reservation for iron, copper, asbestos, and manganese ore, he hastened to add that the tribe was a "fully organized, charter corporation." The superintendent's assertiveness succeeded, and the Bureau of Mines agreed to explore for the reportedly ninety-six percent pure manganese ore, which was designated as a critical wartime metal.[28]

Whether the process was initiated by the tribe or the government, leases on Indian land deposits produced several essential war materials, including oil, gas, lead and zinc. Reservations also yielded lesser amounts of copper, vanadium, asbestos, gypsum, and coal. By the war's end, the government had negotiated 6,500 oil and gas leases, had covered more than two million acres, and had yielded 11,400 producible oil wells for 251,052,000 barrels of petroleum on Indian lands. During the war, Native Americans realized an annual income of six million dollars for minerals valued in excess of thirty-nine million dollars. Furthermore, lead and zinc deposits on 3,726 acres of the Quapaw Reservation provided the country with 415,000 tons of these materials, valued at over thirty-eight million dollars.[29]

The Navajo Reservation in Arizona and New Mexico possessed great diversity in mineral deposits. Among their assets, they counted liquid gas, high gravity oil, vanadium, and a surprising wartime discovery of helium. According to the Navy, this helium played a vital role in the nation's wartime effort. Well before the beginning of hostilities, the Navy announced its intention of expanding its blimp facilities, which caused the Bureau of Mines "to accelerate the continuing search for new sources of helium-bearing gas." One such search occurred near the Navajo Rattlesnake Oil Field, and the government considered the result to be of sufficient importance to build a plant at Shiprock, New Mexico. The Navajo plant contained "the highest helium content of all wells operated by the Bureau of Mines." Although the United States government paid the cost of plant construction, the tribe contributed the plant site location and rights of way "without cost to the government," and received royalties for mineral leasing.[30] Operating from 1944 to 1945, the Navajo helium plant contributed to the Navy's employment of helium blimps to escort surface crafts overseas and to reduce the effectiveness of enemy submarines, its use of helium to reclaim defective magnesium castings, and the Army's use of helium in the Manhattan Project to develop the atomic bomb.[31]

Unfortunately, the intense government search for wartime resources failed to consider the future needs of many tribes. On the one hand Ickes made public pronouncements about conservation for future generations, while on the other hand, he privately allowed some tribal resources to be depleted. "The successful conclusion of this war," the Secretary announced in 1942, "requires that our peacetime and defense jurisdiction over resources . . . be placed upon a basis best suited to serve our military and naval forces without waste and with a view to saving all that we can of such resources for future generations." Ickes's perception of conservation seemed to extend to encouraging agency superintendents and tribal members to use horses as transportation rather than utilizing fuel for automobiles. He failed to intervene, however, when the Blackfeet Tribe was induced by the government to deplete its oil reserves.[32]

In 1944, concerned about the conspicuous wartime oil consumption and the eagerness of oil owners to earn a profit, Bureau of Mine officials recommended to Ickes that oil royalties on public land leases be reduced from thirty-two percent to twenty-three percent. "Even with greatly restricted civilian consumption of oil and gas," warned R. R. Sayers, Director of the Bureau of Mines, "the present need for these minerals is so great that our known reserves are being depleted more rapidly than they are being increased by new discoveries."[33] Sayers's doomsday philosophy became a reality in 1945 when the Blackfeet Tribe discovered that its oil field "had practically reached the peak of its productivity." Predicting a relatively short life span and a rapid productivity decline, William Zimmerman, Assistant Commissioner of Indian Affairs, conceded the fact that the oil revenues derived from nonrenewable tribal assets. Furthermore, he worried that the loss of this revenue would hurt the operation of tribal affairs, which cost more than five thousand dollars per year. In a more urgent and self-serving vein, the assistant commissioner displayed concern that this affair might mean poor publicity for the Indian Bureau. Because the Blackfeet held the distinction of being the first tribe to attain almost complete autonomy in the handling of tribal funds under the Indian Reorganization Act, Zimmerman thought that the inability to properly manage its business could discredit the Blackfeet and "bring into disrepute the entire movement toward self-government of Indian tribes."[34]

Governmental requisition of Indian lumber also provided problems similar to the oil situation. After the war declaration, the War Production Board designated lumber "as one of the half-dozen most critical materials," and the Department of the Interior earmarked a billion board feet of timber to be cut from Interior land. The Secretary intended that Indian timber would supply a substantial portion of this amount. Ultimately, Indian forests furnished five percent of the nation's total lumber need, and tribes sold ninety-five percent of this amount to the federal government. Because timber had been designated a critical material, the Forest Service and the Office of Land Utilization pointed out to the Office of Price Administration that any attempt to control stumpage prices might result in the withholding of lumber from the market. This warning referred particularly to Indian tribes who preferred to sell their lumber at competitive market prices.[35]

Several tribes substantially aided lumber production, including the reservations of Fort Apache, Hualapai, Warm Springs, Colville, and Klamath. Although Congress authorized the Office of Indian Affairs to conduct tribal operations and the administration of forests on Indian reservations, Native Americans on the Menominee, Red Lake, and Navajo Reservations independently operated and sold their timber. Throughout the war years, the Indian Service consistently maintained that the annual wartime cut of lumber only exceeded the 1939 cut by one percent. A minority of Indian Service officials, however, voiced concern at the amount of timber usage. In 1944 Walter Woehlke, Indian Service employee, warned Collier that "sooner or later, probably sooner, we shall be confronted by a slump in the lumber market." As did his colleague Zimmerman, Woehlke worried that any losses sustained by the Menominee or Navajo would be attributed to governmental carelessness and reflect badly on the Indian Bureau. The Menominee, for example, had legislation pending against the government for accounting mismanagement. Woehlke, however, blamed the tribal councils of each tribe for any economic discrepancies.[36]

Increased crop production constituted the final area of Indian contribution to the nation's war effort. Despite a severe manpower drain on all reservations, tribal members markedly increased food production for both the market and reservation use throughout the war years. This commendable achievement owed its success to several factors. First, the Indian Office disseminated educational material on war needs prior to the outbreak of hostilities. Through the Division of Extension and Industry, the bureau provided families with land, livestock, equipment, and seeds for farming and stock raising. Furthermore, the Extension Service instructed families in the processes of growing Victory Gardens in order to can and preserve fruits and vegetables. Finally, the Indian Service claimed that this increased food production resulted from the financial policies of the Indian Reorganization Act, particularly the revolving loan fund and tribal funds which supplied credit to farming families. These policies resulted in the following statistics:

Families	*1941*	*1940*	*1943*	*1944*
Estimated no. reservation families	74,630	83,859	65,947	66,666
No. doing farming, livestock raising	45,019	45,037	46,036	44,045
Total Indian Agricultural Value	19,297,000	25,443,000	27,442,000	31,876,000
Total Agri. Value Marketed	12,985,000	17,457,000	18,077,000	22,298,000[37]

Efforts to increase food production continued throughout the war. In 1943, six Interior bureaus, including the Indian Office, submitted a five-year program to increase the production of five major critical war foods, including meat, fish, dairy products, beans, and potatoes. Among other recommendations, they suggested that the department bring under cultivation 60,000 acres of idle land; increase the Indian livestock quality, farms, and gardens; encourage prudent utilization of fish and wildlife resources; and expand dehydration and canning facilities. A final factor which encouraged food production resulted from increased prices for farm goods, which coincided with decreased government financial aid. Ultimately Indians planted a total of 36,200 Victory Gardens to fulfill both their own needs and the government's obligations.[38]

Personal considerations also encouraged food production. In Arizona, Zuni schoolchildren, worried that their tribal members in the armed forces might tire of "white man's food," sent packages of dried meat and corn to their servicemen. Another Arizona tribe, the Havasupai, numbering only 200 people, viewed photographs of conditions in Poland, and then plowed a gulch bottom to raise crops for "the starving people across the sea." In 1943 the military of Fort Bragg, North Carolina, furnished horses for the Cherokee Reservation during their spring planting season, which was dedicated as the Food for Victory Campaign.[39]

By the war's end, an accounting ledger of combined national tribal activity would have revealed both losses and gains. If nothing else, the wartime activity and feverish search for resources generated a renewed interest in reservation commodities. While Dillon S. Meyer cooperated with an increasingly conservative Congress in their efforts to justify terminating federal guardianship of Indian tribes, tribal resources furnished yet another justification for the movement. The outstanding achievements of Native American servicemen and the wholehearted participation of American Indian defense workers proved to Congress that a reservation population existed which was competent and willing to assume responsibility for a tribe's economic future without further protection from the federal government. Unlike the rest of American society, however, which would experience economic growth in the postwar years, most Native American reservations discovered that this prosperity had bypassed them. For American Indians, the "Great Give-away" failed.[40]

---

[1]In 1942 half of all Indian families earned less than $500 yearly as compared to $900 for the average white family of five. "Tribes Sound a War Cry for Liberty," *Business Week*, 1942, 40; Excerpts from "Postwar Program for the Pima Jurisdiction," U. S. Indian Service, 1944, 21–22, Manuscript A348, Arizona State Museum, Tucson, Arizona.

[2]Ickes Order No. 1636, January 14, 1942, Record Group 70, entry 12, box 3819, folder "War Resources"; Document Outline Number 11, "Mobilization of Natural Resources for War," Record Group 48, entry 858, box 1, folder "Summary of War Records Projects," National Archives, Washington, D. C.

[3]*Indians at Work*, Vol. IX, No. 8 (Washington, D. C.: Department of the Interior, Bureau of Indian Affairs, April, 1942): 7; New York *Times*, January 23, 1945, 6:1, December 22, 1942, 17:4.

[4]*Indians at Work*, February, 1942, Vol. X, No. 6, 26; *Annual Report of the Commissioner of Indian Affairs*, 1944 (Washington, D. C.: Government Printing Office, 1944): 238; New York *Times*, April 22, 1942, 12:5.

[5]Undated Resolution, Record Group 75, entry 184, box A–M, Office Files of Assistant Commissioner William Zimmerman, folder "Menominee Agency," National Archives, Washington, D. C.

[6]New York *Times*, May 9, 1942, 20:8, January 30, 1942, 15:2d; *Indians at Work*, Vol. IX, No. 9–10 (May–June, 1942): 31.

[7]New York *Times*, January 23, 1945, 6:1, December 22, 1942, 17:4; *Indians at Work*, Vol. IX, No. 8 (April, 1942): 7.

[8]New York *Times*, December 22, 1942, 17:41, January 8, 1942, 44:7; *Indians at Work*, Vol. X, No. 2d–6 (October–January, 1942): 8–9, Vol. IX, No. 7 (March, 1942): 5, Vol. IX, No. 8 (April, 1942): 7; *Congressional Record*, 77 Cong., 2d sess., A4385.

[9]Ibid.

[10]"Repealing the So-Called Wheeler-Howard Act," Senate Report 1031, 78th Cong., 2d sess. (10842), June 22, 1944, 16; John Collier, "Indians in a Wartime Nation," *Annals of the American Academy of Political Science* 223 (September, 1942): 29–35; New York *Times*, May 10, 1942, 20:8, December 22, 1942, 17:4; *Annual Report of the Commissioner of Indian Affairs*, 1942, 239–40; *Indians at Work*, Vol. X, No. 2d–6 (October–January, 1942): 20, Vol. X, No. 8 (April, 1942): 12; *Final Report of the Japanese Evacuation from the West Coast Secretary of War Reports* (Washington, D. C.: Government Printing Office, 1942): 250.

[11]Indian Office History, Record Group 48, entry 858, box 7, folder "Indian Office History," National Archives, Washington, D. C.

[12]Indian Office History, 33–35.

[13]Indian Office History, 31.

[14]Indian Office History, 34; Simmons to Zimmerman, November 17, 1942, Record Group 75, entry 189, box A–M, folder "Crow Agency."

[15]Indian Office History, 37–39.

[16]"The Capture of Attu as Told by the Men Who Fought There" in *The Infantry Journal* (Washington, D. C.: The War Department, 1944): 2d; Pamphlet 36–5, "The U.S. Army in Alaska" (Washington, D. C.: The War Department, July, 1972): 89; File OPD 370.05, Alaska Defense Command, Record Group 165, Record of the War Department, National Archives, Suitland, Maryland.

[17]Richard Drinnon, *Keeper of the Concentration Camps: Dillon S. Meyer* (Berkeley: University of California, 1987): 40–41. After a few months, Milton Eisenhower, unable to cope with the concentration camp environment, resigned. Collier, who originally wanted the position as Director of War Relocation Authority, would eventually be replaced as Commissioner of Indian Affairs by Dillon S. Meyer.

[18]Memorandum of April 15, 1942 Concerning Executive Order 9102, Record Group 210, National Archives, Washington, D. C.; Collier, "The Indian in a Wartime Nation," 31; Elizabeth Shepley Sergeant, "The Indian Goes to War," *New Republic* 107 (November 30, 1942): 711; *Annual Report of the Commissioner of Indian Affairs, 1942*, 233.

[19]*Colorado River Indian Tribes v. United States*, August 1, 1951, Manuscript 369, 2–3, Arizona State Museum, Tucson, Arizona.

[20]*Colorado River Indian Tribes v. United States*, 4–11.

[21]*Indian Office History*, 112, 114–15.

[22]Muck to Collier, March 31, 1943, Record Group 48, entry 860, box 423, folder "Office of Indian Affairs, 1943," National Archives, Washington, D. C.

[23]Muck to Collier, April 5, 1943, April 7, 1943, Record Group 48, entry 860, box 423, folder "Office of Indian Affairs, 1943."

[24]Muck to Collier, June 2, 1943, Kavanagh to Collier, June 26, 1943, Record Group 48, entry 860, box 423, folder "Office of Indian Affairs, 1943."

[25]*Indians at Work*, Vol. VIII, No. 11 (July, 1941): 29; Document on Indian Oil Reserves, Record Group 70, box 4465, folder "Indian Lands," National Archives, Suitland, Maryland.

[26]*Indians at Work*, Vol. IX, No. 1 (September, 1941): 10.

[27]*Indians at Work*, Vol. IX, No. 8 (April, 1942): 33; Ickes Order No. 1740, September 26, 1942, Record Group 70, entry 12, box 3519, Indian Office History, 75–76.

[28]McCray to Bureau of Mines, June 25, 1942, R. R. Sayers to Commissioner, July 18, 1942, Record Group 70, entry 12, box 3819, folder "X112."

[29]*Indian Office History*, 77–82.

[30]"Helium Production Expands to Meet Wartime Demands," Record Group 70, entry 12, box 3819, folder "Draft History, Bureau of Mines," 1–3; *Indian Office History*, 31.

[31]Ibid.

[32]"Helium Production Expands to Meet Wartime Demands," 4–5; *Indians at Work*, Vol. IX, No. 9 (April, 1942): 33.

[33]Sayers to Ickes, August 7, 1944, Record Group 70, entry 12, box 4465, folder "Indian Lands."

[34]Zimmerman to F. H. McBride, February 20, 1945, Record Group 75, entry 190, box I–M, folder "Memoes from Staff."

[35]*Indians at Work*, Vol. X, No. 2d–6 (February–July, 1943): 9; *Indian Office History*, 60; Muck to Arnold, February 16, 1944, Muck to Collier, May 25, 1943, Record Group 48, entry 860, box 423, folder "Indian Office, 1943."

[36]Kavanagh to Endersbee, February 1, 1943, Kavanagh to Endersbee, April 1, 1943, Record Group 48, entry 860, box 423, folder "Indian Office, 1943"; Indian Office History, 60; Woehlke to Collier, September 19, 1944, Record Group 75, entry 19, box D–M, folder "Memoes from Staff."

[37]*Indian Office History*, 45–49.

[38]*Indians at Work*, Vol. X, No. 7–8 (1943): 29; Vol. VII, No. XII (August, 1941): 29.

[39]*Indians at Work*, Vol. IX, No. 7 (March, 1942): 5; Vol. IX, No. 8 (April, 1942): 11; *Congressional Record*, 77th Cong., 2d sess., A4385.

[40]The Great Give-Away, a ceremony practiced by many tribes, served many purposes. Traditionally a leader could prove his worth and gain stature by collecting goods only to give them all away in a single social event. This procedure not only ensured the welfare of the poorer, dependent tribal members, it also focused on tribal virtues such as generosity and communal responsibility. Tom

Holm, "The Crisis in Tribal Government," in *American Indian Policy in the Twentieth Century*, Vine Deloria, Jr., ed. (Norman: U of Oklahoma P, 1985): 136.

A great deal of the justification for termination of Indians was based on their tribal resources and potential economic self-sufficiency.

Dillon S. Myer, Director of the War Relocation Authority, and Eleanor Roosevelt, inspect Japanese internees quarters at the Gila River Corporation. Gila River was one of the three Japanese Relocation Camps established on Native American reservations during WWII. National Archives 210-G-6B-469.

Zuni school children in New Mexico held Red Cross drives during snowstorms. State Records Center and Archives, Santa Fe, New Mexico, SWAIA File 4 #32832.

Zuni school children sent corn pollen to servicemen stationed overseas so that they could continue to perform ancient religious ceremonies. State Records Center and Archives, Santa Fe, New Mexico, SWAIA File 4 #39834.

Publicity, Persuasion and Propaganda: Stereotyping the Native American

A 1942 *Saturday Evening Post* article concerning Native American enlistment in the armed forces featured a cartoon with a feathered tribesman shouldering a rifle and marching determinedly in the direction of Berlin, as indicated by an arrowed sign. Although tactless and obvious imagery, the symbolism nevertheless indicated an acute awareness of the American public toward the role played by the American Indian in World War II. This awareness, occurring not by chance but by design, stemmed from several sources. Clearly, the outstanding response of Native Americans to Selective Service registration generated curiosity from other Americans.[1]

During World War II, Native Americans contributed handsomely to the American war effort in military service and in defense work, but, unknown to most Americans, they played another vital role as media figures designed to promote the war effort. This publicity role developed from a conscious effort on the part of the Indian Bureau, the media and politicians. The hard-earned reputation of the Indian as self-sacrificing, hardworking, and patriotic implied that the Indian Bureau had successfully transformed reservation Indians into citizens capable of merging into mainstream society. Furthermore, the media willingly cooperated in publicizing Native American war efforts, because they furnished good copy. By presenting Indians as unassimilated and self-sacrificing, newspapers and magazines created exotic images for public consumption. Finally, Congressmen and other politicians, always sensitive to public attitudes, also exploited the media value of patriotic tribal members from their home districts and states. While this propaganda onslaught certainly captured the public's attention, it also reaped unexpected results in the form of new Indian stereotypes and a Native American population that discovered its powerlessness in generating its own publicity image.[2]

For centuries Native Americans have generated evolving viewpoints from white Americans—from James Fenimore Cooper's eighteenth-century image of the noble savage, to the dying Indian presented in mid-nineteenth century tracts, to the twentieth-century cinematic portrayal of warlike tribes. A recent study of Native Americans in World War II suggests that Indian participation in military duty resulted in their desire to assimilate into white society and adopt white cultural values. An earlier study, however, emphasized that World War II regenerated tribal practices and customs, creating more pride, not less, in Native American traditions. Both views, the assimilationist versus the traditionalist, were exploited during the war by the Commissioner of Indian Affairs, the media, and politicians.[3]

Throughout the 1930s, Secretary of the Interior Harold Ickes and Commissioner of Indian Affairs John Collier made extensive use of the media and encouraged positive publicity toward the Interior Department and the Bureau of Indian Affairs. Ickes particularly maintained a high profile by making speeches to such diverse groups as the North American Wildlife Conference, the Indian Rights Association, and the American Civil Liberties Union. The secretary proved to be a powerfully effective speaker, as constituents often requested copies of his speeches, and a few groups reprinted his remarks in pamphlet form.[4]

Most speeches, however, reached only a limited audience, so beginning in 1933, departmental policy focused on disseminating material to the press. The Interior Department proposed hiring "qualified persons from each department to write specialized news and feature material." In addition, Ickes maintained access to every major newspaper in the country, local newspapers, press associations, magazines and specialized publications. Stuart Godwin, Director of Information, claimed that the Interior Department's manipulation of the media was so successful "because the Secretary was a newspaper man and completely familiar with all aspects of that business." In addition, Ickes "insisted on spot news being handled while it is news." Furthermore, the press department maintained a policy of promptly answering newspaper queries, which assured the department of good relations. As a result of these policies, Godwin believed that their "publicity machine" functioned "smoothly and swiftly."[5]

From 1934 to 1941 the Indian Office issued press releases which, according to Special Agent Floyd La Rouche, "combined facts, both solid and dramatic, with propaganda." The agent claimed that this material, which usually appeared in local newspapers, conveyed a positive picture of Indian Service accomplishments and favorably impressed Congressmen in these districts. This publicity culminated in 1938 with a semi-historical, semi-propagandistic pamphlet entitled "The New Day for the Indians." Financed by Roger Baldwin of the ACLU and researched by Baldwin, the Indian Bureau, and the Solicitor General Nathan Margold, the pamphlet reviewed the results of the Indian New Deal policy. "It represents the most objective and comprehensive appraisal of the present administration of Indian Affairs thus far consummated," claimed Collier. He envisioned a long range publicity campaign for the document which would last for months and "embrace many outlets" including magazine articles, newspaper stories, and a presentation to the President of the United States.[6] Newspaper and magazine coverage evidently interested Collier and Ickes, but they seemed even more intrigued by radio, the medium which Franklin Delano Roosevelt so effectively exploited. Although the Department of the Interior lacked a radio station, it boasted a studio from which recorded programs traveled over ordinary telephone lines to regularly established broadcast stations.[7]

With these resources at their disposal, the Indian Office searched for unusual events to publicize their tribes. Because many of the tribes in California, known as Mission Indians, generally lacked both reservations and tribal costumes, they seldom received the press attention granted to those tribes displaying both colorful clothing and "exotic" backgrounds. In April, 1933, Indian Agent Clyde Hall, employed at the San Francisco, California, Indian Court, developed an ingenious plan to promote California Indians at the Golden Gate International Exposition. Hall explained to Michael Straus, the Interior Department's director of public relations, that although he had managed to obtain publicity with *Time* Magazine and a New York newsreel company, further publicity had been hampered by the lack of Indians attending the exhibit. In one month, however, Hall expected "several demonstrators" to attend the Exposition, and he suggested that Straus arrange to have a national hookup for an air show.[8]

Although the success or failure of the Golden Gate Exposition could not be verified, Straus certainly made credible efforts to stimulate sympathetic Indian interest among radio listeners. Born in Chicago in 1896, he had attended the University of Chicago, worked on newspapers as both a reporter and editor, and served as director for information of Federal Public Administration in 1933 before joining the Interior Department. In September, 1939, his national broadcast concerning the New Mexico Pueblo Indians prompted Collier to remark that the script "moves the story through the essential facts, and in such a way that the dramatic interest doesn't lag at all." After this Collier requested a future broadcast on New Mexico's Indian land crisis.[9]

Collier found another sympathetic colleague in Shannon Allen, director of the Radio Section in the Department of the Interior. In 1940 Allen interviewed Collier for a program entitled "The Indian: Past and Future Roles in National Defense." With such a favorably-disposed interviewer directing positive questions, Collier was able to emphasize the democratic nature of Indians, their loyalty to America and aversion to suppressive dictatorships, and their achievements under the Indian Reorganization Act. The Commissioner cited Native American contributions in World War I and lauded the high registration rate for Selective Service in the current conflict.[10]

Although radio programs captured large audiences, the press generally responded more enthusiastically to activities which incorporated visual stimuli such as tribal customs, traditional costumes, and historical pageantry. In 1940 La Rouche decided that the 1794 Treaty with the Six Nations of New York, renewed annually, fulfilled all these criteria and would make an ideal subject for a media feast. At this time only the Six Nations of New York, a confederacy, and three other tribes, including the Oklahoma Choctaw, the New York Seneca, and the Oklahoma Pawnee, held perpetual annuities by treaty (amounting to an annual sum of approximately $51,020). The latter three tribes had long since opted to receive cash payments in lieu of "blacksmiths" or "light horsemen" promised under the Choctaw Treaty. "Only the Six Nations," explained La Rouche in a July press release, "stick to the precise original method of expending the treaty money." He added that on December 14, 1940, in a ceremony known as "The Calico Treaty," the United States Government would once again give each tribal member six yards of calico. In return the tribe would renew vows of "peace and friendship."[11]

La Rouche followed the press release with a radio interview by Jerry Kluttz of *The Washington Daily News*, WJSV. He began with a statement attributed to Will Rogers, Cherokee humorist and Oklahoma Congressman, who had once quipped that "the United States never broke a treaty with a foreign government and never kept one with the Indians." Agreeing that the government had broken too many treaties, La Rouche described the provisions of the Six Nations "Calico Treaty" which the United States still honored. In a subtle maneuver, he then began to defend the position of the Indian Bureau by stating that the government failed to adequately compensate the Indians with these annuities. "In fact, it could very well be argued," he asserted, "that the Indians support the United States." The field agent based this reasoning on the fact that the Indians had relinquished their land temporarily or in return for land of comparable value. When they failed to regain this land or lost other property, the tribes then brought "claim suits of billions of dollars." As evidence he cited the New York Seneca claim on the Niagara River and the North Dakota claim in the Black Hills. La Rouche ended the broadcast with a plea for sympathy: "He [the Indian] just wants a place to live for himself and his descendants and a chance to earn a living and to live his own life."[12] La Rouche's statement may have been a reaction to recent press releases by both the Democratic and Republican parties, who had, just two days before the radio interview, adopted platform planks advocating early settlement of Indian claims. As usual the Indian Office hastened to offset any idea that settlement of Indian claims would include abolishment of the Indian Bureau. Rather than aiding Indians in retaking the country, La Rouche assured radio listeners during the interview, the Indian Bureau helped American Indians to survive.[13]

La Rouche's press release and radio interview paved the way for an elaborate winter celebration of the Canandaigua Treaty. Held in the Tonawanda Community House near Akron, New York, the historical pageant included a ceremony covering the treaty signing and distribution of calico to tribal chiefs. After speeches, it concluded with tribal dances and songs. Arthur Parker, the curator of the Rochester Museum and a Seneca tribesman who wrote the pageant's script, included many female Indian participants, because "women always spoke at important meetings." In addition to using women wearing traditional costume, La Rouche favored presenting young children dancers who seemed "very Indian in appearance."[14]

The field agent's seven weeks of advance preparation proved fruitful, as three newsreel companies photographed the ceremonies for release to all the motion picture theatres, and the New York *Times* printed one article while promising several more.

"More photographers were present than I have ever seen at any public function in my life," boasted La Rouche to Collier. Encouraged by this success, he planned a documentary film of the ceremony and justified his request by claiming that the Indians "enjoyed the whole affair thoroughly" and "all Indian Service officials are much pleased with the total result." Furthermore La Rouche promised: "In addition to the immediate and tangible results, I believe that the interest aroused amongst editors and others is carrying over into many phases of Indian Service effort and will bring continuingly satisfactory results."[15]

The publicity experiences of the 1930s proved especially useful during wartime, when Collier and Ickes utilized their media knowledge to disseminate personal viewpoints and encourage Indian contributions to the war effort. As early as 1940 the commissioner recognized the necessity of organizing, preserving, and disseminating data for the general public. To obtain the necessary material, he urged cooperation from superintendents and field-office heads in furnishing "information for news releases and *Indians at Work*, an interdepartmental newsletter. Deeming this "a matter of priority," the commissioner also requested that superintendents supply photographs of Indians in all branches of defense work and that they send regular, fresh, complete stories to newspapers and press associations.[16]

Encouraging Native Americans to register for the draft took top priority, and Collier discovered the perfect vehicle for reaching the tribal population with *Indians at Work*. Published monthly and distributed to Indian reservations, agencies, and employees, the magazine always featured an editorial by the commissioner. His first, on Selective Service registration, appeared in November, 1940. "The Government of the United States will find no more loyal citizens than the Indians of this country," predicted Collier. "Theirs is still the ideal of defending liberty and self-government." He further added that Indians had always "practiced selective service universally."[17]

Approximately a year later, Collier turned his attention to persuading Indian Service personnel and their charges to purchase government bonds. In an essay approaching eloquence, he outlined the Nazi design on Europe which consisted of destroying democracies, imperiling freedoms, and transforming the population into slaves. Because he perceived a similarity between former American policy toward its Indian tribes and Nazi policy toward European nations, he urged compassion:

> We ought to be more prepared, more sensitive, to understand the horror of Nazism . . . than workers in most government service . . . and we can't care deeply enough, feel enough, think enough, do enough to help in the supreme effort of our country now.[18]

Two months later Collier further expanded on Nazi policy and ideology while appealing to a basic fear among Native Americans concerning slavery. Responding to the German declaration that American Indians were considered to be Aryans, Collier vehemently denied this assertion and proclaimed that as "Mongoloids," American Indians would become slaves under Hitler. He praised the Indian passion for freedom and confidently applauded their American patriotism. Clearly this message reached Native Americans; one Celilo tribesman, asked why he served his country, reiterated Collier's sentiment almost verbatim. "We know that under Naziism we should have no rights at all," said the young man. "We are not Aryans, and we [would] be used as slaves."[19]

The attack on Pearl Harbor moved the Commissioner profoundly, and in an editorial in January, 1942, he declared that Americans would win the war with their values of self-respect, justice, and freedom. He added that they had nothing to fear in the conflict if they remained faithful to these values. "Who should know all of this . . . better than the Red Indians?" he concluded, alluding to Native American persistence and perserverence. In an effort to boost morale, he mentioned noteworthy accomplishments, stating that he believed, albeit without proof at this time, that Indians had volunteered for the armed forces in larger proportion than any other group in the nation.[20]

Secretary Ickes, who had recently and successfully resisted a bid to allow logging in the National Parks for the war effort, immediately joined Collier in urging the entire Interior Department to coordinate, expend, and also conserve its natural resources for the war effort. In an April, 1942, issue of *Indians at Work*, Ickes announced that the department had established a War Resources Council, with Michael Straus as director. Relying on his past positions as publicity director in the department and temporary member of the War Production Board, Straus possessed intimate knowledge of Indian reservation resources which Ickes intended to fully utilize. "Our immediate and primary function," he declared, "is the full mobilization of the nation's natural resources for war."[21]

By the following year, Collier admitted publicly that Indian Service morale had slumped, caused by reduced appropriations, halting land acquisition, irrigation projects, and new construction. Furthermore, war demands had reduced Indian Service personnel and reservation members. Despite these sacrifices and hardships, Collier worried that the general public failed to appreciate the Indian war effort. "Many of us yearn for a more dramatic identification with the crisis of the world," he mused, perhaps self-analytically. He then urged his readers to dispel negative attitudes, because "collapse of morale is contagious."[22]

In the next issue of *Indians at Work*, Collier gleefully reported that his appeal had worked. "On the home grounds of the tribes, the stresses increase," he informed his readers. "Morale goes up, not down." He then exhorted his readers to more sacrifice and "to hold nothing back." Appealing to a combination of pride and vanity, the commissioner claimed that Indians possessed a history of perserverance which resisted "a crushing of the spirit" and acted as "a light for all the peoples of the world."[23]

By 1943 Collier could feel confident that his messages had influenced both the Indian Service personnel and Native Americans, because the Selective Service reported a ninety-nine percent registration rate, the National Congress of American Indians claimed that Indians purchased more war bonds per capita than any other racial group, and newspapers carried stories of reservations offering their entire resources to the war effort. "The Crow Indians offer Uncle Sam their buffaloes, their oil and mineral deposits," reported the New York *Times* on January 8, 1942, "all the resources of their 2,500,000 acre reservation to help win the war." Collier then turned his attention to utilizing these results for publicity and propaganda efforts, in particular to justify the success of the Indian Reorganization Act.[24]

Because the Indian Bureau believed Congress had adopted a negative attitude toward their agency, many officials urged Collier to push for a more aggressive publicity policy. Special Agent Floyd La Rouche personally believed that former propagandistic methods prevented "adverse criticism" and gained "solid public support." He referred not only to press releases but also to *Indians at Work* and to *As Long as the Grass Shall Grow*, a history book written in cooperation with the Indian Bureau by Oliver La Farge, noted anthropologist, historian, and author. La Rouche envisioned the utilization of celebrities, tribal leaders, and academics to educate the public about Indian Service accomplishments through skillful speakers as well as radio programs and local press releases. The agent deemed the last method, aimed specifically at Congressmen, to be extremely important. He also blamed an absence of favorable news items in the preceding several months for the persistent negative attitude in the House and Senate committees.[25]

Actually La Rouche appeared to be only half right, because local newspapers occasionally carried stories about Selective Service Registration on the reservations, defense training, and war bond purchases which, from time to time, national newspapers reprinted. In the early months of war fever, the commissioner found the New York *Times* and the Washington *Post* to be especially receptive to upbeat stories on Native American contributions. Collier and Educational Specialist Willard Rhodes took the opportunity created by this interest to stress the hardships American Indians endured while contributing manpower, funds, and resources.[26]

In addition to newspaper coverage, the Indian Bureau and Interior Department intended to utilize magazine publications. From 1942 to 1944, Interior Department personnel published articles on American Indians in both scholarly and popular journals. Exhibiting his more scholarly nature, Collier wrote a 1942 article for *The Annals of the American Academy of Political and Social Science*. Pursuing his usual theme of Native American patriotism despite discrimination, he also exploited this opportunity to push a topic of vital importance to him: the Indian franchise. He urged New Mexico and Arizona to extend voting privileges to tribes within their borders, including the Navajo who, in an ironic twist of fate, had exercised their voting privileges within the Indian Bureau to reject the Indian Reorganization Act, the prime focus of Collier's administration. That same year the Indian Bureau Health Director, J. R. McGibony, also gained exposure in a professional journal, *Public Health Reports*, concerning Selective Service registration and American Indian military rejection rates. Eager to reach a wider audience, in 1944 Ickes published in the more popular magazine, *Collier's*. Complete with photographs, the article contained the most recent statistics concerning Indian contributions.[27]

Believing that Indians could induce other countries to become America's "active allies," Collier also intended to publicize their exploits to other countries, because "our Indians are an important symbol to colonial peoples all over the world." He believed that Egypt, India, Iran, China and South America, in particular, felt "strong, cultural bonds with our Indians," making this claim of cultural bonding because of previous responses from these countries. When the Middle East needed American engineers for railroad and irrigation construction, they specifically requested specialists from the Indian Office. After reading newspaper accounts about unfortunate conditions among the Navajo in the 1930s, the nation of India conducted special prayers for the tribe. In 1942 Collier returned the favor by promising that "to the millions of native men and women in the Orient and . . . South American countries, the Indians of the United States send a message of prayer and hope and bravery." The Office of War Information agreed to cooperate with Collier's plans by sending to those countries radio reports and printed pamphlets concerning Native American enlistment.[28]

Although these stories, generally factual and unabashedly self-congratulatory, furnished publicity for the Indian Bureau, another type of article grabbed the public's attention even more. In their efforts to exploit the media, Collier and his colleagues overlooked an important factor in American propaganda dissemination: that one of the primary functions of a free press is to sell the product. During World War II newspaper and magazine publishers discovered that an audience existed for stories about Native Americans, but judging from the types of articles published, they preferred colorful, amusing anecdotes rather than substantive pieces on Indian policy.[29] These popular stories usually stressed the exotic aspects of Indian life, including tribal costumes, traditions, or unique Indian traits. Accompanied by terms such as "braves," "warriors," or "warpath," these articles evoked strong, graphic images of a by-gone era. Magazine articles held the advantage of creative illustration, and publishers often accompanied their stories about Indians with cartoon characters dressed in typical tribal costume and assuming a comic pose. Newspapers, hampered by a lack of space, relied on creating visual imagery. Any Native American who publicly appeared wearing tribal costume, even for such a mundane activity as voting, generated a press story. When Chief Crazy Bull, Sioux grandson of Sitting Bull, voted in Long Island wearing "full tribal regalia," the press described his costume in detail. Stories about Indian soldiers performing actual war dances, thus combining both ceremony and costume, clearly intrigued readers. In July, 1943, the New York *Times* published an article about the departure of the Forty-Fifth Infantry Divison, a unit containing 1,500 Indians from twenty-eight tribes. Prior to their invasion of Sicily, tribal members performed traditional war dances and, emphasizing the religious aspect of the rite, prayed for a successful landing. The *Times* referred to this ancient ritual as a "Redskin war ceremonial."[30]

Whites often overlooked the religious aspect of these Indian rituals, believing that after decades of reservation life, Indian religions had long been defunct. While one historian has asserted that Native Americans became more susceptible to Christianity and conversion and only held traditional dances to gain more acceptance by their white colleagues, Native American accounts dispute this theory. Former Navajo Codetalker Thomas Begay claimed that the war actually strengthened his belief in Indian ceremonies:

> I was very lucky to have gotten through that time. Maybe because I believe in the traditional Navajo ways and felt that the Great Spirit was protecting me. My parents, both very traditional Navajos, had ceremonies for me using clothes that I had worn before I left home to go in the service. These ceremonies protected my well-being so I could survive.[31]

Furthermore, the majority of Zuni military men carried sacred prayer meal or amulets into combat and prayed often during their wartime experience. "The result of all this," claimed anthropologist Evon Vogt, "was an increase in religious activity during the war years and later and a wider participation in ritual than before the war."[32]

Because Indians supposedly possessed special abilities, Americans expected tribesmen to excel as soldiers, and news coverage fulfilled these expectations. Writer Jack Durant's article for the Washington *Post*, reprinted in the *Congressional Record*, quoted Major Lee Gilstrap of Oklahoma, who had trained 2,000 Native Americans at his post. "The Indian is the best damn soldier in the Army," claimed Gilstrap. Their particular talents included bayonet fighting, marksmanship, scouting and patrol work. Half of Gilstrap's Indian recruits held expert rating for rifles, and he claimed they proved particularly adept at scouting, because of their acute sense of perception, their "long, sleek muscles" which were "built for endurance" and superior coordination. Historian Stanley Vestal, who specialized in Native American history, wrote in the May, 1942, *Saturday Review* that Indians excelled at military duty, because they believed in "offensive warfare . . . they invented the blitzkrieg . . . [and] they never gave quarter or expected it."[33]

Other journalists seized the opportunity to publicize the Indian soldier's war effort and to portray him as particularly eager to fight for his country. Writer Estelle Webb Thomas, the wife of a farm supervisor on the Navajo Reservation, published "America's First Families on the Warpath" in *Common Ground*, praising Navajo loyalty, contributions, and military prowess. "They are itching to fight 'He-Who-Smells-His-Moustache' and 'Man-With-Gourd-Chin'," she wrote, respectively referring to Hitler and Mussolini, "and most of all do they long for a crack at the 'Slit-Eye-People'."[34]

Richard Neuberger's stirring article on Native American contributions appeared in the Washington *Post*, the New York *Times*, the *Saturday Evening Post*, *Asia and the Americas*, and twice in the *Congressional Record*. The ex-correspondent for the *Portland Oregonian* and the New York *Times*, who also served as a representative in the Oregon state legislature and became aide-de-camp to Brigadier General James A. O'Connor in Yukon Territory, praised Native American enlistment rates, war bond purchases, and defense work. He wrote, "Army officials maintain that if the entire population was enlisting in the same proportion as Indians there would be no need for Selective Service."[35]

The reading public obviously relished the image of Native Americans as unacculturated, different, and a little naive about white civilization. This fascination extended to Indian names, which offered whites unusual angles for articles. When Sioux tribesman Charles "Kills the Enemy" Jones, "a descendant of a long line of famous chieftains," enlisted in the army, officers supposedly ordered him "to skip the fighting talk and just give them his name." Private Paul Bitchenen, "Chief Two Hatchet," reputedly invaded Italy with the words, "We've come to return the visit of Columbus in 1492." Furthermore, regardless of their tribal standing, Native Americans discovered that they were considered "chiefs" by most Americans. Captain Joseph J. Clark, the first Indian appointed to Annapolis, gained honor as an executive officer of an aircraft carrier and also earned the nickname, "The Chief."[36]

While one historian has suggested that Native Americans exhibited no displeasure at this "nickname," which did not reflect a "Sambo" mentality, some World War II participants, out of respect for a ranking officer, never used the appellation. World War II veteran Vidal Franco served under a Native American, Sergeant Green, and recalled that the troops never dared address him as "Chief." "We never called him that," remarked Franco, "because we wanted to respect him." Remembering his sergeant as a quiet man, Franco claimed that he was a good officer who never talked much with the privates.[37]

As the Indian role deteriorated to glib clichés in the American press, so did the fundamental concept of tribal sovereignty. In June, 1942, a council of Iroquois chiefs from the Mohawk, Onondaga, Cayuga, and Oneida tribes signed a resolution urging war on the Axis powers and presented it to President Franklin Roosevelt and the House of Representatives for "approval." The following month this resolution became a war declaration when Seneca and Tuscarora chiefs joined their fellow Iroquois. Garnering much public attention, the action of the Six Nations elicited praise for the tribes' patriotism but little comprehension of their underlying motives. Newspaper accounts never mentioned tribal sovereignty or pending court cases concerning tribal rights and the draft.[38]

Similar stories about other tribal declarations of war and peace also focused more on symbolism and less on substance. In September, 1945, when the Sioux sent a peace pipe to President Harry S. Truman as a "tribute to the greatness of the President as a leader in war and peace," the Associated Press picked up the story from Pine Ridge, South Dakota. Senator John Gurney, Republican from

South Dakota, presented the pipe to Truman from the Sioux "in the hope that it would be symbolic for future peace." That same month an article in the New York *Times* announced that the Osage Tribe "remained technically at war with the former Axis powers" and would proclaim the peace in October, 1945.[39]

Traditional Indian ceremonies furnished white Americans and at least one foreigner with symbolic honors as well as tangible publicity when Native Americans revived an ancient custom of adopting outsiders into their tribes. In February, 1942, the Indian Federation of America named Joseph Stalin as "the outstanding warrior of 1941." Awarding the Soviet premier a war bonnet and the title of "Chief," Chief Fallen Trees, a.k.a. Paul Horn, warned Edward Carter, President of the Russian War Relief and Emissary to Stalin, that "no one is permitted to wear the bonnet but Chief Stalin."[40] American recipients soon followed Stalin's recognition. General Douglas MacArthur reaped praise and titles from the Wisconsin Winnebago Tribe and the Indian Confederation of America. In June of 1942, "high atop a cliff in the upper dells of the Wisconsin River," the Winnebago named MacArthur "Chief of all American Indians." The following year the Indian Confederation of America chose the general as "the greatest example of an American warrior in 1942." MacArthur clearly appreciated the recognition, because he took advantage of a photographic opportunity by later posing with five Bushmasters. An elite Indian fighting unit in the Pacific trained in hand-to-hand combat and small asssault weapons, this photograph included tribal members from the Pawnee, Pima, Chitmatcha and Navajo tribes.[41]

Naval officers, politicians, and celebrities also received adoption honors. The Sioux inducted Admiral William Leahy, who claimed Cherokee heritage, into the tribe and named him "Leading Eagle." The seventy-year-old admiral endeared himself to the tribe when he then joined in their dance. Wendell Willke, Republican presidential contender in 1944, received the name "Flying Eagle" when the Blackfoot Tribe adopted him. Finally the Penobscot Tribe of Maine ceremoniously adopted Eleanor Roosevelt and aptly renamed her "Ow-du-sees-ul," meaning

"Princess of Many Trails." After placing a wampum headdress on the First Lady, Princess Watawoso told her, "My song is for your protection on your many trails."[42]

Politicians took advantage of the public's interest in Indian affairs to associate themselves whenever possible with Native American achievements. Senator Gurney's willingness to serve as emissary for the Sioux to President Truman furnished an example of effective use of the media. New York politicians seemed especially sensitive to the timeliness of American Indian publicity. In 1942 Governor Herbert Henry Lehman, who later served as Director General of the United Nations Relief and Rehabilitation Administration, designated September 26 as American Indian Day and praised the Native American war effort. Furthermore he credited the Iroquois Confederacy for "influencing the formation of our Federal Union." During the third annual American Indian Day, New York's Lieutenant Governor Joe R. Hanley sent a message to the American Indian Council in honor of the celebration, stating that "in proportion to population there were more American Indians in military service, in industry, and among buyers of war bonds than any other racial group."[43]

On the Congressional level, politicians frequently utilized the *Congressional Record* to submit remarks on Native Americans. Displaying a preference for newspaper stories and magazine articles, Congressmen requested that several local and national articles be reprinted in the *Record*. Senator Elmer Thomas, Democrat from Oklahoma and Chairman of the Senate Committee on Indian Affairs, submitted the Washington *Star* article by Jack Gilstrap entitled "Indians Called Best Soldiers in the Army." Richard Neuberger's story on "Our Indians at War" appeared in the Washington *Post* before Congressman Charles McNary of Oregon asked "unanimous consent to have the article printed in the *Record*." Neuberger's popular writing style earned him a second printing when Representative John Coffee, Democrat from Washington, introduced a similar article, "The American Indian Enlists." Praising the Sioux, Gros Ventres, Mandan and Arikara from North Dakota, Representative Usher Burdick turned to a different source—family letters—for publication in the *Record,* "to let the public know the mental attitude of these Indian warriors."[44]

Collier and Ickes clearly welcomed these insertions into the *Congressional Record* because the articles, particularly Neuberger's story, reflected well on the Indian Bureau. Referring to Collier as "a champion of extended rights and privileges of the American Indians," Neuberger further credited Native American performance to "the enlightened administration of Commissioner Collier." The journalist quoted Representative Coffee as declaring, "America's Indians are fighting for America, because America has made a conscientious effort to right old wrongs and improve the life of our Indians."[45]

The commissioner also utilized the Indian war record when called before congressional committee hearings to justify the success of his program. In 1944, testifying on *Senate Report* 310, an act to repeal the Wheeler-Howard Act, before the House Committee on Indian Affairs, Collier lauded the effort of Native Americans who, he claimed, had sent 43,000 people into war industries or military service. Describing this as an "excellent record," he attributed their contributions to technical skills taught by the Indian Service and Indian schools. Furthermore he reminded Congressmen that the Indian Bureau had been the agency responsible for endorsing the Indian franchise. During his testimony before the same committee, Secretary Ickes supported his colleague's record and argued against abolishing the Indian Bureau by stating, "This cure turns out to be nothing less than the ancient remedy of hanging the doctor." Such a remedy, he continued, ignored the progress made on behalf of the Indian and also failed to consider "the willingness of another agency to assume difficult and complicated responsibilities."[46]

Because of the progress made by the Indian Bureau and other agencies, President Roosevelt decided to document and publicize the war record for his entire administration. In March, 1942, the President informed Harold D. Smith, Director of the Bureau of the Budget, that he was "very much interested" in preserving "an accurate and objective account of our present experience." When he urged the necessity of keeping "systematic records," Smith assumed the responsibility for obtaining a comprehensive history from all agencies. Two years later, Roosevelt appeared to be pleased with Smith's procedures, particularly with the establishment of a Committee on Records of War Administration which had gained the voluntary cooperation of thirty different agencies. Aggressively optimistic, the President declared, "I feel sure that a careful recording of this experience not only will help win the war but also will serve the needs of the postwar era."[47] The President clearly indicated that he saw nothing wrong in advertising his administration's achievements through these war histories. "It is a well-established practice," he asserted, "for officials to make a public accounting of their stewardship." For his part Smith endeavored to fulfill his Chief Executive's expectations. Intending that these war histories should be appropriate for publication, the Director notified department heads to provide funds for this purpose. By the war's end, the Department of the Interior, fully cognizant of the potential publicity value, had submitted a twenty-two-chapter manuscript along with typewritten reports from nine bureaus.[48]

Appointed by Ickes to serve as Supervisor of the War Records for the Department of the Interior, Sylvia Altman stressed that since the history would "be the official and confidential war record, none of the usual restrictions and taboos necessary for security reasons in time of war would apply here." While Altman hoped to receive an honest and accurate report of each agency's contributions, problems and difficulties, she usually received only positive reports. Furthermore she conceded that when necessary, departments could insert prewar activities which had "some bearing on the progress of the war." Along these lines, the Office of Indian Affairs prepared a 119-page document.[49]

In the "Indian Office War History," Native Americans and the Indian Bureau shared the credit for "an unprecedented release of Indian energy during the war years . . . [because] the activities of the Indian Office are inseparable from those of the Indians themselves." The untitled, anonymous report specifically cited as contributions such things as "conspicuous gallantry on the battlefront," war industries work, and increased crop production, all achievements made possible by the Collier administration. Reviewing federal government policy from the publication of the 1928 Merriam Survey through the Collier administration, the historical document followed the same general format as "A New Day for the Indians" in delivering a positive image of the Bureau.[50]

The war history compiled by the Indian Office chiefly concerned contributions on the home front, because a frustrated Collier encountered endless difficulties in obtaining records on Native Americans in the armed services. Although Selective Service kept separate records on registration, the military did not segregate Indians. This integrationist policy, initially endorsed by Collier, presented obstacles in documenting tribal military activity. Unless a unit had a significant number of tribesmen, such as the Navajo Codetalkers, the Forty-fifth Infantry Division, or the Bushmasters, Indians simply blended in with other recruits, and important historical facts went unrecorded. While tribal rolls furnished some accuracy in reporting Indian enlistment, the Indian Office continually pressured Selective Service officials to cooperate in obtaining more data on Native Americans.[51]

In 1942 Collier informed General Lewis Hershey, executive director of Selective Service, that reservation superintendents had complained about the lack of information on draftees. "In view of the patriotic and historic part played by the American Indian in the past and earlier wars," he sternly lectured, "it is hoped by this plan our Service will not be deprived of the opportunity of obtaining the necessary statistical data." The Commissioner then revealed his intention to maintain historical records on the Indian role in the war. Three months later, Collier repeated his request and again met with disappointment. William Zimmerman, the assistant commissioner of Indian Affairs, next tried his luck by implying that if Selective Service failed to keep records on Indian recruits, the information would be lost forever. He also received no response.[52]

Despite an inability to acquire records on Native Americans from the Selective Service, the Commissioner refused to admit defeat. In 1945, desiring to leave a positive legacy of both his administration and the Indian war record, the Commissioner compiled *Indians in the War*, an inter-department pamphlet drawing on material collected from the 1945 memorial issue of *Indians at Work*, the pamphlet admitted that the war record remained incomplete but expressed the hope "that when the peace has come" the whole story could be told. *Indians in the War* printed casualty lists, awards, and decorations presented from 1943 to 1944. It also carried photographs of soldiers, loaned by Indian families, and personal, often poignant war stories.[53]

With justifiable pride the Indian Service pamphlet boasted about its many heroes. These included the two winners of the Congressional Medal of Honor, Lieutenant Ernest Childers, a Creek, and Lieutenant Jack Montgomery, a Cherokee. Other articles mentioned recipients of the Distinguished Flying Cross, Silver Star, and Bronze Star. This document also reported on prisoners of war as well as Indian Service employees who served in the war. Even *Indians in the War*, however, could not resist the occasional stereotypical imagery. One article, "A Family of Braves," informed readers about the Reverend Ben Brave's six grandsons, Sioux tribesmen, who had served in the military. "No doubt we shall hear brave stories of them," punned the anonymous writer.[54]

Special wartime correspondents allowed their stories to be reprinted in the document. Master Sergeant Murrey Marder, Marine Corps Combat Correspondent, wrote about the Navajo Codetalkers. The distinguished wartime correspondent Ernie Pyle described how the Navajo, Sioux, Comanche, Apache, Pima, Kiowa, Pueblo, and Crow Indians joined forces to dance before "a grave audience" of several thousand Marines just prior to an invasion of Okinawa.[55] The pamphlet also honored the efforts of those who stayed at home through narratives provided by officials such as Lieutenant Frederick W. Sleight, United States Naval Reserve. Recalling his experiences with Indians at the Naval Supply Depot in Clearfield, Utah, Sleight asserted that the Indians gave one hundred percent and "were always on the job." Other articles furnished information about Indian women and their contributions to defense work, food production, and military service.[56]

Encouraged by the outpouring of stories and the public's reaction to this publicity, by the middle of the war Collier could feel fairly assured that his endeavors to generate a positive Native American war effort had been successful. While attributing this success to achievements generated by the Indian Reorganization Act, Collier and his colleagues did not rest on their laurels or take a fickle public for granted. Made wary by past errors in dealing with Congress, the American Indian Federation, and other critics, the Indian Bureau continuously attempted to discourage negative publicity.[57]

Before the war's end Special Agent La Rouche had begun to express more reservations than others concerning an excess of positive wartime publicity, because he feared the end result might be undesirable and at odds with Indian Service policy. While he conceded the usefulness of war information, the easy access to newspapers, and the impact on the public, the special agent sensed a danger in overexposure, and he warned Collier:

> Unless such material is linked with some kind of appeal for tangible postwar considerations, and unless the contributions of the Indian Service before the war, and the problems after the war, are sufficiently emphasized and reiterated, the war publicity actually is harmful to our objectives. The idea is spreading that if the Indians can do so well in civilian and military war service, there may after the war remain no need for supervision.[58]

La Rouche's fears proved justified. During the war the remarkable exodus of Native Americans to an off-reservation society could not escape the attention of Bureau critics, who attributed this migration to a dissatisfaction with the Indian Office and a desire to acculturate. In 1943 Bertha M. Eckert, secretary for Indian work at the National Young Women's Christian Association, estimated that 12,000 young Indian women had left their reservations to work in the defense industries. According to Eckert, the Y.W.C.A. had assumed responsibility for aiding the assimilation process of these girls, because government schools had concentrated on Indian traditions rather than American culture. Lauding the "deep patriotism" of these women, the secretary predicted that Native Americans would "probably choose the responsibility of a citizen to the security of a ward after the war." Such declarations would then result in "the vanishing reservation."[59]

Similar articles, complimentary to Native American individualism and critical of Indian Bureau paternalism, were published in newspapers and articles. Writer O. K. Armstrong published one of the most extreme of these critiques in a 1945 *Reader's Digest*. In "Set the American Indians Free!" he argued that the wartime government policy intended to perpetuate Indian poverty and dependence. In this article he cited particular issues of property restriction, segregation, and special exemptions. "One effect of the Indian Reorganization Act," wrote Armstrong, "has been to force a collectivist system upon the Indians with bigger doses of paternalism and regimentation." The present policy, he predicted, would soon be challenged by Indians themselves, because those who had left to serve in military or defense work had encountered new opportunities. "There can be no doubt," he asserted, "that all who return from the service will seek a greater share in America's freedom."[60]

Criticism of Indian Bureau policy, which many believed perpetuated a stifling existence on the reservations, continued after the war's end and focused on the veterans. Representative Francis Case, Republican from South Dakota, reiterated Armstrong's ideas in a 1946 editorial from the *Journal* of Pierre, South Dakota. "Heartily in agreement" with the sentiments expressed, Case introduced the article for the *Congressional Record* which stated that because of their wartime performance, Native Americans "are never going to accept a tribal existence willingly in the future." Without openly insisting on abolition of the Indian Bureau, Case argued the merits of individual effort, higher education, and competition with whites.[61]

Case's colleagues, predominantly Republican, evidently agreed with this assessment. After the war the Senate and House Committees on Indian Affairs convened several hearings to discuss bills meant to release Native Americans from property restrictions. Meeting in May, 1946, the House listened to testimony concerning *House Report* 3680, "a bill to provide for the purchase of restricted Indian lands from heirs or from any Indian over sixty years of age"; *House Report* 3681, "a bill to provide for removal of restrictions on property of Indians who served in the armed forces"; and *House Report* 3710, "a bill to emancipate the Indians of the United States." Case, who introduced all three bills, brought six Sioux witnesses to testify and presented petitions with dozens of Indian signatures on behalf of his legislation.[62]

That same month the Senate conducted hearings on *Senate Joint Resolution* 79, a bill by Harlan John Bushfield, Republican Senator from South Dakota, to establish a committee to study Indian claims and administration of Indian affairs. A Navajo delegation spoke at this hearing, and while most seemed content to plead for more education, John E. Hamilton, President of the National American Indian Defense Association, deplored their wardship status. "I am sure that without federal supervision over the American Indian," testified Hamilton, "he would develop sufficiently to take care of himself in every respect." A continuous adversary of the Indian Bureau throughout Collier's administration and Chairman of the Republican National Committee, Hamilton had severely criticized the economic, health, and educational conditions of the American Indian, which he attributed to their continuing wardship status.[63]

In a concurring opinion, Bushfield introduced *Senate Bill* 1194. Similar to *Senate Bill* 1093, it provided for the removal of property restrictions for Native Americans who had served in the armed forces. At this hearing Indian veterans gave impassioned statements concerning their past wartime accomplishments and their present difficulties with the G.I. Bill, which they blamed on their wardship status. Most witnesses, white and Native American, blamed the Indian Bureau for perpetuating this wardship status, which they felt the Indian had outgrown. Congressmen also credited the war experience and not the Bureau for developing a spirit of independence.[64]

The wartime propaganda and publicity accorded the Native American produced diametrically opposed results. In one respect, the American public came to view Indians as patriotic and sacrificing while still primitive and exotic. To many others, however, the Native Americans emerged as self-sufficient, independent, and extremely eager to completely assimilate into mainstream America. Powerless during wartime to generate their own publicity image, Native Americans now had to grapple with the problem of these new postwar stereotypes. While the first doomed many to what critics claimed was a forgotten, thankless existence on their reservations, the second stereotype resulted in a badly-construed policy, known as the Termination Acts of the 1950s, which would reverse progress and advancements for many tribes. Once again Native Americans discovered themselves depicted as stereotypical caricatures, now viewed in movies and the most recent medium, television. Their wartime heroism and sacrifices forgotten and ignored, they existed throughout the 1950s primarily as a foil for John Wayne in western adventures.[65]

---

[1]*Saturday Evening Post*, October 24, 1942, 79.

[2]For a discussion on white viewpoints of Native Americans, see Robert Berkhofer, *The White Man's Indian: The History of an Idea from Columbus to the Present* (New York: Alfred A. Knopf, 1978). Alison Bernstein provides an assimilationist viewpoint in *American Indians and World War II: Toward a New Era in Indian Affairs* (Norman: U of Oklahoma P, 1990), 58–59; Tom Holm presents a traditionalist viewpoint in "Fighting the White Man's War: The Legacy of American Indians in World War II," *Journal of Ethnic Studies* 9 (Summer, 1981): 69–81.

[3]Collier to All Superintendents and Other Heads, February 20, 1941, Record Group 75, entry 195, box 3, folder "National Defense," National Archives, Washington, D. C.

[4]Charles Schwartz to Ickes, December 24, 1937, Record Group 48, entry 849, box 3, folder "Miscellaneous Correspondence," National Archives, Washington, D.C.

[5]Stuart Godwin to Stephen Tyree Early, November 13, 1933, Record Group 48, entry 849, box 3, folder "Miscellaneous Correspondence."

[6]Collier Memorandum, December 22, 1938, Record Group 75, entry 178, box 11, folder "The New Day for Indians"; La Rouche to Collier, December 1, 1943, Record Group 75, entry 178, folder "F. W. La Rouche."

[7]Shannon Allen to Herbert Mancini, September 6, 1938, Record Group 48, entry 854, Information Division, Radio Section, box 11, folder "Public Correspondence."

[8]Clyde Hall to Michael Straus, April 28, 1939, Record Group 48, entry 854, Box 8, folder "Indian Office."

[9]Collier to Straus, September 27, 1939, Record Group 48, entry 854, box 8, folder "Indian Office"; *Indians at Work* (Washington, D.C.: Government Printing Office): Vol. X, No. 7–8, 15, 1943.

[10]Undated Radio Interview Between Collier and Shannon, Record Group 48, entry 854, box 8, folder "Indian Affairs . . ."

[11]Office of Indian Affairs Press Release, July 8, 1940, Department of the Interior Information Service, Record Group 48, entry 854, box 8, folder "Indian Office."

[12]Material for Radio Interview of F. W. La Rouche for Jerry Kluttz, July 20, 1940, Record Group 48, entry 854, box 8, folder "Indian Office."

[13]La Rouche to Kluttz, July 18, 1940, Record Group 48, entry 854, box 8, folder "Indian Office."

[14]La Rouche to Straus and Memorandum in Connection with Proposed New York Treaty Ceremonies, December 18, 1940, Record Group 48, entry 854, box 8, folder "Indian Affairs."

[15]Ibid.

[16]Collier to All Superintendents and Other Heads, February 20, 1941, Record Group 75, entry 195, box 3, folder "National Defense."

[17]*Indians at Work*, Vol. VIII, No. 3 (November, 1940): 28–29.

[18]*Indians at Work*, Vol. IX, No. 2 (October, 1941): 1–6.

[19]*Indians at Work*, Vol. IX, No. 4 (December, 1941): 3; *Congressional Record*, 77th Cong., 2d sess., December 16, 1942, A4385.

[20]*Indians at Work*, Vol. X, No. 5 (January, 1942): 1–3.

[21]*Indians at Work*, Vol. IX, No. 8 (April, 1942): 33.

[22]*Indians at Work*, Vol. X, No. 1 (January, 1943): 1–2.

[23]*Indians at Work*, Vol. X, No. 2–6 (February–May): 1–3.

[24]New York *Times*, January 23, 1945, 6:1; January 8, 1942, 44:7; J. R. McGibony, "Indians and Selective Service," *Public Health Reports*, No. 1 (January 2, 1942): 57:1.

[25]La Rouche to Collier, December 1, 1943, Record Group 75, entry 178, box 6, folder "F. W. La Rouche."

[26]Each volume of *Indians at Work* carried a special section called "Indians in the News" concerning local items. Furthermore, many of the articles quoted in the New York *Times* were reprints of local newspaper articles; thus Indians received both local and national press coverage. New York *Times*, April 22, 1942, 12:5; January 8, 1942, 44:7; December 22, 1942, 17:4; August 23, 1942, II, 6:1.

[27]Harold Ickes, "Indians Have a Name for Hitler," *Collier's* (January 15, 1944): 58; John Collier, "The Indian in a Wartime Nation," *The Annals of the American Academy of Political and Social Science* 223 (September, 1942): 28; McGibony, "Indians and Selective Service," 1.

[28]*Congressional Record*, 77th Cong., 2d sess., A4385, December 16, 1942; *Congressional Record*, 77th Cong., 2d sess., A3160, August 25, 1942.

[29]Often such news items appeared as "tidbits" rather than as hard news.

[30]New York *Times*, November 8, 1944, 6:7; July 25, 1943, 30:5.

[31]Kenji Kawano, *Warriors, Navajo Codetalkers* (Flagstaff, Arizona: Northland Publishing Company, 1990): 28; Bernstein, *American Indians and World War II*, 58–59.

[32]Evon Vogt, "Navajo and Zuni Veterans: A Study of Contrasting Modes of Cultural Change," *American Anthropologist* 51 (October–December, 1948): 548–49.

[33]*Congressional Record*, 77th Cong., 2d sess., A4125, November 30, 1942; Stanley Vestal, "The Plains Indian and the War," *Saturday Review of Literature* 25 (May 16, 1942): 9–10.

[34]Estelle Webb Thomas, "America's First Families on the Warpath," *Common Ground* 2, No. 4 (1942): 95–99.

[35]New York *Times*, August 30, 1942, IV, 7:6; Richard Neuberger, "On the Warpath," *The Saturday Evening Post* (October 24, 1942): 79; *Congressional Record*, 77th Cong., 2d sess., A3160, August 25, 1942; *Congressional Record*, 77th Cong., 2d sess., A4385, December 16, 1942; Thomas, "America's First Families," 95–99.

[36]New York *Times*, February 26, 1944, 6:4; January 30, 1944, 26:4; September 16, 1943, 5:2.

[37]Oral interview with Vidal Franco, World War II military veteran, April 28, 1992, El Paso, Texas. Transcript in possession of the author.

[38]New York *Times*, June 13, 1942, 17:5; July 26, 1942, II, 9:4.

[39]New York *Times*, September 25, 1945, 27:3; September 9, 1945, 18:4; September 16, 1945, 27:3.

[40]New York *Times*, February 21, 1942, 21:8; February 16, 1942, 19:7.

[41]New York *Times*, June 9, 1942, 3:2; February 14, 1943, 32:4; January 20, 1944, 3:3.

[42]New York *Times*, September 4, 1945, 7:2; February 17, 1944, 34:1; February 9, 1943, 15:1.

[43]New York *Times*, September 24, 1944, 47:4; September 21, 1942, 15:2.

[44]*Congressional Record*, 77th Cong., 2d sess., A4125-412, November 30, 1942; *Congressional Record*, 77th Cong., 2d sess., A3160, August 25, 1942; *Congressional Record*, 77th Cong., 2d sess., A4385, December 16, 1942; *Congressional Record*, 78th Cong., 2d sess., A3587, August 14, 1944.

[45]*Congressional Record*, 77th Cong., 2d sess., A4385-86, December 16, 1942.

[46]Congressional Committee Hearings, House Resolution 166, 78th Cong., 2d sess., February 2, 1944, 37–39, 46, 50.

[47]Franklin Roosevelt to Harold D. Smith, March 4, 1942, Record Group 48, entry 858, box 1, folder "XYZ General"; Roosevelt to Smith, January 25, 1944, Record Group 48, entry 858, box 1, folder "War Records Project Key Data."

[48]Smith to Heads of Executive Departments, November 29, 1945, Record Group 48, entry 858, box 1, folder "XYZ General"; Summary of Agency Historical Publications and Plans, September 13, 1946, Record Group 48, entry 858, box 1, folder "War Histories."

[49]Memorandum for Agency Directors, Bureau Chiefs and Heads of Divisions, May 9, 1944, Record Group 48, entry 858, box 1, folder "War Record Project Departmental."

[50]Indian Office History, 1–2, Record Group 48, entry 858, box 7, folder "Indian Office History."

[51]Lewis B. Hershey, Executive Director, Selective Service, to Denver State Director, Selective Service, December 5, 1940, Record Group 147, entry 1, box 33, folder "105. Races. Alabama-Wyoming," National Archives, Suitland, Maryland.

[52]Collier to Hershey, January 22, 1942; Collier to Hershey, March 19, 1942; Zimmerman to Hershey, September 23, 1942; Record Group 147, entry 1, box 426, folder "214. Indian Reservations. General. Alabama-Wyoming, 1942."

[53]*Indians in the War* (Haskell: Haskell Printing Department, 1945): Table of Contents. This was also published as the *Indian Record*.

[54]*Indians in the War*, 1–11, 50–52.

[55]*Indians in the War*, 12–13, 25–27.

[56]*Indians in the War*, 42–43, 49.

[57]For a discussion of Indian Bureau criticism see Kenneth Philp, *John Collier's Crusade for Indian Reform, 1920–1954* (Tucson: U of Arizona P, 1977).

[58]La Rouche to Collier, December 1, 1943, Record Group 75, entry 178, box 6, folder "F. W. La Rouche."

[59]New York *Times*, February 6, 1943, 16:3.

[60]O. K. Armstrong, "Set the American Indians Free!", *Reader's Digest* 47 (August, 1945): 47–52. It is entirely possible that this article was written by Collier critic and American Indian Federation leader O. K. Chandler, using a pseudonym. Not only are the initials identical, but the literary style and ideas are similar.

[61]*Congressional Record,* 79th Cong., 2d sess., April 17, 1946, A2254.

[62]Congressional Committee Hearings, House Committee on Indian Affairs, Hearings on *House Report* 3680, *House Report* 3681, and *House Report* 3710, 79th Cong., 2d sess., May 6, 1946, June 13, 1946, 1, 47.

[63]Congressional Committee Hearings, House Committee on Indian Affairs, Hearings on *Senate Joint Resolution* 79, 79th Cong., 2d sess., May 14, 1946, 1, 25; *Biographical Directory of the United States Congress, 1774–1989,* 716.

[64]Congressional Committee Hearings, Senate Committee on Indian Affairs, Hearings on *Senate Report* 1093, *Senate Report* 1194, June 12, 1946, 1, 10–13.

[65]Holm, "Fighting the White Man's War," 69; Theodore W. Taylor, *American Indian Policy* (Mount Ary, Maryland: Lomond Publications, Inc., 1983): 105.

Harold Ickes, Secretary of the Interior, 1933–1946, came from a journalism background. During Roosevelt's administration, he wrote several articles on Native Americans. National Archives 208-PU-98-K-2.

Lt. Ernest Childers, a Creek, being congratulated by Gen. Jacob L. Devers after receiving the Congressional Medal of Honor in Italy for wiping out two machine-gun nests. U. S. Army Signal Corps photograph, July 13, 1944. National Archives 208-N-24772.

Mrs. Franklin D. Roosevelt, much-traveled First Lady, receives a bead headdress and the name Ow-Du-Sees-Ul, or "Princess of Many Trails," from Princess Wetawaso of the Penobscot tribe before Mrs. Roosevelt christens the 194-foot wooden fuel barge "Pine Tree" at Camden, Maine, February 8, 1943. Chief Bruce Poolaw, whose tribe members built the lifeboats for the barge, looks on. AP / Wide World Photos.

Three of six Indians named in a tribal pow-wow at Stamford, Connecticut, June 16, 1946, to petition the U. N. for a seat on its Security Council, for Indians in the United Nations, sit in front of a tepee. Left to right are: Chief Swimming Eel, General Representative of Chiefs' Grand Council; Princess Red Wing of Seven Crescents, President of the Women's General Council of the League of Nations of the Narragansett Indians; High Chief Night Hawk. AP / Wide World Photos.

Dan Waupoose, a Menomini chief; kneeling with a rifle and wearing a feathered headdress, Algiers, Louisiana. U. S. Navy photograph, August 24, 1943. National Archives, 80-G-153531.

Across the Blue Waters: The Santa Fe Indian Club

"Greetings from an unknown place across the blue waters," wrote Private Paul Duncan in August, 1943, to Margretta Dietrich, Director of the Santa Fe Indian Club and the New Mexico Association on Indian Affairs. "I write to you folks again [after] not hearing from you folks so long. I forgot where we left off. It's a great pleasure of hearing from you who makes it possible for us to have the news like this."[1]

During World War II, individuals from hundreds of different tribes enlisted in military service, and thousands of servicemen and women wrote to friends and family from "across the blue waters." Although each tribe represented a unique and sovereign nation, Native American servicemen and women experienced certain situations which were unique to them. In many instances, American Indians reacted in remarkably similar ways. While the majority of tribesmen lacked a social agency or network through which they could share their wartime stories, the Santa Fe Indian Club in New Mexico proved the exception to this rule. During the war this club underwent a transformation from a social club for high school students into an institution which served as a lifeline between servicemen and women, their friends back home, and their friends in the military.[2]

Directed by Margretta Dietrich and Mr. and Mrs. Don Secrist, the club had originally been established to provide a wholesome leisure-time environment for Native American teenage boys and girls attending such educational facilities as the Santa Fe Indian School and the Albuquerque Indian School. When the necessities of war interrupted the normal activities of the club, the leaders and members immediately responded to the exigency by channeling the resources of the group to serve the needs of their fellow members, or non-members in some cases, now in the military service. These resources included the continuing operation of the club for servicemen and women on furlough and sending "care" packages to military men and women. The most important contribution of the Santa Fe Indian Club, however, involved the publication of a newsletter. Originally intended to furnish service people with news of the home front and vice versa, the newsletter evolved into a vital lifeline for New Mexican Indian servicemen and women who had dispersed throughout the world.[3]

New Mexican Indian males served in every branch of the armed forces and trained as deep-sea divers, paratroopers, aerial gunners, radio operators, and medics, while New Mexican Indian women enlisted in the WACS and WAVES or worked in defense factories around the country. With only one known exception, they entered the service as enlisted personnel or non-commissioned officers. They came from a number of different tribes, cultures and languages. The servicemen and women claimed tribal ties to nineteen different pueblos as well as four other reservations: the Navajo, the Mescalero Apache, the White Mountain Apache, and the Hopi Reservation. Although all service personnel spoke English, each tribe spoke a different language and adhered to different customs. While the Navajo and Hopi tribesmen primarily practiced their tribal religions throughout the war, the Pueblo and Apache service people often reported attendance at Catholic Mass. Common factors included education and military training. While a few of the young men and women had college plans, the majority of the service men and women belonging to the Santa Fe Indian Club had only recently completed high school. For this reason, their military record, with one exception, indicates rankings as enlisted personnel and noncommissioned officers.[4]

Being from the state of New Mexico evolved as the major common bond for the different tribal members. During the war these young people, raised in a state heavily populated by Native Americans, primarily attending Indian schools, and accustomed to dealing with whites quite familiar with Indian cultures, traveled to different places, encountered new experiences and met numerous people who had never before seen an American Indian. While their educational level, family background, and unique personalities dictated their individual responses to these experiences, the majority of Native Americans revealed a high level of adaptability, curiosity, and youthful adventure as they functioned within white military institutions and were transferred to foreign cultures. Although many white observers viewed this acculturation process as a desire on the part of Indians to assimilate, it can be argued instead that this attitude was in fact the result of over three hundred years of acculturation and sophistication developed in response to European colonization in New Mexico.[5]

Native Americans entering the armed forces first dealt with physical training and classroom instruction, the former of which presented very few problems to most Indian servicemen. Private Augustine Lavato, training to become an army medic, described the obstacle course as fun. "You should have seen the boys fall from the swings into ditches that were filled with water," he wrote. "I laughed at them till I was exhausted. I came thru [sic] without a scratch and it was my first time." Private Ben Quintana, a Cochiti Pueblo artist who had recently won first place in both a New Mexico and national art contest featuring over 58,000 other contestants, was stationed with the cavalry at Fort Bliss, Texas, and also felt amusement at his colleague's efforts. "I had the fun of watching some guys saddle up backwards," he told friends, "and others running after their horses." After training on helium balloons at Camp Tyson, Tennessee, Private Johnnie Cato, San Juan Pueblo, began training with a paratrooper outfit. "Today our first day of training began," he stated, "and seem to me it's [a] pretty rugged outfit and tough." A few Native American servicemen, such as Private First Class Narcisso Abeyta, a talented Navajo artist who had to forego an art scholarship to Stanford University when he enlisted, admitted that infantry training included "the most strenuous series of physical feats ever."[6]

Classroom instruction sometimes presented more difficulty than physical instruction, and New Mexican Indians obviously felt a great obligation to achieve high standards. Private Reyes Lovato, who considered the physical training to be easy, admitted that his courses in the Medical Replacement School challenged him:

> I won't be surprised if I flunk this course. It's really tough going. It really covers a great space, and I guess I would say it's a little beyond me. Nothing like Indian schools. Here's a place where you have to stand on your both feet [sic] and put my poor undeveloped brains to a real task. Lots of times I would sit and listen real carefully and won't understand half of what is been [sic] discussed, but I'm in there pitching like never before.[7]

Nevertheless, the majority of men who kept in touch with the Santa Fe Indian Club successfully completed both their training and their courses and regarded these achievements in their specific fields as great accomplishments. Clearly the military forces welcomed the young men who had received a solid educational background, because the different branches assigned many to advanced training courses. When Lawrence Reyes completed an advanced firing course, the navy accepted him for submarine training. The navy also trained Clarence Chiago in chemical weapons. "Learning the formulas and equations are interesting," he admitted, "as they are a little different from those I used to have in my chemistry classes when I was in school." Nevertheless, he promised that he was studying hard for his tests and "so far I haven't failed any of them." Having completed his training as a paratrooper, Private Thomas Thompson also proudly reported that his commanding officer had recommended him to communications school as a radio operator. Corporal Steven Herrera, Cochiti Pueblo, reported that he had graduated from aerial gunnery school with a final grade of eighty-five which earned him an above average rating.[8]

Throughout their training and military careers, New Mexican Indians traveled to dozens of American towns and several different countries, and in doing so, like all other soldiers, they generally judged a place and its population according to friendliness and entertainment value. In Washington, D. C., both Private Juan Pino, stationed at the Engineers Replacement Training Center, and Private First Class Philip Cosen, a trombone player in the United States Army Band, enjoyed the monuments, museums, and outdoor cafés of the capitol. Indians agreed that even smaller cities such as El Paso, Texas, had its share of attractions for sightseeing. Corporal Pierce Harrison, Navajo, and Connie Harrison, Acoma Pueblo, visited nearby Juarez, Mexico, followed by a trip to the El Paso Zoo "to see monkeys." Several towns received accolades for sensitive treatment, including Scottsbluff, Nebraska. Sergeant Mark Chee, Navajo, expressed his gratitude to the Nebraskans for organizing a Soldier's Day and inviting the servicemen to dinner and a show in town. "This is the best town I ever came across," he wrote. Seaman First Class Paul Barton, Navajo, also raved about Los Angeles, California. Describing the Friday night dances at the Hollywood Canteen, Barton emphasized that he had "seen lots of Hollywood stars serving donuts and coffee to the service men and women that comes [sic] to visit the canteen. They really are nice, swell people." And Corporal José R. Roybal, San Ildefonso Pueblo, claimed that Harrisburg, Pennsylvania, was the friendliest city he had ever visited and added, "I hope that I will be stationed here in Harrisburg for awhile."[9]

On the other hand, Native Americans also criticized some towns for negative attitudes towards servicemen and for dullness. Private First Class Faustin Trujillo pointedly mentioned that Virginia was the "only place they didn't care about soldiers or sailors." In Washington, D. C., Philip Cosen enjoyed the sights, but he condemned the people as unfriendly. Although Seaman Second Class Reyes Lovato, Santo Domingo Pueblo, liked San Diego "just a little," he noted that "I see nothing but servicemen in town." Writing from Sheppard Field, Texas, Private First Class Salvadore Romero complained that not only was the area dry, flat and dusty, but "the town is so dead that it don't pay to go on days off."[10]

Native Americans also traveled to foreign countries around the world, including the Pacific islands, India, Burma, Iran, Africa, and Europe. Again tribesmen formulated their impressions of a particular country from the population's reception, its standard of living, and its cultural attractions. Based on these criteria, New Mexicans held the European countries in high regard as they overwhelmingly related incidents involving friendly people and interesting sights.[11] Among the European nations, England especially received large amounts of praise. "This place is really a wonderful country," wrote Corporal Steven Herrera. "Everywhere we turn it's just as green as the front yard back in the States." In London, Herrera rode horseback in Hyde Park and toured historic St. Paul's Cathedral. Private First Class Marcus Cariz II, Santo Domingo Pueblo, agreed that "it's really a pretty country." Private First Class Antonio Menchego, Santa Ana Pueblo, visited Northern Ireland and "so many English towns that I can't mention them all." First Lieutenant Linda Asenap, stationed as a nurse in England, spent time in both London and Scotland, where she was photographed in a Scottish kilt.[12]

Judging from their letters, New Mexican Indians obviously felt at home with the English population. "I do like this country," admitted Staff Sergeant Carl Tsosie, Navajo, "and the peoples [sic] over here are very friendly." Private First Class Pat Martinez agreed that "of course they are very friendly people and treated me nicely, even inviting me to their homes to drink tea with them, for they love their tea as we love our coffee." John José summed up the Native American sentiment for England by observing that although things were different, the country seemed the same as America. Sergeant Riley Freeland, Navajo, seemed to corraborate this belief by ending a letter from England with a hearty "cheerio."[13]

After the Sicilian and Normandy invasions, Native Americans trekked through the European mainland. Italy and France impressed them so much that many endeavored to learn the national languages. "Finally, I found myself a home here," wrote Private Simon Archuleta, San Juan Pueblo, from Italy. "I hope to speak their language before too long." Sergeant Joseph Martyns, Laguna Pueblo, related that he was also quickly learning the Italian language. Staff Sergeant Robert Dorame had a special reason for learning the French language. He found that in France there were "plenty of very beautiful girls . . . crazy about American soldiers."[14] Rome and Paris, in particular, fascinated the New Mexicans. "I had the most wonderful experience in all my life," stated Private Alfred Kayitah, Mescalero Apache. "I got to see the city of Rome." He told of visiting Mussolini's balcony and St. Peter's Cathedral, where he heard the Pope speak. Sergeant Martyns also agreed that Rome was "the most beautiful city I've ever seen. . . . The people are clean and well-dressed. . . . The girls are very beautiful too." In Paris, Antonio Menchego viewed the Arc de Triomphe, Napoleon's Tomb, Notre Dame Cathedral, and "beaucoup mademoiselles."[15]

Those New Mexicans who traveled to Alaskan territory, India, China, Iran and the Pacific islands experienced the dual opportunity of observing native populations as both an American and as a member of an indigenous population themselves. Their reactions ranged from disdain to sympathy to admiration. Often sounding reminiscent of nineteenth-century anthropologists or missionaries visiting American Indian reservations, Native

Americans compared and contrasted these cultures with both mainstream American norms and their own Indian values.[16] While he was stationed in Alaska, Private First Class José Roybal, San Ildefonso Pueblo, became interested in the history of its natives. Much to his surprise, he learned that the United States government, which had outlawed Alaskan tribal ceremonies for years, had only recently attempted to restore the indigenous cultural traditions. But, he explained, because so many of the older generation had left the area, the knowledge had been lost. It seems that Roybal was unaware that, in the nineteenth century, the United States Government had also outlawed many Indian dances and ceremonials—including the Ghost Dance on the Sioux Reservation and the Snake Dance on the Hopi Reservation. He expressed his opinion on the injustice of the Alaskan situation:

> In my opinion I think it's a pity that fate has stepped in and this should come their way. After learning their situation, I can feel myself saying that I should be thankful that I come from the adobe land, where I hope that in future years to come no ill-thinking white man will attempt to change our way of living or even our ceremonials in the Southwest, the land I wouldn't trade for any part of the world. Since the other boys feel the same, I say this because now I know the significance of the pueblo land.[17]

Native American servicemen stationed in the South Pacific were struck by the similarities between themselves and the islanders, but also noticed the islanders' low standard of living. "The natives of this island," wrote Albert B. Hardy from Mindanao, "are more like our Indians. I mean the look and color but not the way of living." Private José Tafoy, Santa Clara Pueblo, emphasized the poverty of the natives when he recalled that for only the price of a cigarette, a Pacific islander would scale a palm tree to pluck a coconut for him. At times Native Americans commented unfavorably on Pacific islander cultural traditions, but in doing so revealed that they were unfamiliar with older Native American customs. When Private James S. Ortiz, San Juan Pueblo, learned of the courtship practices on his island, he decided that the natives had "funny ways of living." In order to get married, he wrote, one need only offer a pig to "buy a native girl. A pig represent[s] a marriage license. Presenting the poor pig one can get married. It is very cheap at that, don't you think?" Ortiz either did not know of the tradition among nineteenth-century Plains Indian tribes, wherein a young male suitor often offered a horse or horses to his intended wife, or he did not see the similarity between the two customs.[18]

New Mexican servicemen discovered conditions of poverty in the Asiatic countries of China and Iran, but instead of being appalled, they fell under the charm of these ancient civilizations. Sergeant Simon Naranjo, Santa Clara Pueblo, found the Chinese people to be very friendly and charmingly described the use of "an old ox-cart still on the job." Private First Class Tony Aguilar, from Santo Domingo Pueblo and a 1940 Santa Fe Indian School graduate who had participated in student government, asserted that the country would be most interesting to an ethnologist or anthropologist. He also admitted that the Iranian claim to being the most beautiful country in the world had much credibility. "The scenery is certainly very beautiful, snow-capped mountains in the north, and in the valley it is just green with grass, trees and etc.," he wrote. "The people here are very similar to that of our Pueblo Indians, especially Taos and Isleta Pueblos." Private First Class Wilson Guerrero, Navajo-Apache, however, felt that the poverty of Iran took its toll on the natives, who had a hard life. "The[ir] clothes look a thousand years old," he wrote. "Really, it's a sorrowful life. Their food is mostly bread and water, but they are really hard workers." Nevertheless, he succumbed to the charm of the country during the holy season: "I think it's nice to spend Christmas here, in part of the country where Christmas really began. I have seen the natives riding donkeys, herding sheep, traveling on Camels at night, often remind[ing] me of Christmas and the life of Christ."[19]

Although the New Mexican Indians often complained of the poverty and harsh conditions, they usually found something positive to say about the locale or the people. India, however, proved to be the exception. "The people are way behind in civilization," remarked Sergeant Clarence Gutierrez, Santa Clara Pueblo. "They all work in their crude primitive ways. The towns are filthy and I believe it's best to stay right here on the Field instead of going to town." Corporal Pierce Harrison also condemned the "lousy country of India" stating that everything was different from the states, including the language, customs, dress, and food. He also had difficulty understanding the rupee monetary system. Even Sergeant Naranjo, who had enjoyed China, could only say about India that the natives were a "lot different than our American Indians."[20]

In military service, Native Americans served in a variety of ways and occasionally encountered the famous and powerful as well as ordinary citizens. On the grounds of the capitol in Washington, D. C., Philip Cosen proudly stated that when the army band played for Franklin Roosevelt, he sat only ten feet from the president. From Iran Wilson Guerrero and Tony Aguilar reported that they had the great honor of guarding the president during the Tehran Conference where they had also seen Josef Stalin, the Russian premier. At an English military hospital, Lieutenant Asenap felt privileged to be present when the Queen of England visited her ward. "She seems quite friendly," wrote Lieutenant Asenap, "and was rather interested in the progress of the patients."[21]

Whether they happened to be stationed in the United States or overseas, Native Americans faithfully adhered to the traditional G.I. pastime of complaining. The nature of their grievances reveal that they viewed military service and its discomforts in much the same way as their white colleagues. In general, New Mexican Indian complaints varied little from the standard subjects of food, weather, and hard work. "You folks are fortun[at]e that you don't get a chance to eat dehydrated food as we do," griped Seaman

Paul Duncan. Private First Class Wade Hadley, a Navajo serving with the 158th Infantry, otherwise known as the Bushmasters, explained that their diet on a Pacific island consisted primarily of coconuts, which were so plentiful that the natives even paved their roads with the shells. "So don't expect we're having bread and butter or fresh eggs," he warned. Private Joseph Pecos claimed that the Ephrate Air Base in the Pacific was "hotter than a frying pan." Sandy Garcia contended that in New Orleans one could sweat "in the heat just for walking around." Several soldiers complained about the long marches and resulting sores. "My blisters get blisters, too," moaned Theodore Suina. Finally, mosquitoes plagued many New Mexicans who had few of these insects in the dry southwestern climate. "I hope these mosquitoes and cheegers don't get the best of me," wrote William Siow from Louisana. "Some [of] these are big as a Flying Fortress." Training in Florida as an aerial gunner, Joseph Martyns agreed that "the mosquitoes are awful, they come by and lift your dog tags to see your blood type. If it satisfies them, then you can expect a stab as big as getting hit with a brick."[22]

Loneliness, however, ranked first among the complaints voiced by Indian servicemen. Like other soldiers, they suffered because they were far from home and missed female companionship, but another contributing factor was that they were often the only Native American in a company or outfit. Private Ellison Bowman, Navajo, who spent three years in the military, most of it overseas, refused to admit he was lonely, but he mentioned in several letters that he was "still" the only Indian in his outfit. When the military transferred a Jemez Indian to his company, they promptly became best friends. Private Clarence Gutierrez, initially sent to the Aero Industries Technical Institute, lamented that "at this school I seem to be the only Indian, and I certainly hope that they will bring some Indian boys soon." Stationed in the South Pacific, James Ortiz also complained that he was the only Native American in his outfit. "I simply have forgotten my native language," he said. "Many a moonlight I stood beneath the Southern Cross to say a few words in Indian just to make sure that I still understand what I'm saying."[23] New Mexican Indians discovered that even brief encounters with friends from home afforded great pleasure and helped ease the sense of isolation. Writing of his surprise at meeting Private Lupe Lavato on a Virginia base, Private First Class Joe Chavez said, "I really did have lots of fun with him." When Philip Cosen learned that Private Juan Pino had been transferred to the Engineer Replacement Center at Fort Belvoir, near Washington, D. C., he spent an hour searching for him after which "we did [have] lots of fun talking about this and that." In turn Pino reported to friends at home that "old Philip Cosen" looked fat and healthy. Sandy Garcia reported that at Fort Lewis, Washington, he met "some Indian boys that I knew since we were little kids." Private Joe Duran marveled that "after all it is a small world" when he ran into Philip Ahidley in Hawaii. And, after Duran ran into fellow tribesman Peter Vigil at a midnight Mass, he wrote: "I am very happy to meet someone who talks Tewa." Also missing the ability to communicate in his tribal language, Private First Class Frank Lujan, from Taos Pueblo and another 1940 Santa Fe Indian School graduate who had participated in student government, served with Wade Hadley in the Bushmasters. This company, which contained Native Americans from twenty different tribes, caused Lujan to remark that "of course there are quite a few Indian boys here in the 158th Infantry, but the trouble is they can't talk to my language so I can't talks [sic] to their language."[24]

Occasionally a few lucky New Mexican servicemen managed to visit with Indian girls from home. When John Harrison Tso, Navajo, received a visit from Emily Montoya and Lucy Cruz, who were working in a Los Angeles defense factory near his air base, he called the girls "life savers" and claimed they cheered up "an old, worn-out soldier." Servicewomen, on the other hand, appreciated visits from Native American men. WAVE Lila Campos, who was sent to the Naval Station in San Diego, received unexpected help from a New Mexican neighbor, Seaman First Class David Keevama, Hopi. "The first day I was waiting for the boat to bring us to North Island," she told friends, "I met David on the main dock. It was good to see someone I knew because I felt so lost that first day." Sometimes family members arranged to meet. Private First Class Ignacio Moquino traveled from Florida to Georgia on leave to see his sister, Lucy Moquino, a hospital WAC. While stationed in Hawaii, Private First Class Joe Trujillo, San Juan Pueblo, wrote friends that he had just met a Taos, New Mexico, girl at a dance. "I think we are going to be good friends while staying here," he mentioned.[25]

Those New Mexicans who had the good fortune to serve with other Indians reflected a sense of well-being. "For my part I'm fine and having a good time with Vincente Cruz," wrote Seaman First Class Reyes Lovato from a naval destroyer. Serving on another destroyer, Seaman Paul Barton felt grateful that he had "an Indian pardner," who was Hopi, and said, "we're getting along swell." Corporal Jose L. Gutierrez, Laguna Pueblo, served with another Laguna tribesman (Franklin Luther), Cochiti Pueblo tribesman Joe Herrera, and Joseph Tree, a Ute. Women, as well, enjoyed the company of other Indian women. Private First Class Lucy Moquino worked with whites at a military hospital in Camp Wheeler, Georgia, but in the evening she ate and socialized with an old classmate from Santa Fe, Private First Class Golda Bigrope. Although the Navajo Codetalkers had the distinction of having the most Indians from a single tribe, Wade Hadley and Frank Lujan belonged to the Bushmasters, 158th Infantry, which claimed Indians from over twenty different tribes. Having another Indian, even someone from a different tribe, allowed Native Americans to socialize in a uniquely cultural manner. Private First Class Fedelino Sanchez, Santa Ana Pueblo, served in a Marine Tank Battalion with a Crow Indian from Montana. "We talked of home," he recalled, "and sometimes sing a song or two." José Roybal also described the relaxed attitude that New Mexicans felt when socializing with other Indians. He asserted that the six Indian boys with whom he served in England were sometimes "hell raisers when we get together, you know talk and sing more than we do back home."[26]

Nevertheless, no matter how many friends a New Mexican serviceman possessed, like all young military men they wanted to meet young women. In their relationships with women in other states and in other countries, Native Americans exhibited great confidence in their own charm. Their relationships varied from casual meetings, to steady dating, to marriage with both Native American and white women. Private Arnoldo Pino sounded definite that the last mentioned institution would not ensnare him. "I assure you that New Mexico does not have all the good-looking girls," he wrote from California, "because some of the colleens over here are really honeys. However, don't get me wrong, because I came over here single, and I'm going home the same way." Private First Class Joe Garcia also claimed the same distinction for Texas. "Really to talk about Texas," he informed friends, "they have everything from nice-looking girls on up to cattle and horses." Private First Class Hubery Yazzi, Navajo, writing from "somewhere in the Southern Pacific" where the natives spoke French, stated that it was "too bad some of us don't talk French as [there are] many good-looking girls run[n]ing around down in the village." European women also received high praise as being extremely beautiful. In Europe Joseph Martyns had a British WAC girlfriend, and Riley Freeland said he fell in love with a girl in Holland but had to leave her behind when his outfit transferred.[27]

A few New Mexicans, especially those stationed in Pacific islands, seemed to have no luck at all in finding girlfriends. "We sailors are supposed to have girls in every port, but we don't," grumbled Reyes Lovato. Also serving in the Pacific, Seaman Second Class George Lente, Laguna Pueblo, described the methods sailors from the U. S. S. *Oakland* used to meet girls. "The only way you can get close to a girl here is to get a picture taken with her," he explained. "That's the only chance a fellow has of holding a girl fore [sic] a short time, then it's all over with, a lot of guys just keep going back, some of them have more pictures than they could look at." By the war's end, Lente's fortune had changed, and he happily reported that he had married a girl from Richmond, California.[28]

Many young men, however, deeply missed girlfriends back home. Private First Class Theodore Suina expressed his desire that "sweethearts could be dehydrated instead of spuds so we can see real eyes." Private First Class Thomas Thompson asked for the address of a certain Indian WAC with whom he wanted to get in touch while on furlough. When Corporal Pierce Harrison received a visit from his Mescalero Apache girlfriend at his base in Fort Bliss, Texas, he felt so grateful that he showed no displeasure when she complained about his G.I. haircut. Sergeant Mark Chee, Navajo, resolved his loneliness by marrying Santana Montoya from San Juan Pueblo. "Now I have someone back home to care for and fight for." He felt so homesick for his wife that she agreed to follow him from base to base until the military transferred him overseas.[29]

Of course Native Americans in the military also eased their loneliness by creating strong bonds with white servicemen and women. Although José Roybal served with six other Indians from San Ildefonso, Santa Clara Pueblo, Cochiti Pueblo, and the Navajo Reservation, he also asserted that "these white boys are really nice and friendly. They treat us as brothers." Training with the Naval Hospital Corps School, Frank Cata informed friends that "our company is one bunch of swell fellows, to say it effectively." Sergeant Salvador Romero, radio operator and an aerial gunner on a B-17 Flying Fortress, agreed that "members of the crew are swell to me, they are the best fellows after a guy gets to know them." Nicholas Cata, assigned to the U. S. S. *Louisiana*, showed that he reciprocated the friendly attitude when he said, "all the shipmates are treating me swell, and I treat them the same."[30] Private Wilfred H. Jones clearly bonded with other members of his bomber squadron as they traveled to their South Pacific destination. "We had more fun with an ancient custom of initiation on our way after pass[ing] the Equator," he related. "We got a lot of kicks out of the ceremonial."[31]

Part of the bonding process in military life is the use of nicknames, and Native Americans were no exception. Many New Mexicans, particularly those who were the sole American Indian in their outfit, earned the nickname of "chief," which they accepted in a good-natured manner. After he was sent overseas to England,

Corporal Steven Herrera's "Hell's Angels" company was treated to a beer party, where he boasted "the fellows call me 'Chief'." In turn, however, the New Mexicans usually called their white friends "palefaces." Jose Roybal claimed that he got along nicely with his "pale-faced brothers." In New Zealand, Private First Class Richard Price, Navajo, wrote that he was having "a lot of fun with my pale-face cobbers," which he explained was a New Zealand word for "friends." Finally, Wade Hadley refused to take offense as did some of the white soldiers when the "Aussies" called the Americans "bloody bastards." He explained simply that the word "means we are quite friendly."[32]

Like their Anglo counterparts, several New Mexican Indians possessed artistic talent which they utilized to create friendships, develop business opportunities, and even contribute to the war effort. After receiving drawing paper from the Indian Club, Theodore Suina wrote to thank the members. "I have been doing a little sketching for my buddies, and they really do get a kick about [sic] sketches and portraits I did," he remarked. "I hope to continue for I like art work very much myself." At Fort Ord, officers noticed Ignacio Moquino's artistic talent and requested that he create Indian paintings for the company day room and mess hall. One Native American woman received a full-time assignment as an artist when the Women's Army Corps assigned Corporal Eve Mirabel the full-time job of cartoonist and mural painter. Ms. Mirabel's cartoons, including an original named "G.I. Gertie," appeared in the Corps publications. In 1944 she completed murals for Wright Field in Dayton, Ohio, and the WAF Air Power Show, and *Mademoiselle* magazine featured her work in a July issue.[33] Another Cochiti artist, Private First Class Joe Herrera, proudly proclaimed himself to be the son of Tonita Penas, "the artist of Cochiti," and informed his fellow tribesmen that his mother had donated some paintings to the Red Cross during their last drive. Having trained with the Aircraft Warning Service, Herrera traveled to Puerto Rico where, to his delight, he remained for much of the war. "Every now and then I go out to make sketches of some of the beautiful sceneries around here," he wrote.

During his valuable leisure time, Herrera and three white soldiers accepted orders for "Indian greeting cards" and had plans to paint murals. A year later a magazine requested some artwork from Herrera. "My Indian painting down here is something unusual," he informed friends. "The beautiful costumes have amazed those who viewed the paintings." In his final year in the military, the army sent Herrera to Hollywood for reasons he could not disclose. There he made additional contacts to further his artistic career.[34]

New Mexicans also discovered that two commodities from the Santa Fe Indian Club which were quite precious to them—the newsletter and the package—also helped pave the way for closer relationships with their colleagues. Many white servicemen eagerly grasped the opportunity to sample new foods and, in doing so, to learn something about another culture. At least a few New Mexicans experienced a temporary rise in popularity when they received their packages. Seaman William Ethelbah, Apache, told his friends, "You can't imagine what a package from home means to one here. I was pretty popular til they emptied the box and that didn't take very long." Writing from England, Corporal Steven Herrera quipped, "I made some new friends when I had the package." Seaman Third Class Miguel Gutierrez reported that although he didn't smoke, "the other boys enjoyed the cigarettes."[35]

Native Americans obviously enjoyed watching the effect that exotic foods such as piñon nuts and hot chili, had on their friends. "It certainly was fun to watch the boys here eating them [piñon nuts]," stated George Dorame. "Some were trying to break them with their fingers, while others stepped on them so you can probably imagine what happened." Joe Herrera also shared his box with fellow soldiers and recalled that he "had so much fun watching these New Yorkers eating the piñon nuts, shells and all. . . . [O]ne of the boys, after eating some of the chili thought his ears were going to pop off. Another drank about a gallon of water." In New Orleans, Frank Lujan received his gifts and said his friends enjoyed the piñon nuts so much that they wanted him to "order some more."[36]

Whites proved even more receptive and far more curious concerning the newsletters which their Indian comrades received from home. "The newsletter is something to be proud of," wrote Private First Class Joe Chavez. "Some of the boys in my gun crew have asked me to pass the letter around, so I did. . . . Boy, I sure did have fun listening to these boys trying to pronounce the names that they never heard before." When Private First Class William Siow shared his newsletter with his "buddies," he stated that they praised it as being "G.I." Referring to the poems which many of the servicemen sent instead of letters, WAC Byrdian Sombrero said that at the Fifth Service Command Laboratory in Fort Harrison, Indiana, all her girlfriends were "interested in the poems."[37] Sharing the newsletter led to further curiosity from white colleagues about Indian culture. David Keevama reported that he loaned the newsletter to a "paleface" friend and "now it's going from bunk to bunk." Because they asked him so many questions about Indians, Keevama said he was doing his "best to bring things clearly out to them." Reyes Lovato received an equally enthusiastic response from his shipmates:

> I let one of my shipmates read the news. And he says he wishes he had one from his home, just like that. He ask[ed] me where I got that news. I told him it's from the club I belong to and there are the boys too they are in the Army [armed] forces. It's call[ed] an "Indian Club." He sure wants to be with that group.[38]

When confronted with this demand for knowledge, a few Native Americans took the opportunity to disseminate cultural information through language. After José Roybal taught "a white boy how to talk my Tewa language," he insisted that the man understood well enough for Roybal to teach him some Indian songs. Seaman George Lente also spoke to his shipmates in his tribal language. "I got a guy on this ship saying hello in Indian to everybody he sees around here," he remarked. "It's fun."[39]

Despite this attention, many New Mexicans obviously experienced some disillusionment over the total lack of knowledge among white Americans and foreigners concerning the modern Native American. In Atlantic City, New Jersey, Steven Herrera asserted that "the people around here know only what they learn from the books on Indians." In other cases, whites appeared to obtain their stereotypes of American Indians from movies, as comments concerning the ferocity of Indians abounded. Private Lawrence Chavez, Cochiti Pueblo, answered many queries from the English about Native Americans such as "if we still fight the cowboys like they see in the picture shows and if I bring my feather with me." After receiving a ride from a white man in the San Diego area, George Lente said the man commented that the Japanese would be hard to beat because they were "just like the Indians we had here in this country." Lente said he "acted big," replying that he was an Indian and "the Japs will still find it hard to beat us Indians." Wade Hadley concluded that too many whites disregarded a Native American's intellect and considered him to be simply "a head with a feather on top." Louis Naranjo finally lost patience when some white servicemen who were questioning him about the Indian Club wanted to know if the club had any pretty girls. "What a silly question to ask," he replied.[40]

At other times, whites told their New Mexican comrades that they also had some Indian blood, but Native Americans evidently doubted their stories. When Private Lucy Moquino told people she was an Indian from New Mexico, many of the WACs also claimed Indian blood. "I believe some of them," she conceded, "but some I don't think are any Indian at all." Seaman Second Class Joe Simon Sando, Jemez Pueblo, who had recently read in a magazine that the American Indian was in demand as subject material, had similar experiences which led him to the conclusion that something should be done about the ignorance of whites concerning Indian cultures:

> It seems funny that these American boys knew so little about the first Americans. A number of the

> boys started to tell me that their grandparents were either full or part Indian and all said they were proud of their Indian blood. I thought a film strip would be a good thing to make up and send it throughout the camps and bases. I believe that will be one way to let them learn about our people.

When Tony Aguilar heard what Sando had proposed, he endorsed the idea, because he had heard a radio broadcast about the American Indian and the war effort. He felt a film strip could also publicize Native Americans in a positive manner.[41]

Throughout the war, these young, intelligent and talented New Mexicans held a realistic and proud image of themselves both as members of a particular tribe and as Native Americans in general. Therefore, whenever American Indians competed with their white colleagues, they competed as both Indians and as members of a particular tribe, although this last distinction was often lost on whites. After Joe Herrera, who planned to attend art school after the war, placed second in an art exhibition by soldiers stationed in the Caribbean, the newspaper article described him as a full-blooded Navajo. He pointedly mentioned to the newspaper that he was a Cochiti tribesman and asked them to correct the error. At Cambridge, England, Steven Herrera participated in a track meet. "The Limeys were surprised," he declared, "to see a Pueblo Indian take second place in a mile run."[42]

During the four years of war, Native Americans expressed these feelings of pride, self-esteem, solidarity and kinship to each other in their letters to the Indian Club. In turn the Indian Club published portions of each letter in the monthly or bi-monthly newsletter. Originally designed to keep members on the homefront informed of service personnel activities and to keep military personnel informed of homefront activities, the newsletter eventually evolved into an informal public forum. Servicemen and women reflected a genuine feeling of community in the gratitude they felt for the newsletter and the packages they received. The fact that people in their hometown cared so much meant far more than any tangible items sent to them. "It sure gives a soldier a lift to know that folks back home are thinking about us," wrote Charles Pushetonequa. Private Santiago Banado expressed a sentiment widely held by men who came from families who could neither read nor write. "I was more than glad to receive a letter," he replied to the Members, "because I never had received a letter from anybody." Private Juan Pinon declared that the newsletters took "his mind off his weariness and loneliness."[43]

Because the Indian Club relied on the people in the armed forces to furnish the news, they sent the newsletter only to those who contributed, forcing members who were either shy or lazy to make an effort. When Private Ned Notah admitted that he would rather read letters than write them, he spoke for many. Others, however, became faithful contributors. Even Wade Hadley, who wrote several times (including v-mail which he called "dehydrated letters,") once apologized for not writing sooner, because his morale was low. Another faithful letter-writer, George Lente, said he could write a book but wondered "how a lot of the letters get by the censorship."[44]

Regardless of their opinion of their own writing skills, everyone agreed that the Indian Club produced an excellent newsletter. Sergeant Myles Martinez insisted that he could "hardly wait to get [his] hands on [the] next issue." In a literary analogy, Richard Price said, "Reading the news about some of the boys I used to know, makes me feel as if I were on a magic carpet and visiting each of them in various parts of the world." The newsletter generated such interest that Native Americans, such as Private First Class Simon Archuleta, who had heard of it through others, wrote to ask for copies, and some, such as Sergeant Carl Tsosie, Navajo, asked that a newsletter be sent to relatives in the military. Newsletters were so anticipated that if one arrived late, servicemen expressed anxiety. "I have been waiting and wondering the last couple of months if you misplaced my address or forgot to send me the newsletter," wrote Nelson Sakyesva. Those serving with friends had less cause for anxiety. When Reyes Lovato lost the

Indian Club address, he simply obtained it from his shipmate Vincente Cruz.[45]

Because the Indian Club members felt an interest in all New Mexican Indians serving in the military, they sent packages and letters to non-members as well as members. Private First Class K. M. Pollazza felt so grateful at receiving his unexpected gift that he apologized for never attending a meeting and promised to go in the future. Private First Class Cipriano Herrera became a regular correspondent after receiving a letter and the package. "I don't know what to say and where to start," he wrote. "I am sure I don't know any of you folks who sen[t] me the package, but I do think that it was nice of you all to think of me." When he received his gift, Private Eugene B. Charles, Navajo, wondered who in Santa Fe "could be thinking of an Indian boy who wasn't known or seen in the club."[46]

Christmas, of course, was a big time for packages. Funded through dances performed at the Governor's Palace by Indians from San Ildefonso, San Juan, Cochiti and Jemez Pueblos, the packages carried "Do Not Open Until Christmas" labels which were often cheerfully ignored. Frank Lujan felt so overwhelmed at receiving his first gift, however, that he needed encouragement to accept it. "I had received the [package]," he wrote the Indian Club, "but I am not quite sure that its for me or not." He refused to open it until the Club wrote back and declared it to be his property. Corporal Sam R. Robbins gave particular thanks for the knitted slippers he received, which he said he had wanted for two years. Private Sam Roans, Navajo, graciously thanked everyone for the playing cards, while briefly mentioning he had been reclassified from military duty to hospital defense work because of poor eyesight. Several appreciative members sent checks to the Club, including Philip Ahidley, Linda Asenap, Paul Barton, Robert Ladabour and Bob Montoya. The Club then used these contributions to provide celebrations for soldiers on furlough in Santa Fe.[47]

Eventually, the most sought-after gift from the Indian Club resulted from a request by servicemen for a "pin-up girl" from the Club. In the October 20, 1944 *Newsletter*, Margretta Dietrich wrote that the Club was sending a photograph of *eight* girls: Rena Dailya, Mae Rose Aragon, Ofelia Sanchez, Pasquilita Archuleta, Victoria Tafoya, Recita Chavarria, Josefita Cordero and Margaret Arquero. This photograph impacted the servicemen with all the force of the Normandy Invasion. Those fortunate enough to receive a copy wanted more photos, and those who did not receive one forgot everything else—including war news, packages and letters from home—in their frenzy to acquire the photograph of the only Indian women many New Mexicans had seen in months or years. "It's so nice to see what a really American Indian girl looks like after having been a long time in the jungle," stated Pierce Harrison. "Wish you could forward more pictures." Joe Herrera asserted that his morale went up one hundred percent when he received the photo. James Ortiz considered the pin-up girls so "charming" that he placed them next to pictures of Martha Raye and Virginia Olivien. In expressing his gratitude, Tony Aguilar could only reply, "Man, oh, man." Private First Class Joe Ignatius Joyola, Isleta Pueblo, hinted that "there were a couple of them I sure would like to know." When Wade Hadley's Christmas box was ruined in the mail, he asked only for another copy of the pinup girls.[48] White soldiers also appreciated the girls, reported Simon Naranjo from China. "The boys over here are going wild over the pictures." Lila Campos, who had obviously seen someone else's copy, inquired why she had failed to receive the photograph and when she could expect to receive a picture of some "pin-up boys."[49]

The parcels from the Santa Fe Indian Club were not merely entertaining. The newsletter in particular acted as a conduit for political action, as an informal message center, and as a public forum for social issues. For example, no issue raised as much controversy and concern as the 1943 Pueblo Dam Bill. On January 6, 1943, New Mexican Representative Clinton P. Anderson introduced *House Report* 323 "to authorize the exploration of proposed dam sites located on Indian lands within the State of New Mexico." The House Committee on Irrigation and Reclamation unanimously recommended that the bill pass, which would have resulted in the construction of two dams on the Rio Grande River. In order to determine the soundness of the action, the Bureau of Reclamation insisted that it was necessary to drill the foundations on the San Felipe and Otowi Sites. As soon as the Bureau of Reclamation commenced drilling operations, a storm of protest arose over the fact that the Bureau had failed to receive permission from the Indian tribes to enter their lands.[50] Overseas, New Mexican servicemen, fearing the loss of their land, tribal ceremonies and tribal culture, joined in this protest by writing to both Congressmen and the Indian Club. Asking for their vote against H.R. 323, Juan Pino sent messages to both Senator Elmer Thomas and Representative Joe Smith. "I realized my Indian people needed my help," he informed Mrs. Dietrich, "to protect and save the people, their pueblos and their tribal ceremonies." Responding to Mrs. Dietrich about his reaction to the dam site situation, Joseph Pecos replied that he would rather keep the land than accept government money. Several of the young men, such as Augustine Lovato, entreated Mrs. Dietrich to "do everything within your power back home to defeat it." Santiago Bailon criticized the government for this attempt to destroy his land and culture while he was fighting "for this country and to protect my people and the people in the United States." Louis Naranjo, who also wrote to his Congressmen, declared that the dam issue appeared to "be a poor reward for our present services in the war." Naranjo reminded everyone that the Pueblo land grants had been recognized as inalienable property by both Spain and the United States and added, "our land, our religion are bound together." Arguing that Native Americans had enlisted in the armed forces in order that everyone could live peacefully after they achieved victory, he declared, "We thought this [was] a free country for everybody, all races. I don't think it's a free country after all."[51]

While the servicemen protested the bill from their various posts, back in the states the bill ran into serious opposition from the Secretary of the Interior, the New Mexican Association on Indian Affairs, and several tribal leaders. On March 17, 1943 the Committee on Irrigation and Reclamation submitted a report which stated that they believed that the Secretary of the Interior possessed the right to grant permits for drilling on Indian lands. Furthermore, the committee declared that drilling had "been halted by this lack of authority to enter Indian lands." Harold Ickes, Secretary of the Interior, responded to the committee with a statement which recognized the "adverse conditions" in the area caused by inadequate irrigation methods and water seepage, but he also incorporated a recommendation to consider the Native American viewpoint. "The Indians have contended that these reservoirs, if built," stated Ickes, "would destroy irreplaceable agricultural lands, their ancestral homes and villages, their clay pits upon which their large pottery industry depends, and their sacred shrines." Ickes added that the San Felipe tribe had expressed special concern over destruction of their sacred kivas. Ever the diplomat, Ickes, on the one hand, assured the Bureau of Reclamation that "the situation in the middle of the Rio Grande Valley is critical and must be viewed in terms of economic survival and future habitation . . . as well as the utilization of agricultural areas." On the other hand, he warned that "no recommendation to Congress will be made by me for the construction of any improvements until full consideration has been given to all interests and to values of every nature including the real and intangible ones of the Pueblo Indians."[52]

Ickes upheld his word, and on May 19, 1943 Margretta Dietrich, Governor Juan Chavarria of Santa Clara, Governor Sotero Montoya of San Ildefonso, Governor Don Sanchez of San Felipe, Telsfor Romero of Taos, and John Bird of Santo Domingo traveled to Washington, D. C. to protest H.R. 323. "We think we were successful in stopping it," Mrs. Dietrich reported in the June 1943 newsletter. In August both Robert Dorame and Augustine Lovato sent grateful thanks for the outcome. "I'm indeed very happy to hear that you had done a swell job opposing the Damsite bill together with our friends," wrote Dorame, who credited the Indian governors with the victory.[53]

The Indian Club newsletter also functioned as an informal "Missing Persons" agency. Almost every newsletter contained a request similar to one by George Dorame, who wanted to learn the address of Bill Ethelbah in order to visit him before being shipped overseas. This request enabled Lino Tapia to ascertain that he was "a near neighbor of George Dorame." Reyes Lovato, who admitted that he missed his friend Reyes Tonorio, asked where he was stationed. When servicemen learned that friends might be in the same vicinity, they sent messages by way of the newsletter to get in touch. From Italy, Justino Herrera demanded to hear from Alfred Kayitah, also stationed in the same country. Although military rules forbade the Indian Club to publish full addresses, they sent individuals' addresses to everyone who requested this information.[54]

Several members used the newsletter to send special messages to friends. Joe Quintana apologized for not answering letters from Ben Quintana, Steven Herrera, and Theodore Suina. In turn Ben Quintana mentioned that he was worried about his brother, Delphine, from whom he had not heard for several months. Seaman Third Class Charles Romero wanted the *Newsletter* to ask George Lente if he had seen Romero's ship, the S. S. *Reno*. He also asked club member Ofelia Sanchez where her boyfriend was stationed, as Larry happened to be "a pal of his." Many servicemen simply sent big "hellos" to everyone.[55]

By the end of the war, the *Newsletter* had evolved into a vital public forum which promoted a discussion of postwar civil rights. When Wade Hadley sent a letter in February, 1945, protesting the fact that Indians were citizens and fighting in the war and yet could neither vote nor purchase alcohol in their home states, he opened a floodgate of opinions which lasted for an entire year. Everyone agreed that Native Americans should have the privilege of purchasing a drink in a bar. "I certainly agree with Private First Class Wade Hadley," wrote GM Third Class N. P. Tom. "I would like to enjoy a few drinks when I return to New Mexico like any other citizen." Justino Herrera stated that the freedom to sit and drink at a bar should be the same as the freedom to fight "for your freedom and mine." Signal Fireman Third Class George Lente asserted that he appreciated Justino Herrera mentioning the subject of drinking at a bar, because he was often asked by his colleagues why Indians could not drink. "What did we fight for?" he demanded. "Indians have been pushed around too much. Why not stand up for our race like men?"[56]

Concerning the issue of the franchise, New Mexican Indians proved to hold various opinions, from indifference to concern. After President Roosevelt was elected for a fourth term, several of Antonio Menchengo's buddies asked what he thought of this unprecedented political event. Menchego shrugged off their questions. "I told them it doesn't make much difference to me," he related, "because I don't vote." Sam Robbins voiced his fear that the vote would mean trouble in the future for the tribes. Agreeing that it could cause political polarization, Jose Roybal suggested that before tribes gained the franchise, there would be a "deep consideration of the question of the vote. If they do get it, it will divide the Indians into various political groups and there will be a slight difficulty in getting the pueblos on agreeing on one thing."[57]

On the opposite side of the debate, Frank Apachito contended that it was time for Indians to handle their own affairs, or else when they returned home, they would once again see signs reading "No Indians Allowed." Although Joe Herrera admitted that citizenship arrived "a trifle too late" for many of the older generation, who failed to understand modern problems, he insisted that segregation and denial of civil rights only aggravated the situation. "I hope that someday we will all work together," he concluded, "and ask for the restoration of a fraction of our rights granted to all American citizens by the Constitution of the United States and the states involved." Santiago Garcia, who had served as guard on the 1939 Santa Fe Indian School basketball team, reported that everyone agreed with Joe Herrera and hoped to find America a better place than it was when they had left it. He proposed that all Indian veterans should receive the same privileges as white people, because they had been treated like brothers in the war.[58]

In many respects, the wartime experiences of Native Americans mirrored those of mainstream America. Through military training and duty, they learned valuable skills, earned medals and citations, and gained exposure to different cultures and regions. They proved that American Indians in the first half of the twentieth century could compete with their white contemporaries, set high standards for themselves, and achieve success outside their milieu. They too intended to take advantage of the G.I. Bill of Rights and attend school for vocational or academic training in order to be prepared for the postwar world. They too lost comrades, like Cipriano Herrera and Ben Quintana, the latter of which was posthumously awarded the Silver Star for "gallantry in action."[59]

In other respects, however, Native Americans proved to have fundamental differences from mainstream America. The Indian Club newsletter highlighted the close-knit, communal ties between New Mexican Indians and their strong identification with other Indian tribes. After the war, these ties generally drew the American Indian back to his reservation or pueblo, his family and tribal ceremonies. Although a few servicemen, such as Joe Herrera and George Lente, relocated for professional or personal reasons, the majority of New Mexican servicemen and women enthusiastically returned to their culture. They returned with a sense of optimism but also with a profound realization that America failed to fundamentally understand the American Indian. These men and women, so instrumental in changing the course of the war, discovered a great struggle in directing not only their future in the United States but also in transforming America's viewpoint of them as just "a head with a feather on top."[60]

---

[1]Duncan to Mrs. Dietrich, August 21, 1943, Southwestern Association on Indian Affairs, File 114, Letters from Native Americans in the Armed Forces, 1943, New Mexico State Records and Archives, Santa Fe, New Mexico.

[2]Santa Fe *New Mexican*, December 11–12, 1939, 2.

[3]Ibid.

[4]Whenever possible military rank and tribal affiliation are given. For an in-depth analysis of the history and culture of the Pueblo Indians, see Edward P. Dozier, *The Pueblo Indians of North America* (Prospect Heights, Illinois: Waveland Press, Inc., 1970).

[5]New Mexican colonization began in 1598 with the Conquistadore Juan de Onate.

[6]Lovato to Friends, November 19, 1942, Quintana to Mrs. Dietrich, December 20, 1942, Southwestern Association on Indian Affairs, File 112, Letters from Native Americans in the Armed Forces, 1942; Cato to Mrs. Dietrich, August 18, 1943, Abeyta to Mrs. Dietrich, July, 1943, Southwestern Association on Indian Affairs, File 113, Letters from Native Americans in the Armed Forces, 1943; *Hello and Many Lucks*, Southwestern Association on Indian Affairs, 64, File 46 [this is a collection of letters later published in pamphlet form]; Santa Fe *New Mexican*, September 18, 1939, 5–6, October 12, 1939, 2.

[7]Reyes to Mrs. Dietrich, October 8, 1943, Chiago to Mrs. Dietrich, January 18, 1943, File 113; Thompson to Mrs. Dietrich, September 26, 1942, File 112; Thompson to Mrs. Dietrich, Undated, Southwestern Association on Indian Affairs, File 115, Letters from Native Americans in the Armed Forces, Undated. Lovato passed the course.

[8]Gutierrez to Friends, January 13, 1943, Southwestern Association on Indian Affairs, File 114, Letters from Native Americans in the Armed Forces, 1943; Abeyta to Friends, January 13, 1943, File 113.

[9]Chee to Friends, July 6, 1943, Pino to Mrs. Dietrich, January 23, 1943, Harrison to Hello!, August 16, 1943, File 113; *Hello and Many Lucks*, 63, 68, File 46.

[10]Trujillo to Mrs. Dietrich, February 28, 1943, Southwestern Association on Indian Affairs, File 114; Lovato to Madam, March 11, 1943, Romero to Mrs. Dietrich, February 17, 1943, File 113.

[11]A close examination of the letters reveals a strong cultural bias toward the Anglo-Saxon country of Great Britain, which was probably a result of the 1930s and 1940s Indian educational system as well as the prevailing wartime sentiment.

[12]Herrera to Members, June 6, 1943, Herrera to Mrs. Dietrich, August 9, 1943, File 113, *Hello and Many Lucks*, 46, 48, File 46.

[13]*Hello and Many Lucks*, 46, File 46; *Newsletter* No. 12, May 27, 1944, 3, New Mexico Association on Indian Affairs, File 98.

[14]*Hello and Many Lucks*, 41, 50, File 46.

[15]*Hello and Many Lucks*, 44; *Newsletter* No. 21, 3, August 1, 1945, File 98.

[16]For the classic appraisal of nineteenth-century American anthropological viewpoints of Pueblo villages, see Lewis Morgan, *Ancient Society* (New York: Henry Holt, 1878).

[17]Roybal to Mrs. Dietrich, January 21, 1943, File 113; Newsletter No. 21, 3,

August 1, 1945, File 98. Roybal seemed unaware that until John Collier's administration in 1933, many Indian ceremonials and dances, such as the Ghost Dance, were outlawed on most reservations.

[18]*Hello and Many Lucks*, 9–10, 14, 20, File 46.

[19]Aguilar to Mrs. Dietrich, July 23, 1943, Guerrero to Friends, August 3, 1943, File 113, *Hello and Many Lucks*, 53–54, File 46, Santa Fe *New Mexican*, September 29, 1939, 2, December 1, 1939, 6.

[20]*Hello and Many Lucks*, 55–57, File 46. Newsletter No. 11, 3, File 98.

[21]Guerrero to Friend, December 17, 1943, File 113; *Newsletter* No. 16, 1, December 10, 1944, File 98.

[22]Duncan to Mrs. Dietrich, April 10, 1943, Siow to Club Members, March 3, 1943, Martyns to Mrs. Dietrich, August 20, 1943, Pecos to Mrs. Dietrich, August 21, 1943, Garcia to Mrs. Dietrich, February 16, 1943, Kirkland to Club Members, January 16, 1943, File 113.

[23]Maloney to Mrs. Dietrich, July 16, 1943, File 114; Bowman to Mrs. Dietrich, March 16, 1942, File 112; Bowman to Mrs. Dietrich, May 9, 1943, Bowman to Mrs. Dietrich, August 8, 1943, File 113; Clarence Gutierrez to Mr. and Mrs. Secrist, November 16, 1942, File 112; Suina to Members, June 20, 1943, File 113; *Hello and Many Lucks*, 20, File 46.

[24]Chavez to Mrs. Dietrich, September 17, 1943, Cosen to Mrs. Dietrich, February 18, 1943, Pino to Mrs. Dietrich, Feburary 28, 1943, Duran to Mrs. Dietrich, April 26, 1943, Garcia to Members, May 30, 1943, File 113; *Hello and Many Lucks*, 36, File 46, Santa Fe *New Mexican*, September 29, 1939, 2.

[25]*Newsletter* No. 5, June 29, 1943, 4, *Newsletter* No. 18, March 18, 1945, 1, 4, 6, File 98.

[26]Lovato to Madam, March 11, 1943, Barton to Margretta, June 19, 1943, Gutierrez to Mrs. Secrist, April 12, 1943, File 113; Hadley to Mrs. Dietrich, December 28, 1942, File 112; *Hello and Many Lucks*, 23, File 46; *Newsletter* No. 19, 4, May 1, 1945, File 98.

[27]Pino to Mrs. Dietrich, December 27, 1942, File 112; Garcia to Indian Club, August 24, 1943, File 113; *Hello and Many Lucks*, 50, File 46; *Newsletter* No. 19, 5, May 1, 1945, File 98.

[28]*Hello and Many Lucks*, 5, 15, 37, File 46; Dorame to New Mexico Association on Indian Affairs, December 15, 1942, File 112.

[29]Suina to Members, June 20, 1943, Thompson to Club Members, October 16, 1943, Chee to Friends, February 16, 1943, File 113; Harrison to Indian Club, December 11, 1942, File 112.

[30]Roybal to Dietrich, March 6, 1943, Cata to Mrs. Dietrich, January 16, 1943, Romero to Friend, September 28, 1943, Cata to Friends and All, June 12, 1943, File 113.

[31]Jones to Members, March 22, 1943, Herrera to Members, March 8, 1943, File

113; *Hello and Many Lucks*, 14, File 46; *Newsletter* No. 11, 1, April 1, 1944, File 98, Santa Fe *New Mexican*, September 18, 1939, 5.

[32]*Hello and Many Lucks*, 16, 45–46, File 46; Hadley to Mrs. Dietrich, February 27, 1943, File 114; Roybal to Mrs. Dietrich, January 21, 1943, File 113.

[33]*Newsletter* No. 11, 4, April 1, 1944, *Newsletter* No. 13, 2, July 15, 1944, *Newsletter* No. 16, 4, December 10, 1944, File 98; Suina to Friend, January 14, 1943, File 113.

[34]Herrera to Dietrich, December 23, 1942, File 112; Herrera to Dietrich, July 14, 1943, File 113; *Newsletter* No. 15, 3, October 20, 1944, File 98.

[35]Ethelbah to Indian Club, Undated, File 115; Gutierrez to Dear Sirs, December 8, 1942, File 112; *Hello and Many Lucks*, 45, File 46.

[36]Dorame to New Mexican Association on Indian Affairs, December 15, 1942, Herrera to Mrs. Dietrich, December 23, 1942, Lujan to Mrs. Dietrich, undated, File 112.

[37]Chavez to Mrs. Dietrich, July 7, 1943, Freeland to Greetings, July 28, 1943, Siow to Club Members, July 8, 1943, File 113, Newsletter No. 18, 5, March 18, 1945, File 98.

[38]Garcia to Friends, January 25, 1944, File 114; *Hello and Many Lucks*, 14–15, 69, File 46.

[39]*Hello and Many Lucks*, 47–48, File 46; *Newsletter* No. 8, 3, November 15, 1943, File 98.

[40]Herrera to Friends, March 28, 1942, Chavez to Mrs. Wilson, December 28, 1942, File 112; *Hello and Many Lucks*, 39, File 46; *Newsletter* No. 8, 3–4, November 15, 1943, *Newsletter* No. 9, 4, January 1, 1944, File 98.

[41]*Newsletter* No. 17, 3, February 5, 1945, *Newsletter* No. 9, 4, January 1, 1944, *Newsletter* No. 11, 5, April 1, 1944, File 98. The inability of the Native Americans to generate their own public image and the exploitation of their war efforts by various groups is explored in the chapter "Publicity, Persuasion and Propaganda: Stereotyping the Native American."

[42]*Newsletter* No. 7, 3, September 30, 1943, *Newsletter* No. 8, 3, November 15, 1943, File 98.

[43]Pushetonequa to Mada, January 13, 1942, File 112; Benado to Dietrich, August 22, 1943, Pinon to Dietrich, September 3, 1943, File 113.

[44]Notah to Members, January 27, 1943, Hadley to Dietrich, April 1, 1943, File 113; *Hello and Many Lucks*, 5, 38, File 46.

[45]Martinez to Dietrich, undated, File 115; Archuleta to Dietrich, February 6, 1943, File 114; Tsosie to Friends, August 1, 1943, Sakyesva to Dietrich, August 3, 1943, Bailon to Dietrich, August 28, 1943, File 113; *Hello and Many Lucks*, 48, File 46.

[46]Pollazza to Members, November 20, 1942, Herrera to Unknown Friends, November 21, 1942, File 112; Charles to Friends, January 20, 1943, File 113.

[47]Lujan to New Mexico Association, November 29, 1942, Robbins to Friends, November 8, 1942, Ahidley to Friends, December 13, 1942, File 112; Ahidley to Mrs. Dietrich, January 20, 1943, File 113; Roans to Mrs. Dietrich, undated, File 115; *Newsletter* No. 5, June 29, 1943, 1–2, *Newsletter* No. 7, September 30, 1945, 3, *Newsletter* No. 14, September 1, 1944, 4, *Newsletter* No. 15, October 20, 1944, 1, *Smoke Signals* No. 22, September 20, 1945, 1, File 98.

[48]*Newsletter* No. 15, 1, October 20, 1944, *Newsletter* No. 16, 3, 6, 7, December 10, 1944, File 98; *Hello and Many Lucks*, 36, 67, File 46.

[49]*Newsletter* No. 18, 1, 3, March 18, 1945, File 98.

[50]*Congressional Record*, 78th Cong., 1st sess., Vol. 89, A1270; *House Report* 254, 78th Cong., 1st sess., March 17, 1943, "Bill Authorizing Exploration of Proposed Dam sites Located on Indian Lands in New Mexico," 1.

[51]Naranjo to Mrs. Dietrich, March 28, 1943, Pecos to Friends, March 31, 1943, Suina to Mrs. Dietrich, April 30, 1943, Pino to Mrs. Dietrich, May 13, 1943, Lovato to Mrs. Dietrich, June 7, 1943, File 113, Bailon to Members, undated Letters, File 115.

[52]*House Report* 254, 2–3.

[53]*Newsletter* No. 5, June 29, 1943, 1, File 98; Dorame to Greetings, August 4, 1943, Lovato to Friends, August 29, 1943, File 113. *House Report* 323 died in Committee.

[54]*Newsletter* No. 2, January 6, 1943, 1, *Newsletter* No. 3, February 10, 1943, 3, *Newsletter* No. 10, February 15, 1944, 3, *Newsletter* No. 11, April 1, 1944, 6, *Newsletter* No. 14, September 1, 1944, 3, 5, File 98.

[55]*Newsletter* No. 10, February 15, 1944, 4, Newsletter No. 11, April 1, 1944, 6, File 98.

[56]*Newsletter* No. 17, February 5, 1945, 2, *Newsletter* No. 19, May 1, 1945, 3, 5, *Newsletter* No. 21, August 1, 1945, 4, *Smoke Signals* No. 22, September 20, 1945, 2–3, File 98. When Mrs. Dietrich requested suggestions for a name for the newsletter, Joe Herrera contributed the winning name. By August 1, 1945, the newsletter officially became *Smoke Signals*.

[57]*Newsletter* No. 16, December 10, 1944, 5, *Newsletter* No. 21, August 1, 1945, 1, *Smoke Signals* No. 22, September 20, 1945, File 98, Santa Fe *New Mexican*, December 1, 1939, 6.

[58]*Smoke Signals* No. 22, September 20, 1945, 1–4, *Smoke Signals* No. 24, March 1, 1946, 3, File 98. A full analysis of alcohol and voting privileges is covered in Chapter Seven, "Empowering the Native American Veteran: Postwar Civil Rights."

[59]*Hello and Many Lucks*, 3, File 46; *Indians in the War* (United States Department of the Interior, Office of Indian Affairs, 1945): 3.

[60]*Hello and Many Lucks*, 39, File 46.

Pvt. Frank R. Apachito was a member of the Santa Fe Indian Club. SWAIA File 2 #35298. State Records Center and Archives, Santa Fe, New Mexico.

Seaman Reyes Lovato sent this photograph of his ship and shipmates to the Santa Fe Indian Club. SWAIA File 1 #3305. State Records Center and Archives, Santa Fe, New Mexico.

Sgt. Mark Chee poses with family members. SWAIA File 2 #35293. State Records Center and Archives, Santa Fe, New Mexico.

This photo of the "pin-up girls" became famous among Native American servicemen. 5th from left is Victoria Tafoya, Santa Clara tribe, and 8th from left is Margaret Arguiero, Cochiti Pueblo. SWAIA File 3 #35642. State Records Center and Archives, Santa Fe, New Mexico.

Margretta Dietrich, Director of the Santa Fe Indian Club, stands between two servicemen. During the war, Ms. Dietrich and club members raised hundreds of dollars to send packages and newsletters to Native American servicemen and women. SWAIA File 4 #35654. State Records Center and Archives, Santa Fe, New Mexico.

Returning servicemen pose for a photograph. Indian Club member Arkti-Burbank-Maes is second from the right. SWAIA File 3 #35633. State Records Center and Archives, Santa Fe, New Mexico.

Empowering the Veteran: Postwar Civil Rights

Both during and after World War II, the franchise assumed great significance for Native Americans. As sovereign nations, Native Americans possessed a rich democratic heritage. Prior to and during white contact, the majority of tribes conducted operations by consensus rather than coercion, and most Native American groups obtained this consensus through the medium of general councils. Afterwards the group would initiate appropriate action.[1]

Unfortunately, this democratic tradition had not resulted in an increase in bargaining power among Native American tribes. For instance, while citizenship was "promised" to Indians in the Dawes Act of 1887, the act postponed the actual bestowing of citizenship for twenty-five years based on the assumption that by the following generation, most Indians would be assimilated, independent farmers.[2] Forty years later it became clear that the goal of assimilation was far from being achieved, and Congress passed the Snyder Act of 1924, again granting citizenship to all Native Americans. In analyzing the passage of this bill, historian Gary Stein rejects the argument of Vine Deloria, Jr., (and recently revived by Alison Bernstein), that Congress passed this legislation as a reward for Native American military participation in World War I. Furthermore he contests the assertion that the act was passed for political reasons, despite the fact that six states possessed a sufficient Indian population to "determine the consequences of the election in 1924 once they received the franchise." Pointing to the fact that this legislation was not "an act to enfranchise all the Indians," Stein credits the seven Progressives (out of eleven members) belonging to the Senate Committee on Indian Affairs with manipulating the act through the House and Senate in order to place restrictions on the Department of the Interior and the Bureau of Indian Affairs.[3] This belief that the Progressives needed to control the Department of the Interior and the Bureau of Indian Affairs validates the assumption that Congressmen and government officials realized that not only had the reservation system failed to disappear, but that in all probability it would continue for some time. Political recognition by way of citizenship conferred a sense of duties and responsibilities while at the same time providing a modicum of protection and privilege by presumably extending to Native Americans access to the Fourteenth Amendment.[4]

In 1940, cognizant of impending war, Congress once again declared Native Americans to be citizens by passing the Nationality Act. Because Selective Service registration had been conducted on Indian reservations since 1938, it appeared that this act intended to reinforce the "duties" aspect of citizenship, namely that of military service. While tribal and individual Native American resistance to the act was minimal, the government initially sought to define American Indian status within a wartime society. The courts soon found this act to be useful. When an Iroquois man claimed draft exemption based on the 1794 Treaty with the Six Nations and charged that the United States held no power to draft members of an independent nation who had twice rejected American citizenship, the federal court "reluctantly" ruled against the young Onondaga man and declared that the interests of the United States overrode any prior treaty status of American Indians. "Where a domestic law conflicts with an earlier treaty, that the statute must be honored by the domestic courts has been well established," ruled Circuit Judge Jerome Frank.[5]

Concerning citizenship, the Courts scrupulously guarded the interests of the United States while for many years overlooking the inherent privileges for Native Americans. Indian enfranchisement varied widely from state to state, and by World War II six states still denied Indians the right to vote. The reasons stated for disenfranchisement varied from residency, to illiteracy, to nontaxation, to wardship status. In some cases officials believed that Native Americans could be American citizens without holding state citizenship. Based on this belief, a New Jersey election board denied a Cherokee tribal member the right to vote in a primary election stating that Indians could vote only in presidential years. Citing the Nationality Act of 1940, Albert Scarvel won the privilege of casting his ballot on the basis that he had recently been declared a citizen for the second time.[6] In the south, Native Americans discovered that, comparable to their African-American counterparts, they risked discrimination when voting Republican in "marginally Democratic counties." Resurrecting the post-Reconstruction Mississippi Plan which based voter qualifications upon literacy, North Carolina courts effectively forestalled many potential American Indian voters. "You couldn't read or write to my satisfaction if you stayed here all day," a 1945 election judge told one astonished Cherokee who held a Master of Arts degree from the University of North Carolina.[7]

Because they considered incidents such as these to be unjust, the Cherokee openly expressed dissatisfaction with the American voting process. In 1940, as they anticipated the drafting of their young men into the military, the North Carolina Cherokee Tribe issued a resolution specifically denouncing voting practices:

> We, as a people, have been unjustly deprived of our right of franchise by the election boards in these counties, even our college graduates being refused by the local county boards, the fundamental right

> to register and vote in elections held in the state. . . . [W]e feel that any organization or group that would deprive a people of as sacred a right as the right of suffrage would not hesitate to deprive them of other constitutional rights, including the three inalienable rights—life, liberty, and the pursuit of happiness.[8]

While North Carolina continued to discriminate against Indians until the 1950s, five other states held constitutional arguments for American Indian disenfranchisement. Utah, for instance, disenfranchised Native Americans on the basis of residency, claiming that Indians who lived on reservations could not vote, because they failed to qualify as residents of the state, spoke different languages, possessed a separate culture, and—in the most curious legal reasoning to be found—were unfamiliar with state governmental processes. Challenged by Utah Indians in *Allen vs Merrell*, the case eventually reached the United States Supreme Court, which remanded the case back to the Utah State Supreme Court for a rehearing. Utah's state legislature refused to repeal the statute until 1957, giving the state the distinction of being one of the last to grant the vote to Native Americans.[9]

New Mexico and Washington disqualified American Indians from voting on the grounds that they did not pay state taxes. Arizona and Idaho disqualified them because they were considered wards under the guardianship of the Indian Bureau, who controlled their lands held in trust. Because New Mexico and Arizona possessed the largest percentage of Native American populations in America, their constitutions disenfranchised a considerable portion of tribes.

Protests against Indian disenfranchisement in these two particular states eventually mounted from the Commissioner of Indian Affairs, missionaries, Native American veterans, and a Presidential Commission.[10] In 1943, irate at America's ingratitude for the Native American war effort, John Collier reminded Congress and the American public that Indians had a Selective Service registration rate of ninety-nine percent and a wartime participation figure of thousands, many of whom came from New Mexico and Arizona. "These states should do the American thing and grant the Indians the franchise," fumed Collier. "All over the world, we are preaching democracy and should grant a little more of it at home."[11]

Missionaries also expressed concern for Native American voting rights. Father Stoner, a Catholic missionary among the Arizona Hopi prior to the war, maintained a steady wartime correspondence with two Hopi brothers, both naval servicemen, while he was stationed at a Tucson military hospital. Severely criticizing Collier for "keeping Indians backward," Stoner often mentioned the importance of joining veterans' organizations and fighting for the franchise.[12]

Native American soldiers were not unaware of the irony of fighting in a war for a country which denied them basic rights. Private First Class Wade Hadley, stationed with the 158th Infantry Bushmasters, marveled that while a member of the armed forces, he could not only vote during elections, he could also "drink in the public bars" any time he wanted. He added: "According to the letters from home my people are being taxed and their livestock being reduced. But still they are not allowed to vote and drink their liquor as they wish."[13]

Indian leaders also took the initiative in the battle for the franchise. In 1944 Pima and Tohono O'Odham leaders approached a congressional committee hearing to discuss the voting issue. This committee refused to consider the matter and determined that the Arizona State Legislature must be the one to grant voting permission to its tribes. Although the Pima and Tohono O'Odham had been unsuccessful in gaining action from Congress, two years later a delegation of Navajo veterans appeared before a congressional committee hearing to protest their disenfranchisement. Citing Native American war achievements, these tribal members gained an important ally with the 1946 Truman Civil Rights Commission. Referring specifically to the Arizona and New Mexico constitutions, the commission's final report argued for enfranchisement of Native Americans by pointing out that Indians paid all federal and state taxes with the exception of lands held in trust:

> The constitutionality of these lands is being tested. It has been pointed out that the concept of "Indians not taxed" is no longer meaningful; it is a vestige of the days when most Indians were not citizens and had not become part of the community of people of the United States.[14]

Faced by this overwhelming mandate, in 1948 the Arizona Supreme Court reversed its earlier decision, thus enfranchising a potential 40,000 Native American voters and setting a legal precedent for New Mexico, which also contained many veterans from Navajo, Hopi, Zuni, Pueblo and Apache tribes. In 1962, New Mexico finally allowed American Indians to vote in state elections, becoming the last state to enfranchise this part of its population. Congress finally took action in 1970 with the passage of the Literacy in English Act, which forbade voting discrimination based on literacy qualifications. Expanded in 1975 to cover twenty-four states, it specifically mentioned Indian languages to further ensure that political conditions which had existed in North Carolina and New Jersey would not resurface.[15]

While the franchise issue enjoyed almost universal endorsement among Native Americans, the issue of purchasing liquor proved to be extremely divisive. As a rule military men supported the right to purchase alcohol wherever they wished, but tribal leaders usually objected to liquor consumption in general and liquor sales on reservations in particular. Many Native Americans returned from the war feeling more than a little patronized when they were still unable to purchase alcohol in stores or taverns. Historically the sale or manufacture of alcohol had been prohibited in Indian Territory, because the Indian Service contended that liquor, not being indigenous to Native Americans, had a profound effect upon tribal members. While under the influence of alcohol, American Indians had exhibited great susceptibility to land usurpation and trade exploitation. In order to keep friendly relations between Native Americans and the United States government, in June, 1834, Congress passed an act forbidding the introduction of "ardent spirits" within Indian country.[16] From this point on, a series of national laws strengthened governmental control over the use of alcohol by Native Americans.[17] The Indian Bureau actively aided in the enforcement of this prohibition. Hiring their own Liquor Suppression Officers, augmented by additional help from special officers in the Civilian Conservation Corps, the Bureau confidently claimed that in 1937 they had seized ninety-two illegal stills in Indian Country. Furthermore, the officers developed 2,936 criminal cases, achieved a ninety-three percent conviction rate, and collected $38,951 in fines. Eventually, the Liquor Suppression Department confiscated 28,247 gallons of whiskey, 258 gallons of wine, and 486 gallons of beer on reservations.[18]

Many observers blamed Indian poverty, a high unemployment rate, and disease on an alcoholism level that reached as high as fifty percent on some reservations. Ira Hayes, the Pima Marine who helped raise the United States flag on Mount Suribachi, Iwo Jima, in 1945, gained national attention when he "drank his way to oblivion and death" ten years later. "Alcoholism is a major affliction to a frustrated and discouraged people," wrote journalist Harold Fey when mourning Hayes' death.[19]

Clearly reservation Indians experienced many problems with alcoholism, and for this reason, most tribal leaders favored liquor control. In 1942 the Acoma Pueblo Indians, who had invested four thousand dollars of their funds in war bonds, implored the government that "we are very glad to let Uncle Sam have the use of our money. But please inform him that we do not wish these funds to be used to buy liquor for the soldiers." When given the local option of abolishing liquor on their reservations and surrounding cities, Alaskan Indians generally voted against alcohol. During the war, the Red Lake Band of Chippewa also opposed a bill which would have repealed their liquor law. In this case the state legislature wanted more liberal game privileges extended to whites on the Reservation in exchange for alcohol privileges on tribal grounds. Chippewa Tribal Secretary Peter Baptiste claimed to speak for the entire tribe when he firmly stated, "we do not want to trade the existing privilege [of limited rights to whites] for a glass of beer."[20]

Despite these sentiments expressed by tribal members, many Native American servicemen desired the same personal and social privileges accorded to white servicemen. For Indians in the military, frequenting bars or drinking with their friends fulfilled much more than a desire for alcohol. Soldiers or sailors often recounted how pleased they were to encounter friends from home at a military or public tavern. Although many military personnel (particularly Indian women) preferred to socialize at USO Canteens and Indian Clubs which served only non-alcoholic beverages, others spoke of visiting nearby towns or base clubs where they experienced chance meetings with other tribal members. Sergeant Sandy Garcia, San Juan Pueblo, mentioned running into two childhood friends at the Main Post on Fort Lewis, Washington. "We sure had a good time together," he fondly recalled. Sergeant Raphael Pino and Sailor Pasqual Cruz, also from San Juan Pueblo, met regularly at a Pacific island beer garden to gossip about friends. "Sometimes we talk of home," he told friends, "and sing some Indian songs."[21]

Others visited bars or taverns to meet with women and other friends when USO Clubs were simply unavailable. Servicemen spoke with admiration about young USO women in Mexico, Italy, France and Holland. Corporal Steven Herrera, Cochiti Pueblo, wrote home about a "swell party" in England with his outfit. "I had a cute British lassy on one hand," he recounted, "and a glass of beer on the other." Sailor Bennie Teba, stationed in Melbourne, Australia, also expressed his gratitude for his host country. "I'm sure having a wonderful time with the Aussie women," he said, "with their beers too." Finally, servicemen went to bars or drank in order to bond with their fellow soldiers, sailors, and marines. Private Wilfred H. Jones, Navajo, related that when Marines played volleyball, they wagered their beer rations on the games.

"We really got scalped," he good-naturedly complained after one game. "I mean alive too. . . . [W]e lost our case of beer."[22]

By the end of the war, servicemen began to voice open concerns about the treatment they expected to receive as veterans. Sergeant Sandy Garcia contended that in battle, white and Indian men fought as brothers, and they should be treated the same in civilian life. Joe Herrera, Cochiti Pueblo, agreed with this assessment. "I'm afraid many people have the wrong impression that all Indians go wild over these intoxicating liquors," he argued. "I have witnessed some of the worst escapades during my career in the army, and they weren't Indians either." Sailor George Lente also spoke of the "privilege of sitting at a bar to drink":

> What did we fight for? To be free is what we fought for and not to be pushed around. Indians have been pushed around too much. Why not stand up for our race like men! I got a lot of buddies on this ship that ask me why they do not let Indians drink. I've told them it's just a law that's been laid down for us.[23]

When these men returned to their reservations or towns, they felt understandable resentment when denied the privileges so freely given them elsewhere around the world. In California, Pomo Indians often dressed, acted, and spoke like Mexicans in order to be served in taverns. While most Native Americans criticized tribal members who drank too much, they also complained of discriminatory treatment against inebriated Indians. Frank Beecher, Hualapai Tribe, claimed that in Kingman, Arizona, local authorities failed to incarcerate whites for public drunkenness, but they quickly jailed Indians for the same offense. A New Mexican Navajo bitterly recalled being incarcerated with two Anglos and several Spanish-Americans after a drinking binge. Authorities almost immediately released the others without trial but held the Indian for ten days.[24]

During the war a movement began to repeal the federal law prohibiting the sale of alcohol to Indians when they were off the reservation. In December, 1943, the House of Representatives defeated a bill which would have allowed Minnesota Indians to purchase beer, but by 1944 this attitude had changed. Congressmen, the American Legion, and the Indian Bureau joined veterans in voicing their disapproval of the liquor laws and calling for an end to the ban. Two years later the Bureau of Indian Affairs and the Secretary of the Interior introduced Senate 2159 requesting that Congress allow off-reservation Indians to purchase alcohol. The 1948 Hoover Commission recommended that "Indian Liquor Law 123 should be reversed. It is discriminatory and widely resented for that reason. The law encourages bootlegging and excessive drinking of bad liquor at high prices." On August 15, 1953, Congress finally passed Public Laws 277, 280 and 281 which repealed the Federal Indian Liquor Law and urged the states of New Mexico and Arizona to follow their example.[25]

According to Public Law 277, the Federal Indian Liquor Law did not apply to "Indian country," the majority of which fell within the borders of New Mexico and Arizona. On September 29, 1953, New Mexico repealed the State Indian Prohibition Laws, but the repeal affected only "those areas under jurisdiction of New Mexico which was not Indian country." Arizona, however, continued to uphold Indian Liquor Laws based on the contention that the citizens of Arizona had not held a referendum to repeal its own state constitution. Some tribal leaders viewed this inaction as nothing less than hypocritical. Loyde Allison claimed that Indian alcoholism derived from the fact that prohibition was repealed for everyone but American Indians. "Today there is more drinking than when repeal came," he stated. "If the State abolished the law, the excessive Indian drinking would stop." Burton Ladd, Indian Service employee on the Tohono O'Odham Reservation, concurred, stating that the law "doesn't stop the traffic. They can get all they want in Tucson."[26]

World War II proved to be watershed years for an increase in civil rights among Native Americans. Many postwar American

Indian groups turned to radical measures which captured the public's attention—such as seizing Alcatraz Island or destroying documents at the Bureau of Indian Affairs to protest tribal conditions. Other Native American groups employed a more enduring, long-range potent weapon: the vote. In 1992, half a century after World War II, a Colorado American Indian, Ben Nighthorse Campbell, won a seat as his state's Senator. At President-elect William Clinton's 1992 Economic Conference, two Native American tribal governors, Peterson Zah representing the Navajo Nation, and Wilma Mankiller representing the Cherokee Nation, spoke on behalf of their people. These highly visible events clearly proved that Native Americans had moved beyond the fringes of American politics and become an acceptable, lobbying interest group. Rejecting acceptance into the mainstream, American Indian political interests still remain particularly tribal oriented.

---

[1]Wilcomb Washburn, *The Indian in America* (New York: Harper and Row, 1975): 85.

[2]"Abolition and Treaty Making," in Prucha, *Documents*, 136.

[3]Gary Stein, "Indian Citizenship Act," *New Mexico Historical Review*, Vol. 47, No. 3 (1972): 257–74.

[4]Charles J. Kappler (ed.), *United States Laws and Statutes, Indian Affairs, Laws and Treaties*, Vol. III (Washington, D.C.: Government Printing Office, 1971): 420; "Citizenship Act," *United States Statutes at Large*, 68th Cong., 1st sess., 253, June 2, 1924; Alison Bernstein, *American Indians and World War II* (Norman: University of Oklahoma Press, 1991): 22; "Nationality Act," *United States Statutes at Large*, 76th Cong., 3d sess., October 14, 1940.

[5]Ex Parte Green, 123, Federal Reporter, 2d Series, 862–63; "Treaty with the Six Nations, 1784," *United States Laws and Statutes, Indian Affairs*, Vol. II, October 22, 1784, 7 Stat., 15, 5–6.

[6]O. K. Armstrong, "Set the American Indian Free!" *Reader's Digest* (August, 1945): 49; New York *Times*, September 22, 1943, 26:6; "1940 Nationality Act."

[7]Charles Weeks, "The Eastern Cherokee and the New Deal," *North Carolina Historical Review*, Vol. 53, No. 3 (July, 1976): 307.

[8]Cherokee Tribal Council Resolution, November 5, 1940, Record Group 147, entry 1, box 33, folder "105.1 Indians—General," National Archives, Suitland, Maryland.

[9]Vine Deloria, Jr. and Cliff Lytle, *American Indians, American Justice* (Austin: U of Texas P, 1983): 224–25.

[10]Armstrong, "Set the American Indian Free!," 49; *Constitution of the United States: National and State,* Vol. II, 25, Vol. II, 23–24, Vol. IV, 26 (Washington, D.C.: Government Printing Office); Theodore Taylor, *The States and Their Indian Citizens* (Washington, D.C.: Government Printing office, 1972): 90.

[11]New York *Times,* September 21, 1943, 26:7; "Revision of Laws and Legal Status," *Congressional Committee Hearings,* House Committee on Indian Affairs, *House Resolution* 166, 78th Cong., 2d sess., December 4–8, 13, 1944 and February 2–25, 1944.

[12]Father Stoner to Byron Homer, April 28, 1944, December 14, 1944, Manuscript Collection A-15, Correspondence of Father Stoner, Arizona State Museum, Tucson, Arizona.

[13]Wade Hadley to Mrs. Dietrich, December 19, 1944, Southwestern Association on Indian Affairs Collection, File 46, *Hello and Many Lucks,* New Mexico State Record Center and Archives, Santa Fe, New Mexico.

[14]*Annual Report of the Commissioner of Indian Affairs, 1946* (Washington, D. C.: Government Printing Office, 1946): 381; Taylor, *The States and Their Indian Citizens,* 91; Truman's Civil Rights Commission, *To Secure These Rights* (Washington, D. C.: Government Printing Office, 1948): 40, 161.

[15]Taylor, *The States and Their Indian Citizens,* 91; Annual Report of Law Division Office of Indian Affairs, June 30, 1946, Record Group 75, entry 190, box D–M, folder "Seminar on Social, Educational, and Religious Work," National Archives, Washington, D. C.; Deloria and Lytle, *American Indians, American Justice,* 226.

[16]*Laws Relating to Indian Affairs,* Vol. I, 18; *Annual Report of the Commissioner of Indian Affairs, 1946,* 381; "Trade and Intercourse Act, June 30, 1834," Prucha, Documents, 67; "Act to Regulate Trade and Intercourse with the Indian Tribes," *United States Statutes at Large,* 29th Cong., 1st sess., June 30, 1834, 729.

[17]"Regulations Regarding Liquor and Annuities, March 3, 1847," Prucha, Documents, 75–76; "An Act to Regulate Trade and Intercourse with the Indian Tribes, *United States Statutes at Large,* 29th Cong., 2d sess., June 30, 1834, 729; House Executive Document No. 1, 52d Cong., 2d sess., (3088): 30; "An Act of 1897 to Regulate Trade and Intercourse with the Indian Tribes," Prucha, Documents, 188; *Laws Relating to Indian Affairs,* Vol. V, 390; "An Act to Modify the Operation of Indian Liquor Laws," *United States Statutes at Large,* 73d Cong., 2d sess., June 27, 1934.

[18]Press Release on Liquor Traffic, Record Group 75, entry 849, box 3, folder "Releases—Disapproved or Rewritten."

[19]Harold Fey, "Our Neighbor, the Indian," *The Christian Century,* Vol. LXXII, No. 12 (March 23, 1955): 39.

[20]House Resolution 166, 129, February 25, 1944; *Indians at Work,* Vol. IX, No. 9–10 (May–June, 1942): 39.

[21]Sergeant Sandy Garcia to Indian Club, May 30, 1943, Southwestern Association on Indian Affairs Collection, File 46, *Hello and Many Lucks;* August 1, 1945, *Newsletter* No. 20, Southwestern Association on Indian Affairs Collection, File 98, New Mexico State Records Center and Archives, Santa Fe, New Mexico.

[22]Corporal Steven Herrera to Mrs. Dietrich, October 10, 1944, Private Wilfred Jones to Members, July 17, 1944, Southwestern Association on Indian Affairs, File 46, *Hello and Many Lucks;* September 20, 1945, *Newsletter* No. 22, File 98, August 1, 1945, *Newsletter* No. 21, File 98, New Mexico State Records Center and Archives.

[23]August 1, 1945, *Newsletter* No. 20, September 20, 1945, *Newsletter* No. 22; March 1, 1946, *Newsletter* No. 24, Southwestern Association on Indian Affairs, File 98, New Mexico State Records Center and Archives.

[24]Evon Vogt, "Between Two Worlds: Case Study of a Navajo Veteran," *American Indian* 5 (No. 1, 1949): 16, 20; Oliver La Farge, "They Were Good Enough for the Army," *Harper's Magazine* 195 (November, 1947): 444; *Annual Report of the Commissioner of Indian Affairs, 1946,* 381; "To Permit Sale of Liquor to Indians," *Congressional Record,* 79th Cong., 2d sess., 4534, May 7, 1946; Burt Aginsky, "The Interaction of Ethnic Groups: A Case Study of Indians and Whites," *American Sociological Review* (February, 1949): 290; Interview with Frank Beecher, June 19–20, 1968, Manuscript 272A, Hualapai Oral History Project, Arizona State Museum.

[25]New York *Times,* December 23, 1943, 13:2; House Resolution 166, 69, 42; "Investigation to Determine if Revision of Laws Regarding Indians is Required," House Report 2091, 78th Cong., 2d sess., December 23, 1944, (10848): 11; *Annual Report of the Commissioner of Indian Affairs, 1946,* 381; *Congressional Record,* 79th Cong., 2d sess., A4533-4534, May 7, 1946; *United States Statutes at Large,* 79th Cong., 2d sess., LXXXII, LXXXXIII, LXXXVI; *United States Statutes at Large,* 83d Cong., 1st sess., 586–90; Taylor, *The States and Their Indian Citizens,* 62; Report of the Committee on Indian Affairs to the Commission on Organization of the Executive Branch of the Government, Hoover Commission, October 1948, 144, Manuscript Collection A356, Arizona State Museum.

[26]Indian Service Discussion, November 3, 1949, Manuscript Collection A478-C, Dobyns Fieldnotes; Interview with Loyde Allison, August 12, 1954, Manuscript Collection A349; Navajo Tribal Council Meeting Proceedings, November 3, 1953, Manuscript Collection A285, Arizona State Museum.

Skilled in the native lore of their ancestors and a match for the Japanese in any fight are these Navajo Indians, serving with a Marine signal unit on Bougainville. Front row, l-r: Pvt. Earl Johnny, Pvt. Kee Etsicitty, Pvt. John V. Goodluck and Pfc. David Jordon. Back row, l-r: Pvt. Jack C. Morgan, Pvt. George H. Kirk, Pvt. Tom H. Jones and Cpl. Henry Bake, Jr. Defense Department photo, Marine Corps, Bougainville. December 1943. National Archives 127-GR-137-69896.

Harrison Begay and Joe Herrera (3rd and 4th from left), Cochiti Pueblo, receive medals in a postwar ceremony, 1954. SWAIA File 3 #35641. State Records Center and Archives, Santa Fe, New Mexico.

Afterword

During the early 1950s Congress initiated the "unilateral termination of the United States' relationship with the tribes," and by 1961, 109 bands and tribes had been released from the guardianship of the federal government. When the government terminated its guardianship over a tribe, that tribe lost federal protection from state invasion in the form of taxation, conservation laws, and innumerable other legal issues with which most tribes were unprepared to cope. "Termination was an unmitigated failure," asserts political scientist Sharon O'Brien.[1]

In recent years scholars have debated the sources of the Termination Acts that followed the aftermath of World War II and signified an end to the New Deal experiment. Historian Larry Burt attributes the roots of termination to both internationalism and regionalism. Citing the postwar super patriotism of the 1950s, he compares the Cold War's antipathy to Communism, to the criticism many Indian Bureau opponents linked to Indian communalism. A conservative reaction to the New Deal's mushrooming bureaucracies, he asserts, gained impetus in the postwar decade. More importantly, he describes a western growth boom that took advantage of this anti-communalism and attempted to gain control of remaining tribal properties for individual enterprises.[2]

Anthropologist James Officer agrees that many critics of the New Deal argued that the Roosevelt administration had failed to make Indians self-sufficient. Consequently, Congress was greatly influenced by the 1948 Hoover Commission Report "which strongly urged the federal government to follow a policy of assimilation." The implied message, concludes Officer, "was that the government should remove itself from the Indian business as rapidly as possible."[3]

While historian Laurence Hauptman agrees that Indian Bureau mismanagement, paternalism, and authoritarianism contributed to an atmosphere conducive to the acceptance of the Termination Acts, he also attributes a growing public awareness of the Native American wartime effort, particularly that of the Iroquois, as part of this impetus for policy reform. "Now the Iroquois were stereotyped as heroic warriors ready to go on the warpath in defense of their Uncle Sam," he writes. Asserting that placing Native Americans in the "context of mainstream America" created a second crisis which would lead critics to view political separatism as unAmerican, he credits extensive wartime publicity with furnishing a political atmosphere for the Termination Acts.[4]

Political scientist Nicholas Peroff agrees with Hauptman's assessment, further asserting that the Indian Bureau, under Commissioner Dillon S. Meyer, cooperated with a Republican Congress, President Dwight Eisenhower, and a national public opinion that "provided indirect support for policies promoting accelerated Indian assimilation. . . . [I]n the 1950s there was a growing unitary conception of the American way of life." Furthermore, Peroff concurrs that this public opinion derived in large part from the wartime participation of Native Americans, which led to the belief that "Indians could fight and work like everyone else and, therefore, should join the mainstream of society and live like everyone else."[5]

Clearly neither the Native American role in the war, nor the implied failures of the Indian New Deal, completely accounted for the 1950s legislation. Terminaton was the stepchild of the Dawes Act, the ultimate conclusion of a badly-construed policy and failed experiment. It was a curious juxtaposition of twentieth-century reactionary statism emulating nineteenth-century reactionary progressivism. In the twentieth-century scenario, however, Native Americans failed to receive even token allotments. While successful in removing badly-needed health, educational and vocational services from reservations, the Termination Acts failed to end poverty or low educational attainment. In fact these problems were often relocated to cities with the dispossessed Native Americans, in a modern equivalent of Indian Removal. Alvin Josephy charges that the government abandonment of relocated Indians in the 1950s led to many of them living on skid rows. "When they lost their jobs or housing," he states, "the Indians tended to become stranded persons in alien societies."[6]

The 1960s, marked by the rise of the American Indian Movement, the capture of Alcatraz, and the vandalism of the Indian Bureau, reflected the vacuum in leadership at the Congressional and administrative levels. Because Native Americans had been rewarded for their participation in World War II with legislation which proved to be more harmful than any which had preceded it, many American Indians in the sixties generation rejected assimilation and experienced instead a resurgence of traditionalism, tribalism and identification with their unique heritage. "Red Power" became the rallying cry for a new generation of American Indians once again demanding to be considered as more than simply a stereotype.[7]

Obviously these are areas of research which must be explored. There are unanswered questions to the causes of Termination, Relocation, and Red Power. The studies and conclusions of the "Wartime Historians" should fill some of the void and should be used to evaluate intergenerational trends, conflicts, and social issues. In particular, the leadership proclivities of surviving veterans should be studied for their impact, direction, and purpose. This is the challenge for future historians.

---

[1]Sharon O'Brien, "Federal Indian Policies and Human Rights," in *American Indian Policy in the Twentieth Century*, ed. Vine Deloria, Jr. (Norman: U of Oklahoma P, 1985): 44.

[2]Larry Burt, *Tribalism in Crisis: Federal Indian Policy, 1953–1961* (Albuquerque: U of New Mexico P, 1982): 4.

[3]James E. Officer, "The Indian Service and Its Evolution," in *The Aggressions of Civilization*, ed. Sandra Cadwallader and Vine Deloria, Jr. (Philadelphia: Temple U P, 1984): 78–79.

[4]Laurence Hauptman, *The Iroquois Struggle for Survival: World War II to Red Power* (New York: Syracuse U P, 1986): 8–10, 63.

[5]Nicholas Peroff, *Menominee Drums: Tribal Termination and Restoration, 1954–1974* (Norman: U of Oklahoma P, 1982): 14–15, 20–21.

[6]Alvin Josephy, *The Indian Heritage of America* (New York: Bantam Books, 1968): 354–55.

[7]For an evaluation of the Native American protest movement of the 1960s, see Alvin Josephy, *Red Power: The American Indian Fight for Freedom* (New York: McGraw-Hill Book Co., 1971).

Bibliography

Government Records

"An Act to Provide Per Capita Payments." *U. S. Statutes at Large*. 77th Cong., 1st sess., 1941.

"An Act to Regulate Trade and Intercourse with the Indian Tribes." *U. S. Statutes at Large*. 29th Cong., 2d sess., 1834.

"An Act to Modify the Operation of Indian Liquor Laws." *U. S. Statutes at Large*. 73d Cong., 2d sess., 1934.

"An Act to Exempt Certain Indians from the Provisions of the Act of June 18, 1934." *U. S. Statutes at Large*. 48 Statute, 984, vol. 891, 164, June 13, 1940.

Biographical Directory of the American Congress. 1774–1971. Washington, D. C.: GPO, 1971.

Bureau of Indian Affairs. Record Group 75. National Archives. Washington, D. C.

Bureau of Mines. Record Group 70. National Archives. Suitland, Maryland.

"Citizenship Act." *U. S. Statutes at Large*. 68th Cong., 1st sess., 1924.

Code of Federal Regulations. Washington, D. C.: Department of the Interior, 1940.

Commissioner of Indian Affairs. *Annual Report to the Secretary of the Interior*. Washington, D. C.: GPO, 1941–1946.

Committee on Indian Affairs. Report to Commissioner on Organization of the Executive Branch of the Government. Hoover Commission. October 1948. Manuscript A357. Arizona State Museum. Tucson, Arizona.

Congressional Committee. Hearings before the House Subcommittee on Indian Affairs. *House Report* 7781. 74th Cong., 1st sess., 1935.

Congressional Record. 76th Cong., 1st sess., 1939.

Congressional Record, 77th Cong., 1st sess., 1941.

Congressional Record. 77th Cong., 2d sess., 1942.

Congressional Record. 78th Cong.,1st sess., 1943.

Congressional Record. 78th Cong., 2d sess., 1944.

Congressional Record. 79th Cong., 1st sess., 1945.

Congressional Record. 79th Cong., 2d sess., 1946.

Federal Bureau of Investigation. Report No. 61-7560-833. Henry Allen.

_____. No. 61-7587-746. American Indian Federation.

_____. Report No. 121-6970-1. Alice Lee Jemison.

_____. Report No. 100-41053-14, Mrs. W. K. Jewett.

_____. Report No. 61-7587-603/605/635/652/675, William Dudley Pelley.

_____. Report No. 101-3-044-5, Mary Heaton Vorse.

Federal Employment Practices Commission. Record Group 228. National Archives. San Francisco, California.

Final Report of the Japanese Evacuation from the West Coast. Secretary of War Reports. Washington, D. C.: GPO, 1942.

House. Investigation of Indian Affairs. *House Report* 2680. 83d Cong., 2d sess., 1954.

House. An Act of 1897 to Regulate Trade and Intercourse with the Indian Tribes. House Exec. Doc. No. 1, 52d Cong., 2d sess.

House. *House Report* 5921, 76th Cong., 1st sess., 1939.

House. Bill Authorizing Exploration of Proposed Dam Sites Located on Indian Lands in New Mexico. *House Report* 254, 78th Cong., 1st sess., 1943.

House. Investigation to Determine if Revision of Laws Regarding Indians is Required. *House Report* 2091, 78th Cong., 2d sess., 1944.

House. Proposed Provision Pertaining to Existing Appropriations for the Department of the Interior. *House Report* 2091, H. Doc. 284 (1055). 79th Cong., 2d sess., 1946.

House. Use of English in Indian Schools, H. Exec. Doc. No. 1. 50th Cong., 1st sess., 1887.

House Committee on Indian Affairs. Hearings. An Act to Facilitate and Simplify the Administration of Indian Affairs. *House Report* 4386. 79th Cong., 2d sess., 1946.

House Committee on Indian Affairs. Hearings. Revision of Laws and Legal Status. *House Report* 166. 78th Cong., 2d sess., 1944.

House Committee on Indian Affairs. Hearings. Emancipation. House 3680, 3681, and 3710. 79th Cong., 2d sess., 1946.

Indian Appropriations Act, 783. *U. S. Statutes at Large*. 60th Cong., 2d sess., 1909.

Indian Appropriations Act, 31. *U. S. Statutes at Large*. 66th Cong., 1st sess., 1919.

Interior Appropriation Act, 356. *U. S. Statutes at Large*. 79th Cong., 2d sess., 1946.

Kappler, Charles J., ed. *United States Laws and Statutes. Indian Affairs. Laws and Treaties*. Vol. I-V. Washington, D..C.: GPO, 1971.

Microfilm Collection 1194, MID, 1917-1941, Roll 176, OCS. National Archives, Washington, D. C.

"Nationality Act." *U. S. Statutes at Large*. 76th Cong., 3d sess., 1940.

Photo Collection. National Archives, Washington, D. C.

"Repealing the Indian Liquor Law." Public Law 720. *U. S. Statutes at Large*. 83d Cong., 1st sess.

Report of the Committee on Indian Affairs to the Commissioner on Organiza-

tion of the Executive Branch of the Government. Hoover Commission. October, 1948. Manuscript A357. Arizona State Museum. Tucson, Arizona.
Secretary of the Interior. Record Group 48. National Archives. Washington, D. C.
Selective Service. Record Group 147. National Archives. Suitland, Maryland.
"Selective Service and Training Act." Public Law 720. *U. S. Statutes at Large*. 76th Cong., 3d sess., 1940.
Senate. *Senate Report* 2206. 76th Cong., 1st sess., 1939.
Senate Committee on Indian Affairs. Hearings. Establishment of Joint Committee to Investigate Claims Against the United States. S. Joint Resolution. 79th Cong., 2d sess., 1946.
Senate Committee on Indian Affairs. Hearings. Property Restriction Removal. *Senate Report* 1313, 78th Cong., 2d sess., 1946.
Senate Committee on Indian Affairs. Hearings. Senate Doc. 1651. 75th Cong., 3d sess., 1936.
Senate Committee on Indian Affairs. Hearings. Senate Doc. 1424 and Senate Doc. 2589. 75th Cong., 1st sess., 1935–1937.
Senate Committee on Indian Affairs. Hearings. Food Stamp Plan Benefit. Senate Doc 1341, 77th Cong., 1st sess., 1941.
Senate Committee on Indian Affairs. Hearings. Property Restriction, Removal of Veterans. 79th Cong., 2d sess., S. 1093, 1946.
Special House Committee. Hearings on Un-American Activities. *House Report* 282, 75th Cong., 3 sess., 1938.
Senate. Report on Indian Conditions. *Senate Report* 310, 6 (10756), 78th Cong., 1st sess., 1944.
Senate. Repealing the So-Called Wheeler-Howard Act. S. R. 1031, (10842), 78th Cong., 2d sess., 1944.
Sixteenth Census of the United States. 1940. Characteristics of the Population. Washington, D. C.: GPO, 1943.
Supression of Liquor Traffic, 413. *U. S. Statutes at Large*. 76th song, 3d sess., 1940.
To Secure These Rights. Truman Commission on Civil Rights. Washington, D. C.: GPO, 1948.
War Department. Record Group 165. National Archives. Suitland, Maryland.
War Relocation Authority. Record Group 210. National Archives. Washington, D. C.

Manuscripts, oral histories, and interviews

Alison, Loyde. Interview. August 12, 1954. Manuscript A-349. Hualapai Oral History Project. Arizona State Museum. Tucson, Arizona.

"Arizona Indian Voting." Manuscript A-663. Arizona State Museum. Tucson, Arizona.

Beecher, Frank. Interview. June 19–20, 1968, Manuscript 272A. Hualapai Oral History Project. Arizona State Museum. Tucson, Arizona.

"*Colorado River Indian Tribes vs. United States*, August 1, 1951." Manuscript 369. Arizona State Museum. Tucson, Arizona.

Cornelius, Ernestine and Carmen Cornelius Taylor. Interview. Undated. Tape OH 1238. Native American Educators Oral History Project. Montana Historical Society. Billings, Montana.

Crook, Viola. Interview. June 17, 1969. Manuscript A375-A. Hualapai Oral History Project. Arizona State Museum. Tucson, Arizona.

"Excerpts from the Postwar Program for the Pima Jurisdiction." Manuscript A348. Arizona State Museum. Tucson, Arizona.

Franco, Vidal. Interview. April 28, 1992. El Paso, Texas.

Harrison, Mike. Interview. August 17, 1967. Manuscript A-80C. Yavapai Oral History Project. Arizona State Museum. Tucson, Arizona.

Hello and Many Lucks. File 46. Southwestern Association on Indian Affairs. New Mexico State Records Center and Archives. Santa Fe, New Mexico.

Letters from Native Americans in the Armed Forces. Files 112–15. Southwestern Association on Indian Affairs. National Archives, Washington, D. C.

Medicine Crow, Joseph. Interview. January 30, 1989. Tape OH 1226. Native American Educators Oral History Project. Montana Historical Society. Billings, Montana.

Navajo Tribal Council Meeting Proceedings, November 3, 1953. Manuscript A285. Arizona State Museum. Tucson, Arizona.

Newsletters No. 1–24. File 98. New Mexico Association on Indian Affairs.

Segundo, Thomas. Interview. June 22, 1949 to September 1, 1949. Manuscript A478-A, A478-C. Hualapai Oral History Project. Arizona State Museum. Tucson, Arizona.

Stoner, Father. Correspondence. Manuscript A-15. Arizona State Museum. Tucson, Arizona.

Newspapers

Courier Express. Buffalo, New York. November 23, 1938. National Archives, Washington, D. C.

Santa Fe *New Mexican*. New Mexico State University, Las Cruces, New Mexico. Microfilm. 1939–1940.

Casper (Wyoming) *Tribune-Herald*. University of Wyoming, Laramie, Wyoming. Microfilm.

New York *Times*. 1942–1945.

Articles

Adair, John and Evon Vogt. "Navajo and Zuni Veterans: A Study of Contrasting Modes of Cultural Change." *American Anthropologist* 51 (October–December, 1949): 547–61.

Aginsky, Burt. "The Interaction of Ethnic Groups: A Case Study of Indians and Whites." *American Sociological Review* (February, 1949): 288–93.

Armstrong, O. K. "Set the American Indians Free!" *The Reader's Digest* 47 (August, 1945): 47–52.

Beatty, Willard W. "Education Offered by the United States Indian Service." *Industrial Arts and Vocational Education* 34 (March 1945): 134–35.

"The Capture of Attu as Told by the Men Who Fought There." *The Infantry Journal* (1944).

Cartoon, *Saturday Evening Post* (October 24, 1942): 79.

Collier, John. "Indians Come Alive." *Atlantic Monthly* 170 (September, 1942): 75–81.

_____. "Indians in a Wartime Nation." *Annals of the American Academy of Political and Social Science* 223 (September, 1942): 29–35.

Cunningham, Clara H. "Adventures Among the Indians." *Public Health Nursing* 33 (July, 1941): 433–36.

Engleman, Grace. "Trachoma Nursing." *American Journal of Nursing* (April, 1942): 383–89.

Fey, Harold. "Our Neighbor, the Indian." *The Christian Century* 72 (March 23, 1955): 361–64.

Holm, Tom. "Fighting the White Man's War: The Legacy of American Indians in World War II." *Journal of Ethnic Studies* 9 (Summer, 1981): 69–81.

Ickes, Harold. "Indians Have a Name for Hitler." *Collier's* (January 15, 1944): 58.

"Indian Education." *Time* (August 12, 1946): 42.

Indian Record. Haskell, Kansas: Department of the Interior, Bureau of Indian Affairs, 1945.

Indian Truth. 16 (April–May, 1939).

Indians at Work. Washington, D. C.: Department of the Interior, Bureau of Indian Affairs, 1941–1945.

Indians in the War. Haskell, Kansas: Department of the Interior, Bureau of Indian Affairs, 1945.

Johnston, Philip. "Indian Jargon Won Our Battles." *The Masterkey* (n.d.): 131–37.

La Farge, Oliver. "They Were Good Enough for the Army." *Harper's Magazine* 195 (November, 1947): 444–49.

"Lo the Educated Indian." *Newsweek* 21 (April 26, 1943): 80–81.

Malouf, Carling. "Observations on the Participation of Arizona's Racial and Cultural Groups in World War II." *The American Journal of Physical Anthropology* 5 (December, 1947): 493.

McCarthy, Dan B. "Samuel Smith and Son Michael . . . Plus 52 Other Navajo U.S. Marines." *VFW Magazine* (January, 1982): 26.

McGibony, J. R. "Indians and Selective Service." *Public Health Reports* 1 (January 2, 1942): 26–31.

Neuberger, Richard. "On the Warpath." *Saturday Evening Post* (October 24, 1942): 628–31.

Officer, James E. "The Indian Service and Its Evolution," in *The Aggressions of Civilization*, Sandra Cadwalader and Vine Deloria, Jr., eds. Philadelphia: Temple U P, 1984.

Peterson, Helen. "American Indian Political Participation." *The Annals of the American Academy* 311 (1957): 116–26.

Platero, Juanita and Siyowin Miller. "A Warrior Returning." *Common Ground* 1 (1945): 41–52.

Ritzenhaler, Robert. "The Impact of War on an Indian Community." *American Anthropologist* 45 (April–June, 1943): 325–26.

Sergeant, Elizabeth Shepley. "The Indian Goes to War." *New Republic* (November 30, 1942): 708–709.

Smith, Sherry. "Lost Soldiers: Re-searching the Army in the American West." *Western Historical Quarterly* 29 (Summer, 1998): 149–63.

"Spanish Schoolbooks for Young Indians." *Science Newsletter* (June 7, 1941): 361.

Stein, Gary. "Indian Citizenship Act." *New Mexico Historical Review* 47 (July, 1972): 257–74.

Tadlock, J. A. "Navajos Respond to Nation's Need." *Manpower Report* (April, 1943): 7–8.

Thomas, E. W. "America's First Families on the Warpath." *Common Ground* 2 (1942): 95–99.

"Tribes Sound a War Cry for Liberty." *Business Week* (December 2, 1944): 40.

Useem, John, Gordon MacGregor and Ruth Hill Useem. "Wartime Employment and Cultural Adjustments of the Rosebud Sioux." *Applied Anthropology* 2 (January-March, 1943): 1–9.

Vestal, Stanley. "The Plains Indians and the War." *Saturday Review of Literature* 25 (May 16, 1942): 9–10.

Vogt, Evon. "Between Two Worlds: Case Study of a Navajo Veteran." *American Indian* 5 (1949): 13–21.

Watson, Editha. "Giving Health Back to the Indians." *Hygeia* 24 (October, 1946): 750–53.

Weeks, Charles. "The Eastern Cherokee and the New Deal." *North Carolina Historical Review* 53 (July, 1976): 303–19.

White, Lonnie. "Indian Soldiers of the 36th Division." *Military History of the Texas Southwest* 15 (1979): 7–20.

Winters, S. R. "Health for the Indian." *Hygeia* 22 (September, 1944): 680–82.

Books

Allswang, John. *The New Deal and American Politics*. New York: John Wiley and Sons, 1978.

Beaver, R. Pierce. *Church, State and the American Indian*. St. Louis: Concordia Publishing House, 1966.

Becker, Thomas E. *Navajo Way*. New York: The Indian Association of America, 1956.

Berkhofer, Robert. *The White Man's Indian: The History of an Idea from Columbus to the Present*. New York: Alfred A. Knopf, 1978.

Bernstein, Alison. *American Indians and World War II: Toward a New Era in Indian Affairs*. Norman: U of Oklahoma P, 1990.

Britten, Thomas. *American Indians in World War I: At Home and at War*. Albuquerque: U of New Mexico P, 1997.

Burt, Larry. *Tribalism in Crisis: Federal Indian Policy, 1953–1961*. Albuquerque: U of New Mexico P, 1982.

Cadwalader, Sandra L. and Vine Deloria, Jr., eds. *The Aggressions of Civilization*. Philadelphia: Temple U P, 1984.

Carlson, Leonard. *Indians, Bureaucrats and Land: The Dawes Act and the Decline of Indian Farming*. Connecticut, Greenwood Press, 1981.

Collier, John. *The Indians of the Americas*. New York: Norton, 1947.

Commager, Henry Steel, ed. *Documents of American History*. 8th ed. Meredith Corporation, 1968.

Deloria, Vine Jr., ed. *American Indian Policy in the Twentieth Century*. Norman: U of Oklahoma P, 1985.

_____ and Cliff Lytle. *American Indians, American Justice*. Austin: U of Texas P, 1983.

Diamond, Sander. *The Nazi Movement in the United States, 1924–1941*. Ithaca, New York: Cornell U P, 1974.

Dippie, Brian W. *The Vanishing American: White Attitudes and U.S. Indian Policy*. Connecticutt: Wesleylan U P, 1982.

Dozier, Edward P. *The Pueblo Indians of North America*. Prospect Heights, Illinois: Waveland Press, 1970.

Drinnon, Richard. *Keeper of the Concentration Camps: Dillon S. Meyer*. Berkeley: U of California P, 1987.

Fourth Signal Company. Baton Rouge, Louisiana: Army and Navy Publishing, 1946.

Hagan, William T. *The Indian Rights Association*. Tucson: U of Arizona P, 1985.

Hauptman, Laurence. *Between Two Fires: American Indians in the Civil War*. New York: Free Press Enterprise, 1995.

_____. *The Iroquois Struggle for Survival: World War II to Red Power*. New York: Syracuse U P, 1986.

Hertzberg, Hazel. *The Search for an American Indian Identity*. Syracuse: Syracuse U P, 1971.

Holm, Tom. *Strong Hearts, Wounded Souls: Native Americans of the Vietnam War*. Austin: U of Texas P, 1996.

Jeansonne, Glen. *Transformation and Reaction: America 1921–1945*. Milwaukee: U of Wisconsin P, 1994.

Josephy, Alvin M. Jr. *The Indian Heritage of America*. New York: Bantam, 1965.

_____. *Red Power: The American Indians' Fight for Freedom*. New York: McGraw-Hill, 1971.

Kawano, Kenji. *Warriors: Navajo Codetalkers*. Flagstaff, Arizona: Northland Publishing, 1990.

Kelley, Lawrence. *The Assault on Assimilation*. Albuquerque: U of New Mexico P, 1983.

La Farge, Oliver. *As Long as the Grass Shall Grow*. New York: Alliance Book Publishing, 1940.

Mitchell, Broadus. *Depression Decade*. New York: Rhinehart, 1947.

Morgan, Lewis. *Ancient Society*. New York: Henry Holt, 1878.

Navajos in World War II. Navajo Community College, 1977.

Parker, Dorothy. *Phoenix Indian School: The Second Half-Century*. Tucson: U of Arizona P, 1996.

Parmer, Donald. *Indians and the American West in the Twentieth Century*. Bloomington: Indiana U P, 1994.

Peroff, Nicholas. *Menominee Drums: Tribal Termination and Restoration, 1954–1974*. Norman: U of Oklahoma P, 1986.

Philp, Kenneth R. *John Collier's Crusade for Indian Reform, 1920–1954*. Tucson: U of Arizona P, 1977.

Prucha, Francis Paul, ed. *American Indian Policy in Crisis*. Norman: U of Oklahoma P, 1976.

_____. *Documents of United States Indians*. Nebraska: U of Nebraska P, 1975.

Ruetten, Richard. "Burton K. Wheeler of Montana: A Progressive Between the Wars." Ph.D. diss., University of Oregon, 1961.

Satz, Ronald. *Tennessee's Indian Peoples*. Nashville: U of Tennessee P, 1979.

Schlessinger, Arthur. *The Almanac of American History*. New York: G. P. Putnam's Sons, 1983.

Smith, Jane F. and Robert M. Kvasnicka, ed. *Indian-White Relations: A Persistent Paradox*. Washington, D. C.: Howard U P, 1976.

Spicer, Edward. *Cycles of Conquest*. Tucson: U of Arizona P, 1962.

Taylor, Graham. *The New Deal and American Indian Tribalism*. Lincoln: U of Nebraska P, 1980.

Taylor, Theodore W. *American Indian Policy*. Mount Ary, Maryland: Lomond Publications, 1983.

_____. *The States and Their Indian Citizens*. Washington, D. C.: GPO, 1972.

Utley, Robert. *The Last Days of the Sioux Nation*. New Haven: Yale U P, 1963.

Washburn, Wilcomb. *The Indian in America*. New York: Harper and Row, 1975.

Index

Page references in *italics* indicate illustrations.

J

K

L

M

Y

Z